Aesthetic nonsense makes commonsense, thanks X

Aesthetic nonsense makes commonsense, thanks X

Lisa Radford

Foreword

For the past twenty years, Lisa Radford has written alongside (and sometimes about) contemporary art and artists in Melbourne. This anthology has been published to coincide with Radford's solo exhibition *Dear Masato, all at once (get a life, the only thing that cuts across the species is death)* showing at West Space from 4 November to 10 December 2016, as part of the organisation's annual commission series. Brought together in *Aesthetic nonsense makes commonsense, thanks X*, Radford's criticism and ficto-criticism captures many local histories that speak to politics, friendship, popular culture and a myriad of other subjectivities.

Speaking recently, Lisa explained that 'Artists, for some reason, have trusted me. I hope they still do. I write by learning through their work. The writing becomes a kind of mapping of this experience. It is a writing through, not about, art.'[1] In contrast to what we might usually expect of art discourse, Radford's writing often reads like a stenographer is recording her thought processes in real time. Subjects jump in, only to be left hanging at the end of a paragraph like a red herring, as another tangent is pursued. All the while, the artwork or exhibition informing every new node of meaning remains unseen, rarely directly referred to.

So here is a map in which aesthetic nonsense makes common sense. One in which an exploration of ancient burial tombs in the Netherlands relates to Irene Hanenbergh's material processes, the biography of a pro skater and the film *Magnolia* speak to Blair Trethowan's *Products that Educate, Inspire and Delight* (2001), and Brazilian wandering spiders, Rasputin and Napoleon tie in with the title of a group show. Collected here, alongside her reviews and catalogue essays, are comment pieces such as Radford's 2013 series for Stamm, a Melbourne writing collective that published monthly, online reviews of contemporary art between 2012 and 2015, and the previously unpublished 'Procrastipainting', which profiles a selection of Melbourne-based painters.

Having practiced as an artist, writer, curator and teacher in Melbourne since the early 2000s, much of Radford's writing features a recurring cast of peers, collaborators and students. Even if not writing about the exhibitions or works of friends such as Masato Takasaka, Lane Cormick, Sharon Goodwin, Colleen Ahern, Ry Haskings, Nicholas Mangan and Blair Trethowan, Radford is referring to them by first name and dropping them into one another's catalogue essays. Members of the collaborative art group DAMP, of which Radford was a member from 1999 to 2010, also make an appearance, including Amanda Marburg, Nat Thomas, Rob Creedon, Sharon Goodwin and James Lynch. And other artists written about here, such as Natasha Madden & Zac St. Clair, Lucina Lane, and Paula Hunt, were Radford's students at the Victorian College of the Arts.

Amongst the divergent topics explored in this collection, we can see a history of Melbourne contemporary art rushing past in fragments: able to be pieced together, or left to blur in with everything else.

Patrice Sharkey and Robert Shumoail-Albazi
Melbourne, Australia, November 2016

Note

1 Lisa Radford, 'Lecture #10', Thursday 12 May 2016, as a part of Season 1 of the *Writing & Concepts* lecture series at RMIT University, Melbourne. See: http://writingandconcepts.com.au/index.php/lisa-radford/

Introductions

Come with me to the sea... of... love

Lisa Radford, the guilty seraph, the one-who-knows and feels bad before writing. She feels bad because she has something to say. It's as if you stole my letters and read each one out loud, and kept right on saying. Combining catholic and protestant and in search of jewish guilt, she alternates between a negative theology and a there-must-be-something. Formerly stuck in a suburb watching the boys tuning the radio in a car in the early evening, at least she had a best friend. She writes like Gin House Blues with resentment and kindness. She gasps as to why what we all know is not included in art? I can only quote Frances Ferguson:

> *formalism… the claim that art necessarily detached itself from the world and its representations*

This art, forever repeated, has been so inadequate and continues to be so and it's not for lack of trying and indie tears. Before this monkey goes to heaven we want something Gigantic. Like a mournful female Job she can stand more but wonders why it has to be this way? When Lisa asked me to write this essay she wondered whether it was too Oedipal to ask me to write, given I was her teacher and mentor for a while. Well, the quote I best remember from the Oracle to Oedipus is:

> *You are the murderer of the king whose murderer you seek*

Lisa understood well that all us dumb people had to read and know more and enter the intellectual terrain, it was no betrayal. Because, like the Oracle says, you never know or understand yourself very well and this becomes the plank of what-we-know that we can stand on (together). Because all the dogwhistles of misbegotten prejudices reside in us. After you go to art school your friends and family can no longer understand you. But the working class and the students used to all be friends; Lisa never lost sight that, even without Marxism, you need a brain, and to understand you need others to live (together).

I think I'm halfway through. How'm I doing here? Let me tell you about it.

After years of A Constructed World talking to live eels and then a copper replica, artist Angelique Buisson suggested she'd like to address some speech to a blue acrobat's ball that had been such an unpredictable presence in our work. She read Donna Haraway then another time Douglas Copeland to a large blue plastic ball in performances. With care. Who knows why? All these essays of Lisa's were written to address what may not have been clear at the time and not being sure that someone would read or listen. 'There must be someone else like me?' The art world is such a racket, especially in an Australia that feigns the tyranny of distance, which was politically reconfigured after we joined the internet. It's different there or it's provincial here. Neither of which are true because those boys in the car in the hood were tuning into Nirvana on the car radio that night and recognised exactly what it meant to them there and then. There are other people in other places who feel exactly the same. There are other people in other places who don't want to be subsumed by a crappy, aloof art world.

A few years ago, in our crumbling studio in Montmartre (yes, like a '50s American movie), we did a writing project with twelve people. After talking for a while, we wrote some reviews, one sentence for each person, going round and around the table in turn. I think we wrote about four, they all made perfect sense and we published them. When Jacqui and I write together, we both just use 'I' and leave it to the reader to decide and often can't remember who wrote what ourselves. This is what Lisa's writing engenders and evokes; there's no art or audience, production or reception, there's simply a sea of voices we all find ourselves in.

A Constructed World (Geoff Lowe with Jacqueline Riva)
Prato, Italy, October 2016

dear Lisa

We must begin wherever we are… (says JD). And where I am being an invitation to write a piece (of sorts) to accompany a collection of essays, letters, texts, written by you, Lisa Radford, between 1996 and 2016, I take this advice. I enter this scene around 2012, just after the colour pages. Some of these texts I know and some I don't. I am not with-in this gathering but sitting somewhere with-out, on a line that leads out from and back to the writing gathered here. This line isn't mine but one of many such lines spun out from the work contained in this volume of texts.

These lines are difficult to name. I hesitate to call them dérives, although they bear some resemblance in their seeming wandering and dismissing of foundational underpinning. I also hesitate to describe them as detours, despite the elision of the authorial voice and the movements made in relation to the immanence of language. These derivation lines are better described by your term 'co-presentation', where the writing achieves a (self-)presence only in the company of others: a letter, a fictional interview or an arrangement of ready-made texts. These lines also trace the practice of the writing within the writing, of the work of defusing and opening a topology of texts, one to another, one to itself, of a reading and writing of proximity that must be reinvented each time. There is no history to be fashioned out of this collection of writing. Without approval, these texts trace lines and notate themselves, they are notations of themselves, they are with-out subject and with-in reading. 'Some of these are shit', you say, 'but that's kind of the point…'.

Writing as I am from the future, as a figure in a thesis yet to be written, I see this company, the milieu of the writing, its context, as the against of the text that is also the *with* of the text; a dialogic contradiction as self-presence that invokes a *with*-out as an omission, as absent speech, or as references communicating both privately and publicly. These are the tricks that envelop your texts in a dialogue with the work they refer to. I might describe this with-out as a necessary void in the text that allows a space outside. Productive contradiction, you might call it. Is this the same productive contradiction as when, in a rhetorical turn, you ask (as you will), 'Who cares?', to elicit what you describe as the dead-end rhetorical response of 'So, what are you going to do about it?', a figure of some rhetorical self-reflexivity? The rhetorical figure that I am in this future nods to yours, and will reply, 'What could be resolved by ending this?' One point opens another…

I have been mining for critical intention and I have found a red herring…

You drop these in the path of critical intention, diversions from taking seriously the seriousness of what follows in your pages. A distraction to another (differing) end. A distraction leading back to the text itself, revolving its coded (your term) references through their socialised narratives, something (political) presented in the guise of another form and words. DISCOURSE — I shout here — remember its (productive) contradictory definitions: (a) a rambling deployment of others' words, and (b) its coherence of iterative acts.

(But now that I have started shouting, I remember that in the future you are going to write a play about this exact contradiction of discourse and its political necessity, and there will be a lot of shouting in it.)

This text I am writing here can only be a red herring placed in the path of the reader to tempt them to take seriously the superficiality in what follows. Red herring — a flash, an intensity, something appearing to no purpose but to mesmerise and introduce aesthetics to the scene. Writing Space / Image Space: distributions into and out of the social, currencies formed by friendship and the political; narratives co-staged as the contradiction and violence of causal relations…

painting / writing / utterance / editing / curating / scripting / exhibitions / books / presentations / plinths / walls / paperclips /

Everything begins with a question to art…

Fiona Macdonald
Melbourne, Australia, November 2016

Writing to my friends

Lisa still sometimes wears a dress over pants.
— Jarrod Rawlins

I think Lisa Radford and I infiltrated the art speak we were being fed as youth. It was not planned, or really even discussed, but it is something that comes from growing up with chips on shoulders. We both came from the West (actually, Lisa is from the North—Coburg, to be exact), with the chips, and the shoulders, into the thing we knew as the art world, and we brought a great deal of bravado — as opposed to confidence — with us (as you probably already know, Lisa doesn't have any confidence).

And with this bravado comes a perfect level of naiveté, which is most useful for presenting one's opinions and ideas. As we were more self-conscious than self-aware we didn't know this was happening, but because we had the burning need to speak for ourselves — to comment, criticise, contextualise, etc. — we had to find a way to do this. Obviously, the most promising results come from just working with what you know, not necessarily what you are told you need to know. So that's what we settled for.

Lisa and I share a methodology for writing about art, which is to not really write about it, not to describe it or make definitions for it. On many occasions I'm sure we weren't even thinking about art: that's the point. We write around it, through it, under it, but not really about it. The way I approach this is to imagine that I am writing notes to my friends, and that nobody really outside of this friendship group will read the text. And maybe this is true, maybe nobody else does read these texts, maybe you're not reading this; either way, I have established a failsafe method of writing all sorts of guff, both cogent and incoherent.

This writing to your friends thing, with its seemingly unstructured, unintentional, aimless strategy of not writing about something directly or with a sense of distanced examination, can easily be seen as an exercise in producing metaphors. But it's not. It might be more interesting than that, because it creates a bigger intellectual space for debate, and that is the goal.

Take 'The Outback Denier' text Lisa and I invented for an issue of *Art & Australia* magazine. If I were to write directly about a specific artwork, or a whole group, using descriptions such as 'a conceptual and moral disability', or 'a politically motivated fraud', I would need to disguise those accusations in a metaphor; hang on, that's what we did. Oh, yeah. Start again.

Art writing to your friends is a version of imagining your audience naked. This methodology means that I am free to make mistakes, understand existing arguments and discourses incorrectly, or not at all. It's not an approach designed to undermine existing discourses, that is simply arrogant and naïve, and you can see this approach a mile off. In fact, that is the essence of what makes bad art—to attack a dominant discourse for no other purpose than to attack or mock it. Pointless. Whereas writing to your friends serves a communicative purpose that most other art writing can't.

This is not a diatribe about outsider writers infiltrating some kind of illustrious intellectual space reserved for others (even though I admit it could easily be mistaken for one), because that shit doesn't really exist anyway. It's an illusion that there is a specialised writing context that dominates a particular art scene, which in our case is white, western-centric art being made in Australia.

What we are talking about here is art writing, straight up—art theory, art criticism, art history. And the purpose of art writing is to describe, explain, and produce meaning for art. Some people writing about art are very good at getting bogged down with looking for the right idea, the magpie approach to using theory and criticism, or at least an interesting idea, and this is where convolution can stem from, which is not to be confused or interchanged with complexity. They are not the same thing. I think. Complexity is to be embraced, but it also needs to be uncluttered. This may be the motive for infiltration. I am not sure, as I am completely unaware of my motives, and I think Lisa's keep shifting.

As you may gather from this text, in my opinion art

writing is often filled with lofty ideas that impose themselves on art in an extraneous and bullish manner. This is what Lisa and I saw when we arrived. At first everything seems shiny: the young bower bird artist heads into the academy, nipping around looking for the plan, and the solution. But you don't need to. The institution needs you to *bring* the plan and the solution. Otherwise, there is nothing there. At all. Except objects.

I have written this to Lisa, nobody else really, except maybe you. And it's dedicated to Blair.

Jarrod Rawlins
Hobart, Australia, November 2016

1996

Recipe for making 'good artists'

Take 20 or so talented yet pretentious, egotistical, highly intellectual and definitely cool people, along with tuition by highly skilled, well read, dedicated, though sometimes elitist and pretentious artists, combined with adequate facilities and a title such as 'Associate Diploma of Art (Visual Art)'; mix well. Let simmer for two years: competent, confident artists. Bon appétit.

Let's not be too cynical, because, in general, studying art at TAFE has been a positive experience; although, when all you have to draw comparisons with is high school and the experiences of 'acquaintances' who study at larger institutions, evaluating your education to date is difficult. Any negative aspects are predominantly concerned with bureaucratic and economical factors — 'Okay, you are good enough to pass, but this could be due to course funding based on pass rates'. Other than that, the training in art that I have experienced is with people who are dedicated to learning the 'how-tos' and 'whys?' from professional, dedicated artists. The course is fairly intense and a lot is left up to the initiative and enthusiasm of individual students. First year involves learning techniques and basics so that in second year you have the privilege, unique to Western TAFE, of studio space with 24-hour access to mature as an artist and person. The only major difficulty I have is that only one to two hours are allocated to art history while two to three hours are allocated to Alan Pease, and that perhaps there is not enough positive critical response.

Overall, the opportunities and doors that TAFE has opened are overwhelming, but until funding criteria are changed, red tape and bureaucratic systems eliminated, as well as some attitudes altered, institution heads will favour football over creativity and schooling in the arts will only be seen as an escape from looking for a 'real job'. But I'm sure there will be those who need simmering.

First published in: Jacqueline Riva & Geoff Lowe (eds), *Artfan 6: Art School Mama*, Summer 1996/7, A Constructed World Inc., Melbourne.

2001

Products that Educate, Inspire and Delight

The film *Magnolia* begins with a series of short stories that function as anecdotes for the rest of the movie. One is the story of a pilot, who, unbeknownst to him, picks up a scuba diver in his plane, which is carrying water from a nearby lake to a local bush fire. The scuba diver of course dies and is found later, suspended in a burnt-out tree. It turns out that, the day before, the pilot was gambling at the local casino. After an inquest and autopsy, the pilot discovers the scuba diver was the dealer at the table where he lost all of his money. Strange coincidence? The pilot takes his own life and *Magnolia* unfolds. A story of groups and individuals: two dying men from different families and their wives, children, friends and associates. The separate stories of each, all seemingly unrelated. As the movie plays, you piece together the relationships and the connections. The stories are different but sometimes they overlap, link and crossover. The stories pass each other. Occasionally, the stories themselves know that they are connected, other times they cross: one with no knowledge of the others' existence. Like the anecdotes, the stories seem like mere coincidence, but with the benefit of hindsight and recollection there is a sense of relativity and meaning. But you wonder if, in the end, the situations have again been reduced to mere coincidence.

I think I remember the Gator graphic in question, from the eighties. Its most popular version was in fluoro green. It originated on a Gator skateboard, eventually surfacing on Vision T-shirts and berets. A spiralling geometric pattern—black triangular shapes or an African tribal reference that doubled as the scales of an alligator's back. Sometimes found in pastel variations or simply in black and white. Spiralling inwards, or maybe downwards—a fluoro op art vortex that, when positioned and read alongside Gator's own story, has interesting and funny connotations.

Mark 'Gator' Anthony Rogowski moved to a suburb in

San Diego County, California, with his mother and brother when he was three. I don't know a lot about the area, although some comparisons have been made with the Western suburbs of Melbourne.

Gator skated regularly from the age of ten and is considered one of the great skaters of the '80s, along with Tony Hawk and Christian Hosoi, also from San Diego County. During the '70s, skating boomed in the California area, it suffered a minor setback in the late '70s, but by the eighties skate parks and ramps were being built across the US. Skateboard manufacturers became multimillion dollar companies, expanding into clothing, sneakers and movies. The first video magazines were skating magazines. The culture very much image-based—frame-by-frame photographs of trick after trick filled pages and pages of various skating magazines, t-shirts, caps, not to mention the graphics on boards. The primary way a skater made money was through sales of the skater's own boards; their name printed somewhere on the deck with a graphic positioned, more often than not, on the underside of the board. The graphic would eventually wear off through use, before the board would finally break and another deck bought to replace it.

In 1980, Gator was 13 and the standard board size was a 10 × 30 inch, seven-ply, maple-laminated deck. At the height of his success in the mid eighties, the Gator spiral deck sold for $50; Gator received $2 from each sale. At their peak, sales would reach 7,000 decks per month—a cool $14,000 in Gator's pocket. This, coupled with high comp winnings and income from Gator's name being lent to various Vision sport products, meant a nice salary for the San Diego teenager. Gator was in every magazine—Gator stories, spreads and full-page ads. It's perhaps safe to say Gator had become a skaters' hero. He had been part of the growth of 'vert' or ramp skating (primarily characterised by a down-up-down motion with tricks interspersed at various ends of the ramp, edge of the pool, spillway or stormwater drain).

'That was a great time for us ... we were making a ton of cash, we flew all over the world, there were skating groupies at every stop. It was pretty cool to see a bunch of guys from San Diego County at the centre of this huge thing. No doubt we were stoked.'[1] The pop star lifestyle. Skate a few comps while the money keeps rollin' in. Gator met a girl in Arizona, Brandi. They bought a house together. Gator was at the height of his popularity.

By the late eighties, vert ramp skating was being overthrown by a newer form of skating: street skating. The obstacles existed in the urban environment—kerbs, garbage cans and stairways. It was characterised by encounters with police and the sounds of boards smacking against the pavement. It was considered more dangerous, more exciting, more anti-establishment. Other vert skaters, like Tony Hawk, adapted. Gator feared fading into skating history and not being able to skate any more.

October 1989 marks the beginning of what may be considered the spiral down. After a competition in West Germany, Gator and the other skaters partied into the night, which in itself was not unusual. Gator leapt out of a second-storey window, convinced he could fly, and landed on a wrought-iron fence, impaling his neck, face and hand. He survived, was patched up in Germany and returned to San Diego, but spent months in plastic surgery trying to save his modelling career. He emerged from a San Diego hospital looking like Gator, but acting and speaking differently. 'Jesus Christ spoke to me through the accident, I was a blind dude and now I can see.'[2] Gator began preaching to skaters and surfers—to anyone who would listen. His boards were now covered with religious symbols. His girlfriend Brandi wasn't into it and left to live with her father and mother. Gator was devastated. Despite his conversion, he would call Brandi's parents and leave abusive messages; he couldn't deal with the fact that Brandi had moved on.

On 20 March 1991, Gator had lunch with Brandi's best friend, Jessica. They ate, went to Gator's house, watched videos and drank wine. As Jessica got up to leave, Gator went to his car and returned, sneaking up on Jessica from behind. With a metal steering lock, Gator hit Jessica several times over the head, handcuffed her, took her upstairs and raped her. Still conscious, he suffocated her, turned over his bloody mattress, put Jessica, the clothes, the handcuffs and the steering lock in a bag, drove to a desolate place known as

Shell Canyon, and buried Jessica's body in a shallow grave. Police questioned Gator a few weeks later about the disappearance — there was no evidence to be found. There were missing persons posters plastered all over San Diego County.

On 10 April, Gator walked into the local police station and confessed to the murder that, at the time, the police were not even aware of. The story became the lead news article — *Hard Copy* did a re-enactment. In the skating community, stickers either read 'Free Mark Anthony' or 'Skateboarding is Not a Crime — Murder Is'.

On 6 March 1992, Gator was sentenced to six years' jail for rape and 25 years to life for the murder; he is serving time in San Diego County jail and is eligible for parole in 2010.

It's funny how, on reflection, there seems to be a parallel between Gator's life and the downward spiral vortex design of the popular Gator deck. That, like Gator's life, the design spins and spirals out of control. There are more anecdotes: Gator was apparently in the INXS clip 'Devil Inside'. When I got the call telling me this, I was on the train. After hanging up, the woman sitting beside me passed over a small book, no larger than a business card. Protected by a small plastic sleeve, I could see the cover was gold. She had handed me the booklet face down; I turned it over and saw the words 'PURE GOLD', printed in bold white type. I removed the booklet from its protective casing, opened to the first page and read… *Words from the Holy Scriptures*. I smiled thinking of the Gator story, turned to the woman beside me and said thank you.

Gator was also in the Tom Petty clip, 'Free Fallin'. Incidentally, it was here where he met his girlfriend Brandi. In *Jerry Maguire*, Tom Cruise sings the same song to the radio in celebration of his newfound success and freedom; the strange thing is that, in relation to the Gator story and the vortex graphic, the song title and lyrics take on a different meaning, more like a loss of control, downwards — a panicked state.

With the benefit of hindsight, the skateboard graphics and the bit parts played by Gator in the (now) aptly named clips, perhaps even his small role in *Gleaming the Cube*, are pointers — to what eventually happens in his life. On their own, they exist just as stories, occurrences that mean nothing they were just what Gator was doing at the time.

The Gator anecdote perhaps parallels the story of images. Some have no meaning, while others are deliberately embedded with meaning. Some images have a history that occasionally you are aware of, like art that references itself, or like advertising that references art. Sometimes the stories of the different images overlap and cross over; other times they never meet.

In *Magnolia*, the audience has the benefit of seeing all sides of the stories from the comfort of a cinema chair.

Full Power Trip was released in 1990, there is not a lot of vertical ramp footage. Gator and some other skaters are causing havoc in a supermarket. The camera is held by Gator, in his other hand a toy aeroplane soars through the supermarket, the shelves like the sides of a canyon. The toy plane spins several times and crashes into washing detergent bottles.

* * *

26.04.01

Dear Blair,

I feel a bit nervous describing my own work but you seem to be persistent enough (I hoped you would forget) so that makes me not worry so much. Here goes.

Last year and the year before I painted and drew several versions of a blue and red triangle motif taken directly from a design from disposable wax paper drink cups. These pictures resembled to me a bit like amateur supremacist pictures, small and domestic in size and with wobbly edges. One of these I eventually presented as part of *Abstract Setting* (2000). Which contrasted alongside one of these paintings two hand drawn drink cups I had also made against a hand painted wood veneer backdrop made from an MDF panel. A high modernist motif (an easy target) assimilated with a popular sign. Conflating high and low was less of an interest than trying to realise how the frame informs and contains our experience. Two different containers a painting and drink cups with the same sign on their exterior both constructed, the support fabricated too.

My curiosity initially led me to produce this work. I wanted to see what it looked like. also thought if I showed it, it might link some of my earlier work with my recent painting shows. Even though now I feel this is way too much like cosmetic surgery not art and I kind of think its way too literal, people still trod allover the work at the opening. Twice! In Melbourne and in Sydney. This always surprises me because ‘everyday life’ has been such a familiar sign for ages in fact institutionalised. Anyway I’m probably underestimating the intentions here. Maybe the discovery isn’t so easy. For some its stretched out, suspended and over looked. Like when those guys from h. at DAMPs G street opening put the computer back together again. They covered up and kept working as though nothing had happened despite you and Martin so obviously had dropped it off the desk and every body was visibly upset. We still need to hunt down and open up the structure these relations of reality. Small gestures like your gouaches, which convey not weight but render the surfaces palpable. Contact, instant and immediate relationships with the work.

Keep real baby
James Lynch

* * *

Yahoo! Mail
Date: Mon, 02 Apr 2001 10:54:50 +1000
Subject: For Blair
From: skoop@████.com | **Block Address** | **Add to Address**
To: amandamarburg@████.com

Hi Blair,

In the early nineties I got a new credit card in the mail. I opened the envelope and inside was not just a new card but a new look. The old card had a printed border on it, running around the edge of the card and the card details were inset from that, in much the same way that a picture frame is put around all sorts of things, ads especially.

Anyway, that border or frame was gone in the new card. The patterned surface ran all the way to the edge of the card, to the edge of the plastic. A small detail, but it fundamentally changed the way I regarded the card. Previously I had thought of it as merely a stiff support for the graphic design and information on it. The card was hidden by the 'picture' on it. After all, that's what a border does; heralds what is within it, as special, designated.

But without it, the card was somehow just a plastic object; its function a matter of plastic, something of exact proportions that gets precisely slotted and run along its magnetic stripe. It presented no representational or pictorial dimension at all (now, you seem to get more of this again, a hologram minimum).

I haven't bothered to inquire, but I'm sure it relates to some fundamental shift in banking or finance practices. I know my own attitude to the card as an object changed, and probably at some other level, my attitude to money too; as if some pretend, illusory thing had been replaced with something real, a curious correlate to the extrapolation of monetary value from materials to graphics to pure information, and no doubt it's all imbricated with my own maturing and burgeoning anxiety about super.

Cheers,
Stuart

Co-authored by Stuart Koop and James Lynch, first published as a catalogue essay for *Products that Educate, Inspire and Delight*, Blair Trethowan, Gertrude Contemporary Art Spaces, May 2001.

Notes

1 Tony Hawk in Cory Johnson, 'Free Fallin', in *The Village Voice* (8 December 1992).

2 Mark 'Gator' Anthony Rogowski in Johnson, 'Free Fallin'.

2004

Thanks Mum: Paintings by Anne Kearney

Blair asks his Mum to do paintings for him.

There are a few things that come to mind.

The first is Pedro Almodovar's film *All About My Mother.* In it, Esteban asks his mother, Manuela, if she would prostitute herself to protect him. It's hypothetical, of course, but Manuela replies that she has already done almost everything a mother could do for him. The movie unfolds and Esteban dies. The hypothesis: perhaps Manuela did do all that she could… except tell Esteban about his father, who happens to be a HIV-positive transsexual prostitute.

Secondly, a longer, personal anecdote. My mother always hated art, primarily because she thought it was about being a good drawer and she wasn't. She thought that she couldn't understand it—that it all went above her head. I suppose I kind of used to think the same thing.

Anyway, my mother dies, and you have to clean a whole lot of shit up. Which is hard 'cause you find things that you didn't know about. And then you have to throw stuff out, which is harder because you've already lost the person they belong to and throwing their possessions out is like negating their existence—even when you know, theoretically, this isn't true—that you have memory and all of that.

Anyway, I kept this book that mum made.

She was sick for a long time and watched a lot of TV. The lounge room was filled with videocassettes of the programs she couldn't watch when broadcast because the show was on at 4:30 in the morning or at the same time as another. I went around there on Sundays—we watched telly and instead of talking about the obvious, we got on to doing crosswords together. We both liked trivia and quizzes and, probably more so, we liked competing against each other (not that this was ever said). Like the obsessive–compulsive she was, crosswords came to occupy much of her time.

The book has a turquoise hard cover and is spiral-bound

in black, the pages within are lined… basically, it's your standard A5 notebook that you can buy from Officeworks for approximately four bucks. Each page in the book is filled with information: a page per TV show, about 60 in all. By no means is it a comprehensive guide to pop culture, but it's reasonably extensive.

For each TV show, the director, producer, shooting location and casts are listed. There is information crossed out and written over, various pens have been used and her handwriting changes in size—each page was added to on a regular basis. I suppose the book is like a self-compiled dictionary or encyclopedia. The order was determined as the information came to hand, not alphabetically or chronologically. Mum had no access to the Internet or reference books. Basically the book sat beside her on the couch and as she read something, watched something or found the answers to last week's crossword, the information was systematically entered into the book. Occasionally, when I was visiting, she would quiz me and my answers would be added. But the book, which had kind of started off as ours, became hers. The pages are well worn and although it seems there is no apparent order, she knew where all the answers were when needed. Inside the book there are also snippets—handwritten notes, clippings from magazines and newspapers with information underlined—waiting to be catalogued.

I had always wanted to do a series of drawings based on this book—like an illustrated dictionary, I guess—not as a kind of tribute but more like my addition to the information, the part I could've played, I suppose—kind of daggy and sentimental, I know. I haven't, though, and doubt that I will. The value in this book, I suppose, is that it is like evidence of an experience. As personal as this is, somehow it transgresses just my own experience. I've shown it to other people (much to her dislike—she used to say to me, already embarrassed, 'I bet you show this to your friends'), and they see a value in it as well. Maybe this is because they know me—but I like thinking that it's not.

It's funny, the book is filled with errors, it's not perfect, it doesn't tell you things you really need to know or information you can't find out somewhere else, so in a way it's kind of wrong and in the greater scheme of things it's not a significant artwork. But it feels like one.

Just before she died, I was trying to do a crossword with her to keep her awake, I was asking her the questions and filling in the blanks, she looked up at me from her dozy state and said, 'Are you stupid or something?'.

Maybe I am.

Thirdly, the book *Vernon God Little* by Peter Findlay under his nickname of D.B.H. Pierre. Vernon has been wrongly accused of a high school massacre. His mother, Doris, refuses to mention or acknowledge that he has been arrested for murder at any point during the novel. The hypothesis: families don't talk about shit. It's all somehow encoded in Doris's persistent questioning: 'Are you eating well? What did you have for dinner?'

Lastly, Sophia Coppola's *Lost in Translation*. Bob Harris whispers something into Charlotte's ear. In the tender gesture, the audience is given the power to make up and interpret the meaning of the unheard words.

'Surrounded by voices of dubious authority we should practice being blind and silent.' Elizabeth Newman quoted it from Eden Liddelow and sent it to Geoff, Geoff sent it to Blair, and then Blair sent it to me. Perhaps Lizzie is right. But… perhaps… not too blind and not too silent.

Maybe.

First published as a catalogue essay for *Thanks Mum: Paintings by Anne Kearney*, Blair Trethowan, Uplands Gallery, March 2004.

2005

Still Lives

Whilst squeezing Sculpey into the shape of a face, I said, 'hello little fella; you are beautiful' (Sculpey—rude in colour, squeezable looking, squishy and bulbous—a great modeling material). I made the face quickly—within a minute. She had scrunched up eyes, a honky nose and a sad little mouth. Her expression touched me, more than any person's image I have seen in quite a while. I photographed her and painted her portrait floating above one of Cel's patterned singlets. The singlet, whilst empty of any body, gives her something to cover her timid soul with—if she had a body.
— Rob McHaffie

At nightfall, to move the vessel out of port, the blow, as Hieronymus Bosch teaches, up the anus of the elect, into the cavity of the sail spun by the ships spider. Hail the Ship of Fools. If it didn't exist, we would have all died of boredom long ago.

Look here, preambler, just who do you think you are? Are you perhaps unaware that to speak of Arcimboldo nowadays you have to be the guardian of the new order, gloomy and psychiatrist, as they say today?[1]

I went to New York for the first time in 1996. I don't remember sleeping much… I don't remember eating much… I didn't need to. For some reason I remember making faces of Norbert Loeffler in salt on tables at bars with Spiros and Masato. I don't know why we made them… it's not like we were bored. It's hard to make pictures about what you haven't already seen. I guess that's why all those realistic futuristic movies like *Blade Runner*, *RoboCop* and even *Star Wars* look kinda corny now—*Blade Runner* was set in a dark, neon-lit, densely populated Los Angeles, but based on the city of Osaka—already there, already existing. Ridley Scott made a wormhole, bent time and transported one world into another. I guess that's what we do—create wormholes to make sense of the world. Semi-imaginary friends, semi-imaginary scenarios, semi-imaginary fears. Forever making faces in the clouds with the other fools on the ship.

First published as a catalogue essay for *Still Lives*, Rob McHaffie, Spacement Gallery, June 2005.

Note

1 Maurice Rheims, 'The Prince of Pictorial Whims', in *The Archimboldo Effect* (Milan: Thames and Hudson, 1987), 111.

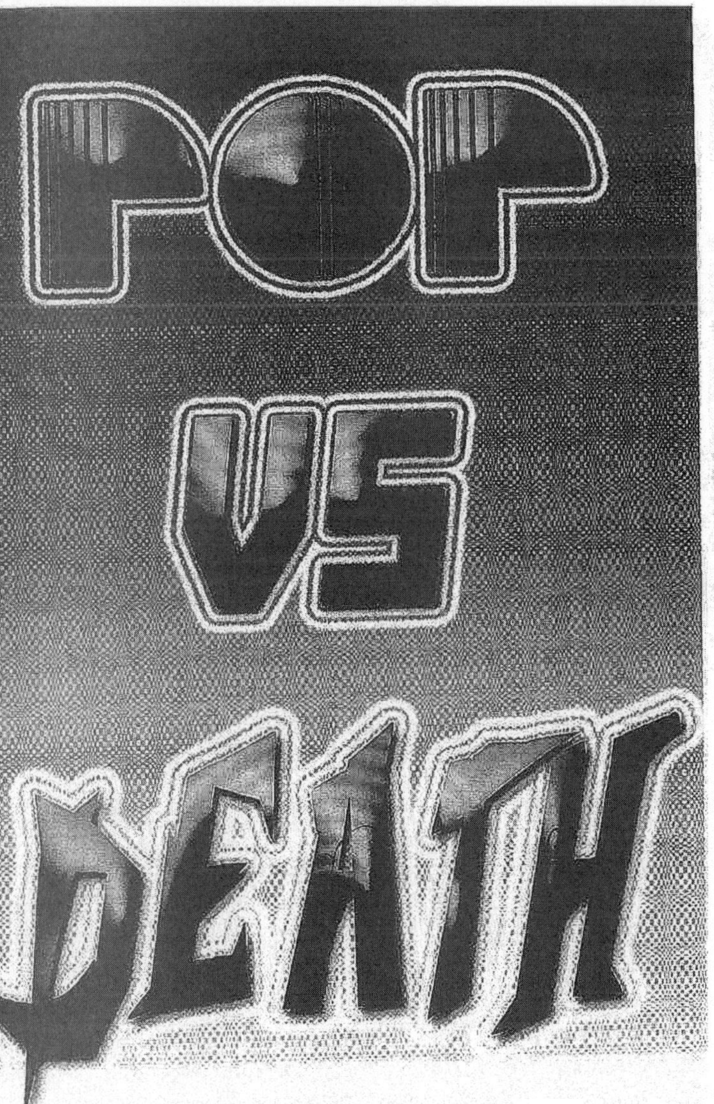
POP
VS
DEATH

AFTER TAKING THE BRASHS BAG HOME THAT I FOUND ON THE TRAIN – I DISCOVERED IT CONTAINED A NAPALM DEATH CD – EARACHE, A PURPLE, PLASTIC CYLINDRICAL OBJECT & A SMALL METAL TUBE AND CONE. I WAS 13, DIDNT HAVE A CD PLAYER AND SO THE CD SAT ON MY SHELF BETWEEN 'KYLIE' AND 'OPEN UP AND SAY AH', MY PARENTS FOUND THE BAG AND THOUGHT I WAS A POT HEAD – BRASHS WENT BROKE.

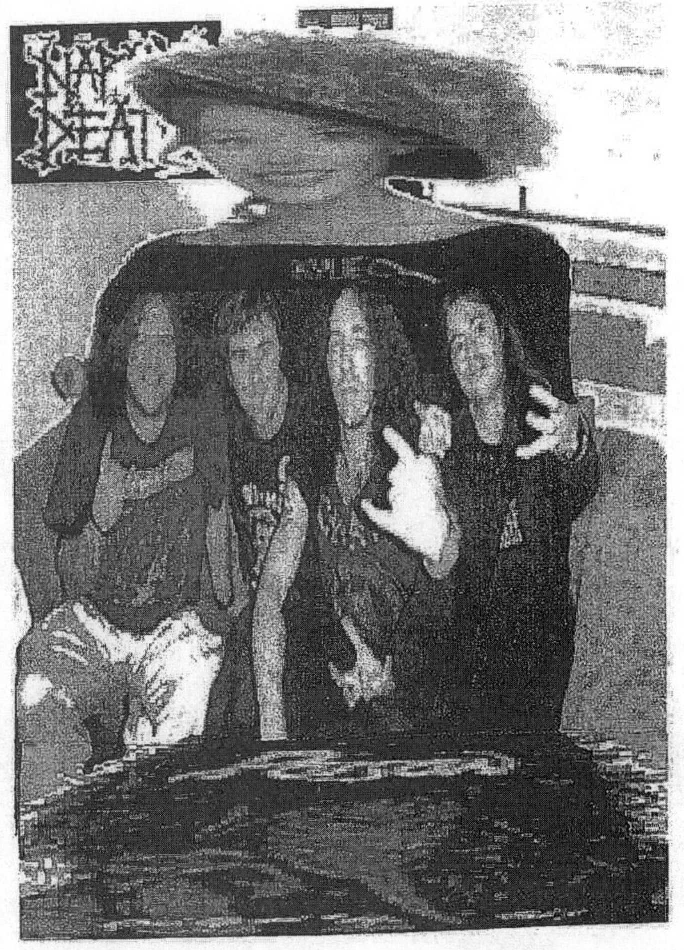

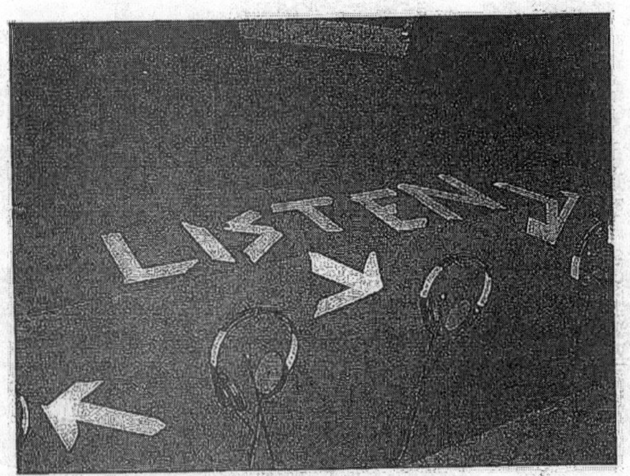
LISTEN

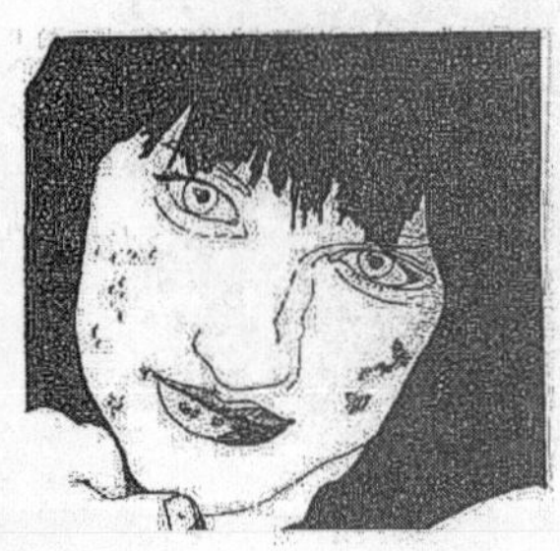

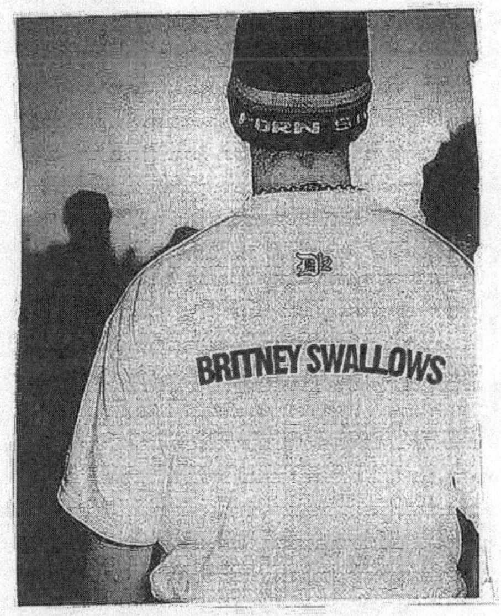
BRITNEY SWALLOWS

666. THE NUMBER OF

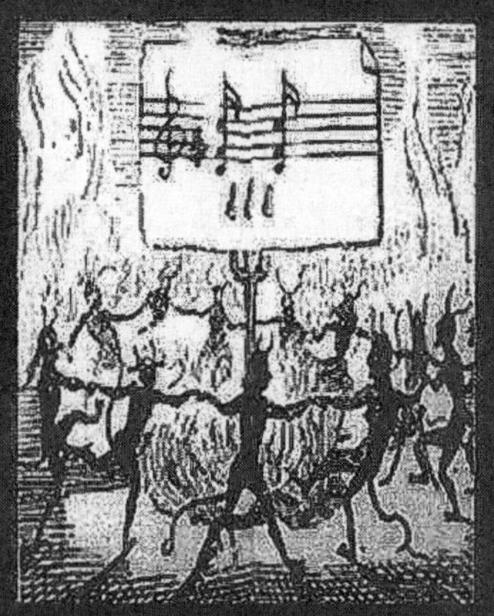

RONALD REAGAN'S HOUSE

True Melbourne No-Metal

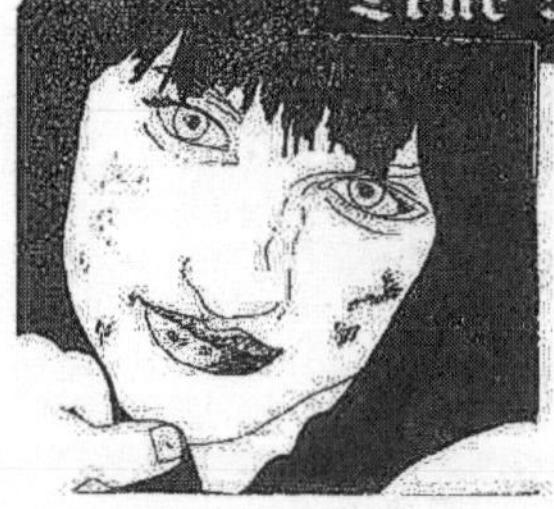

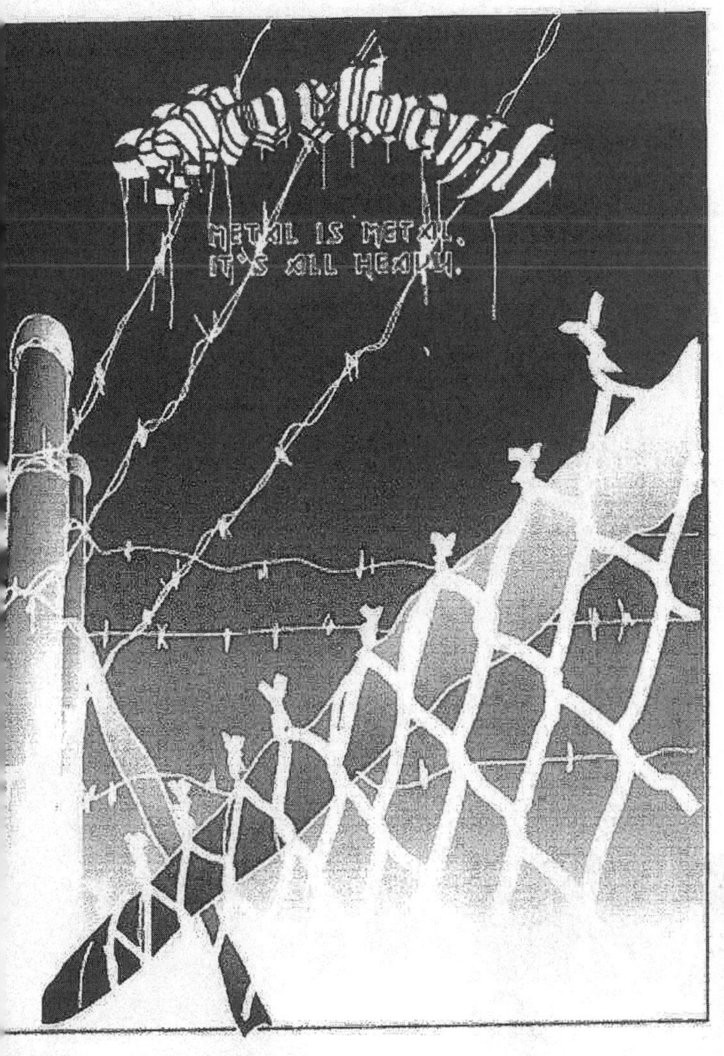
METAL IS METAL.
IT'S ALL HEAVY.

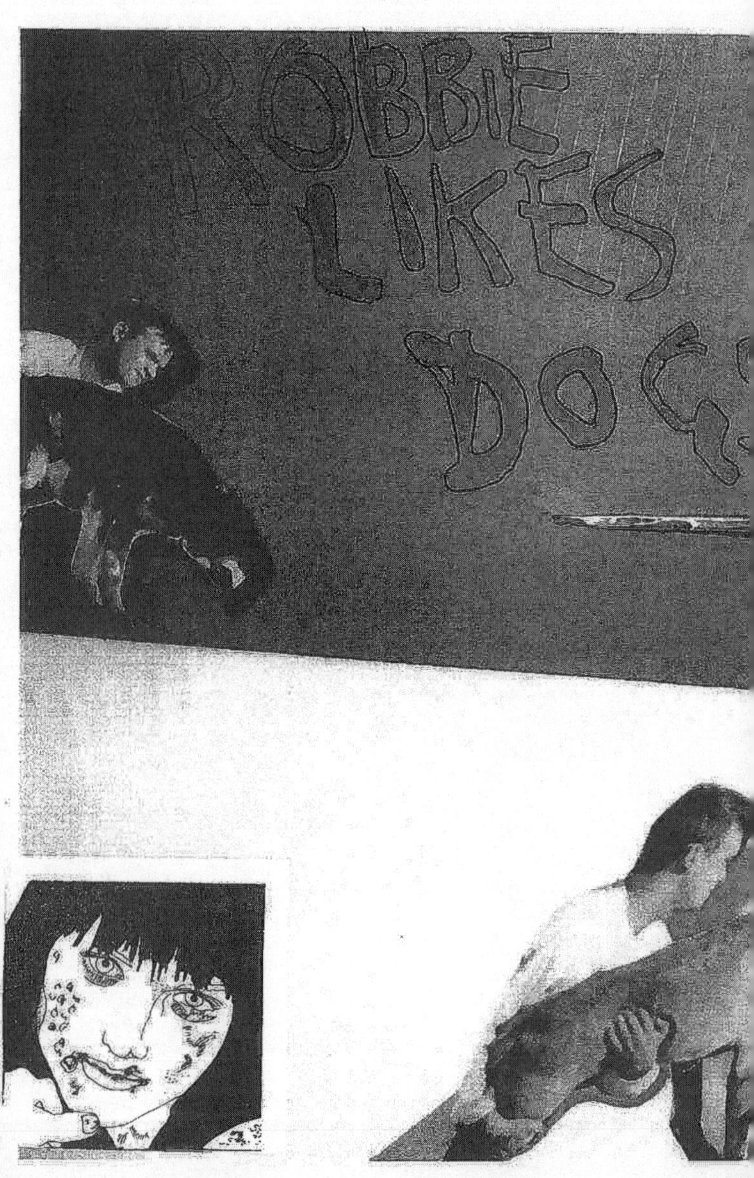
ROBBIE
LIKES

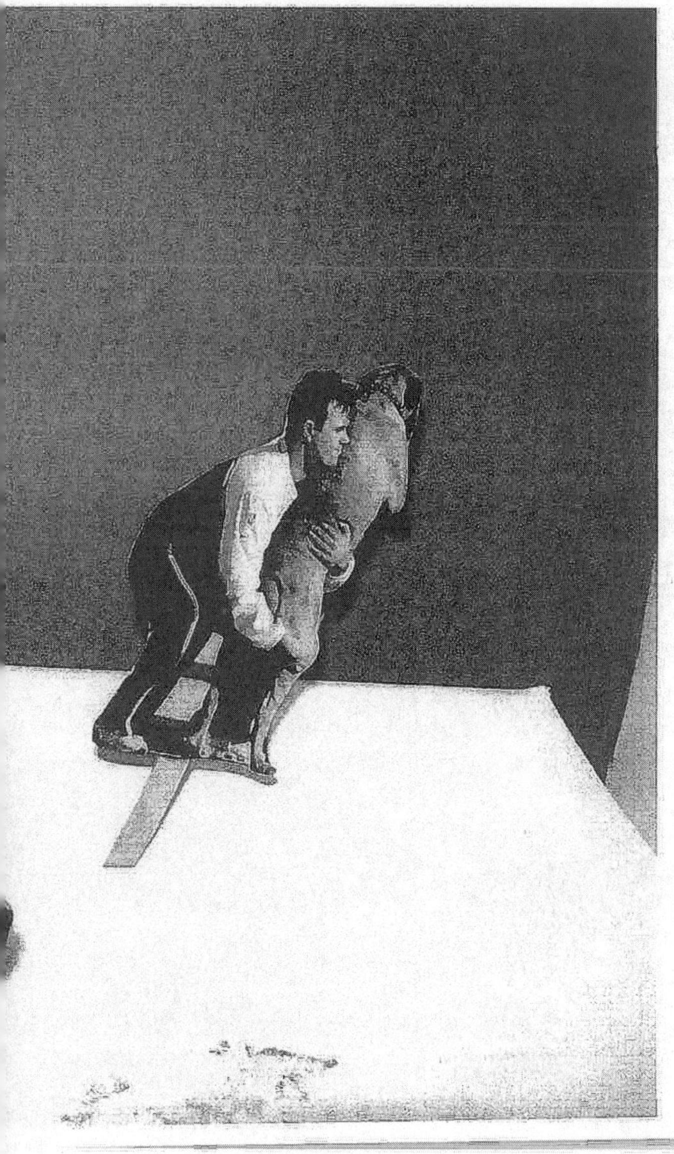

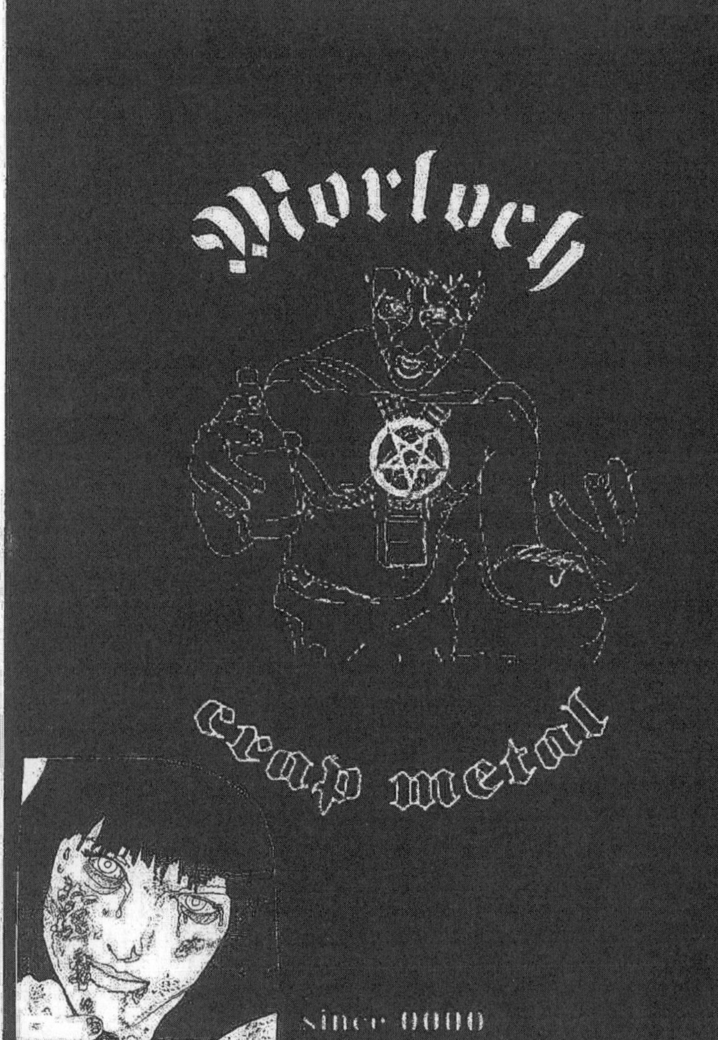
crap metal
since 0000

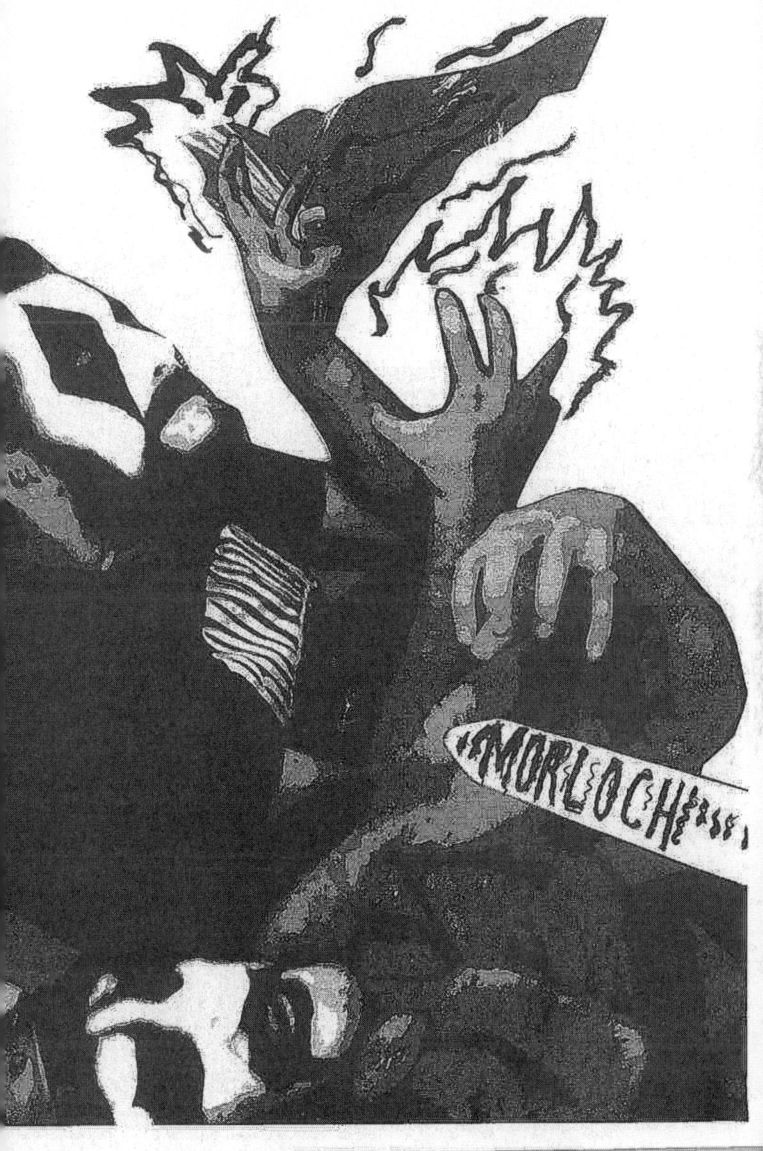
MORLOCH

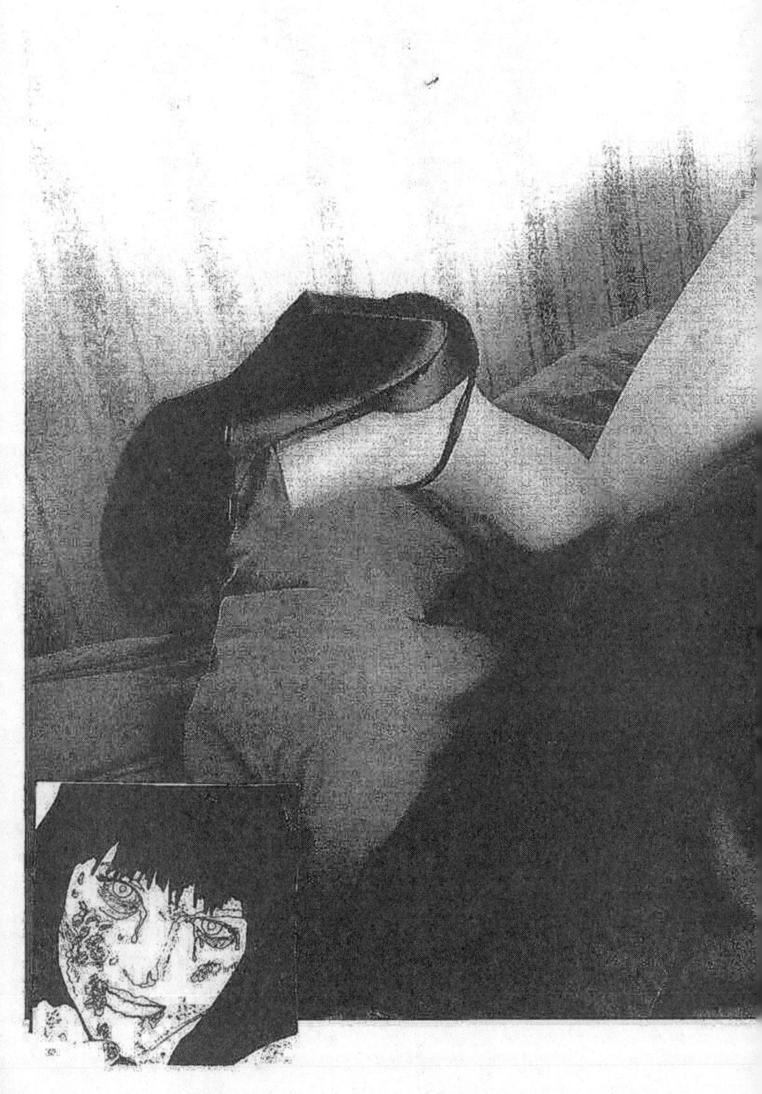

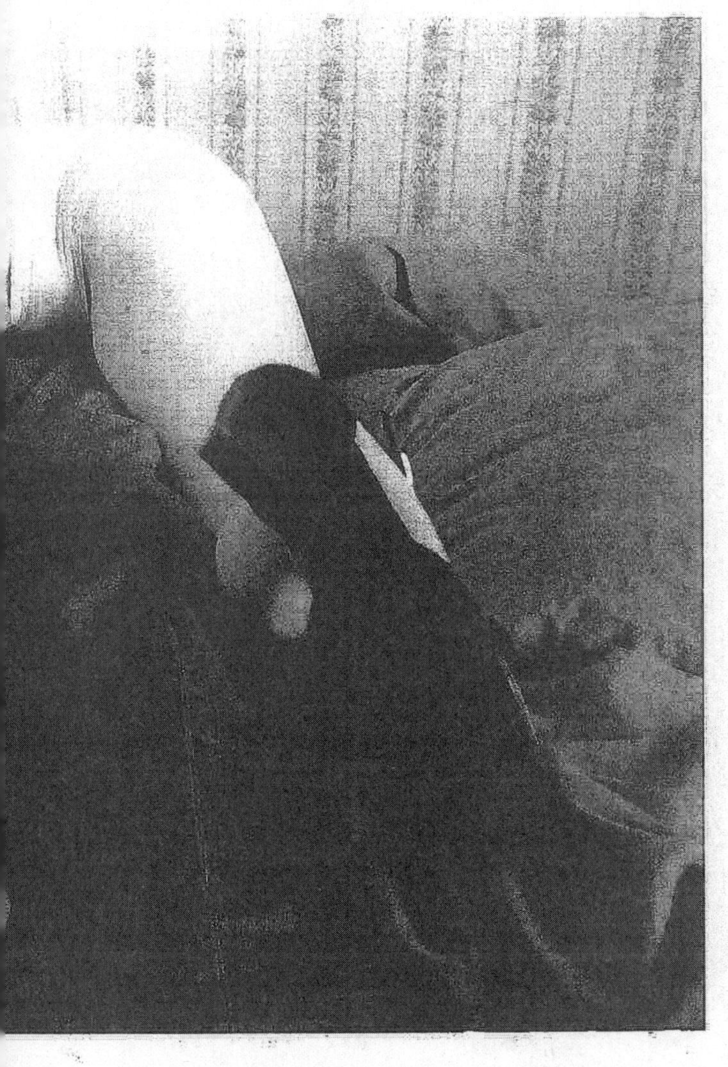

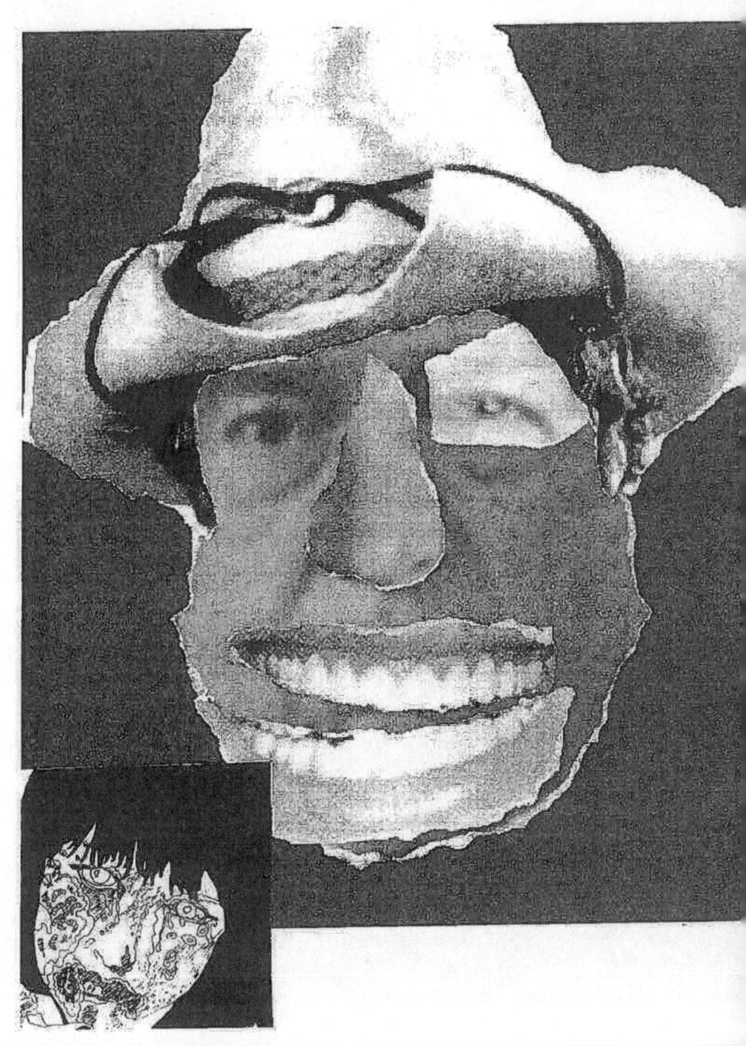

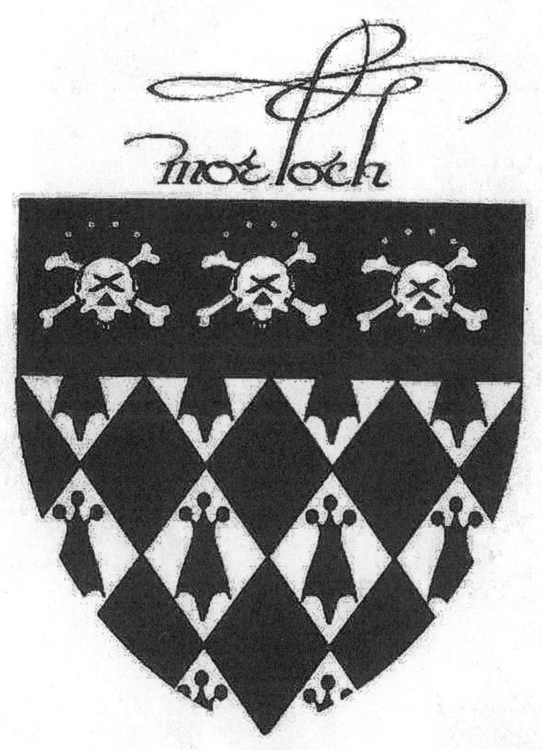
motloch

2005

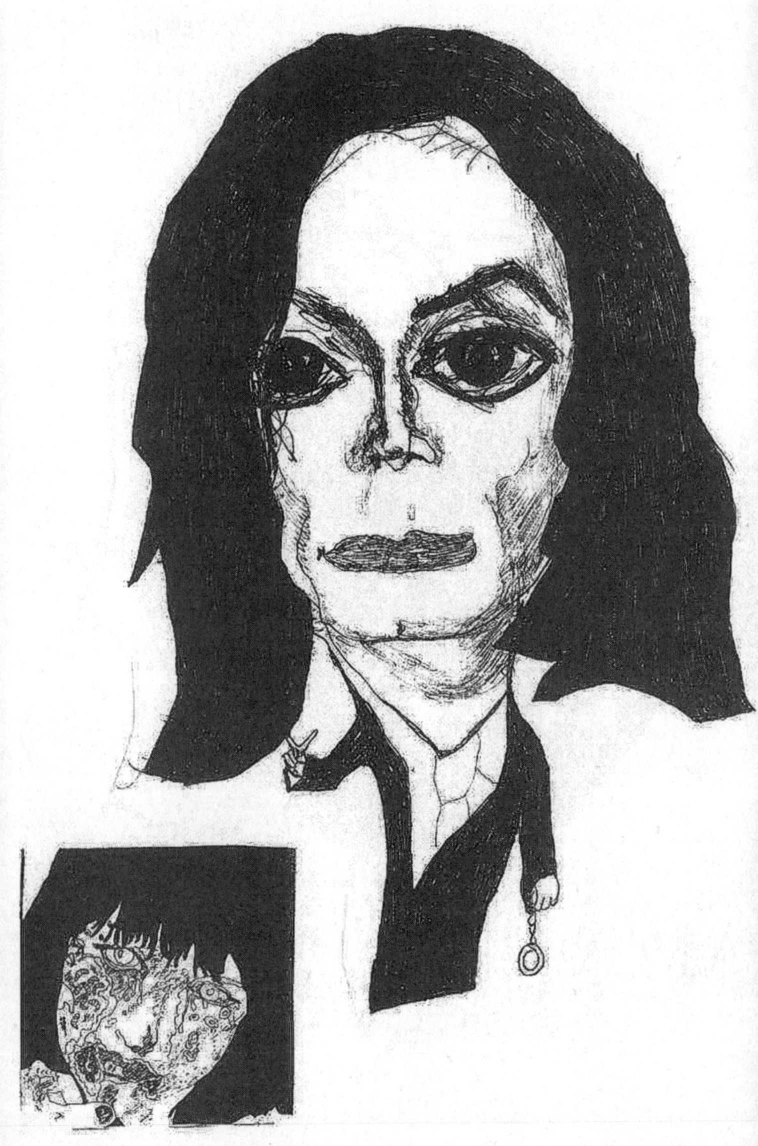

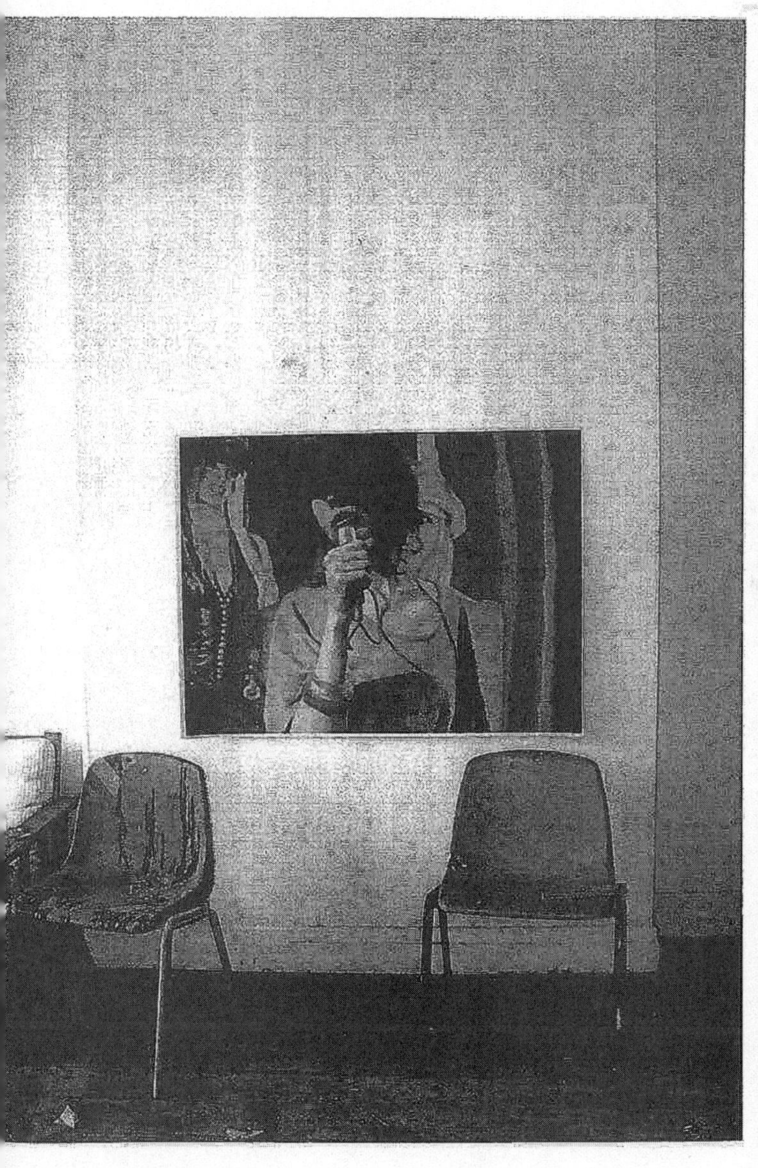

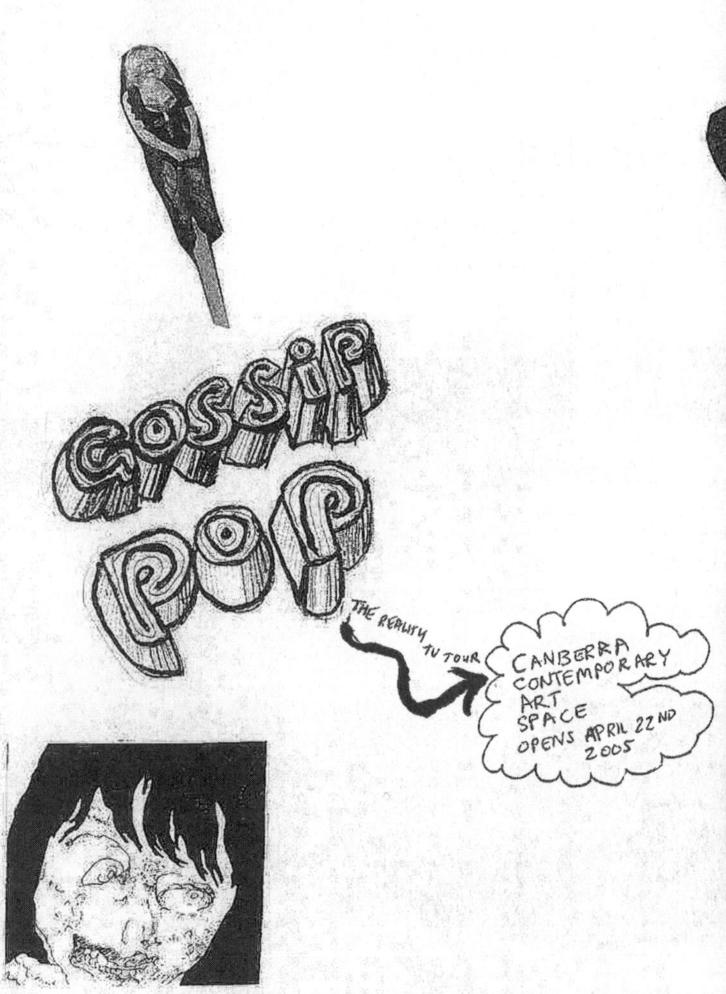
GOSSIP POP
THE REALITY TV TOUR
CANBERRA CONTEMPORARY ART SPACE
OPENS APRIL 22ND 2005

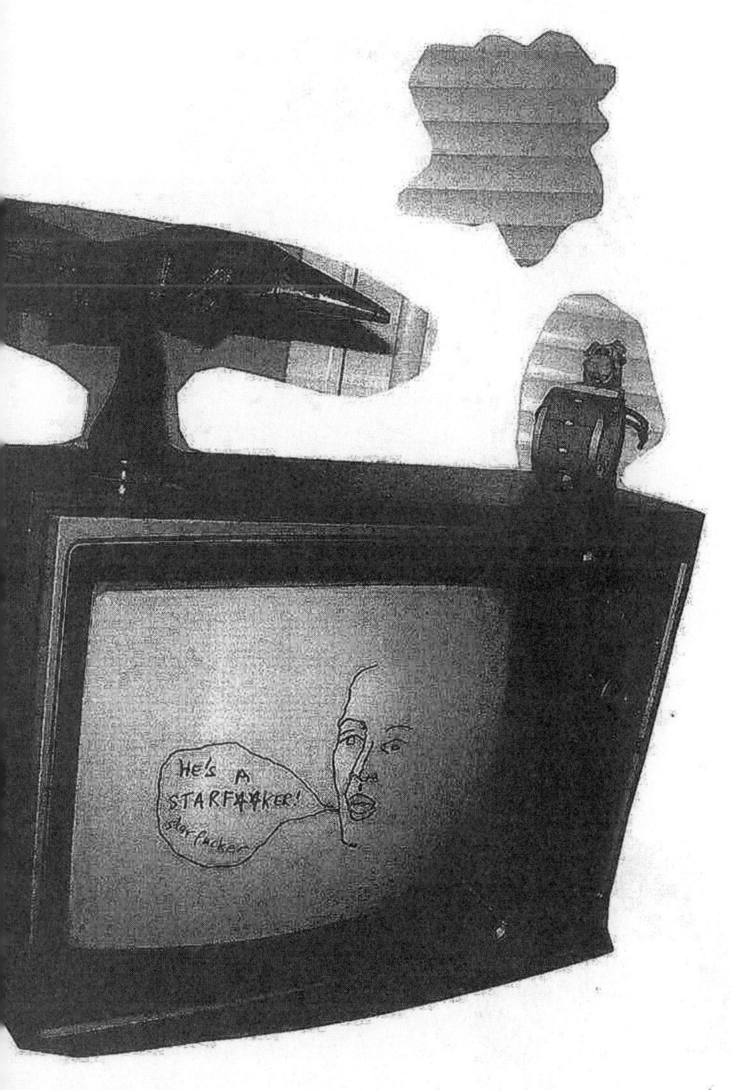
He's A
STARF**KER!
starfucker

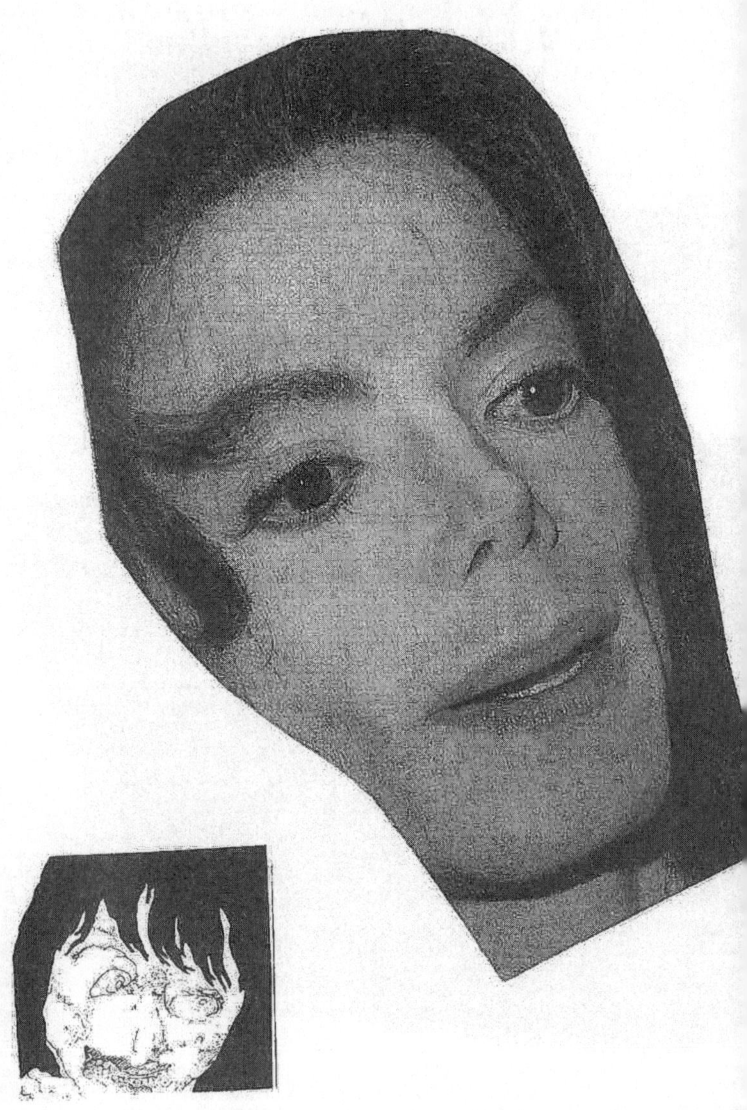

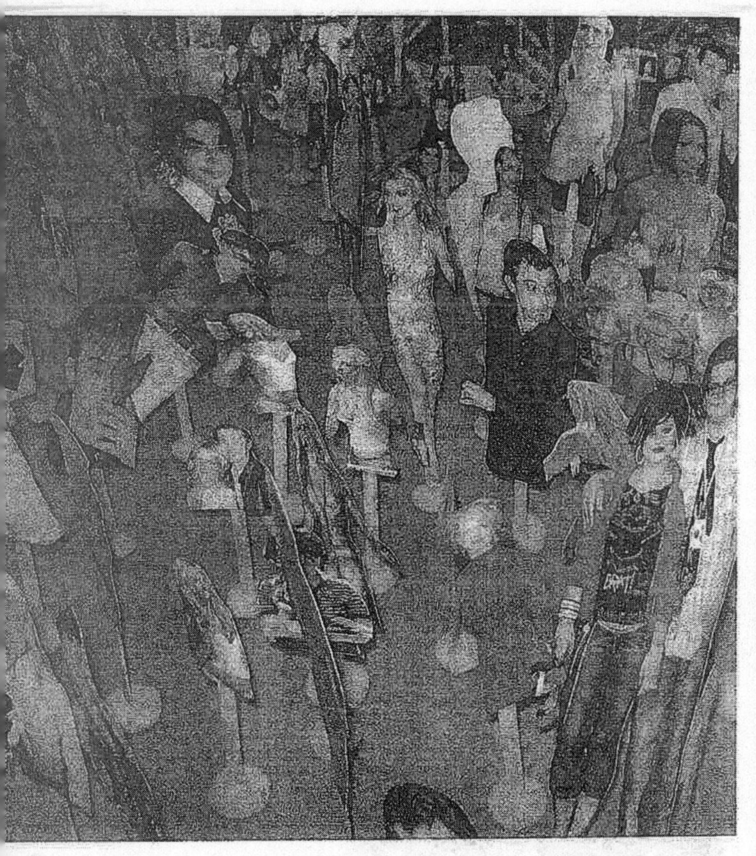

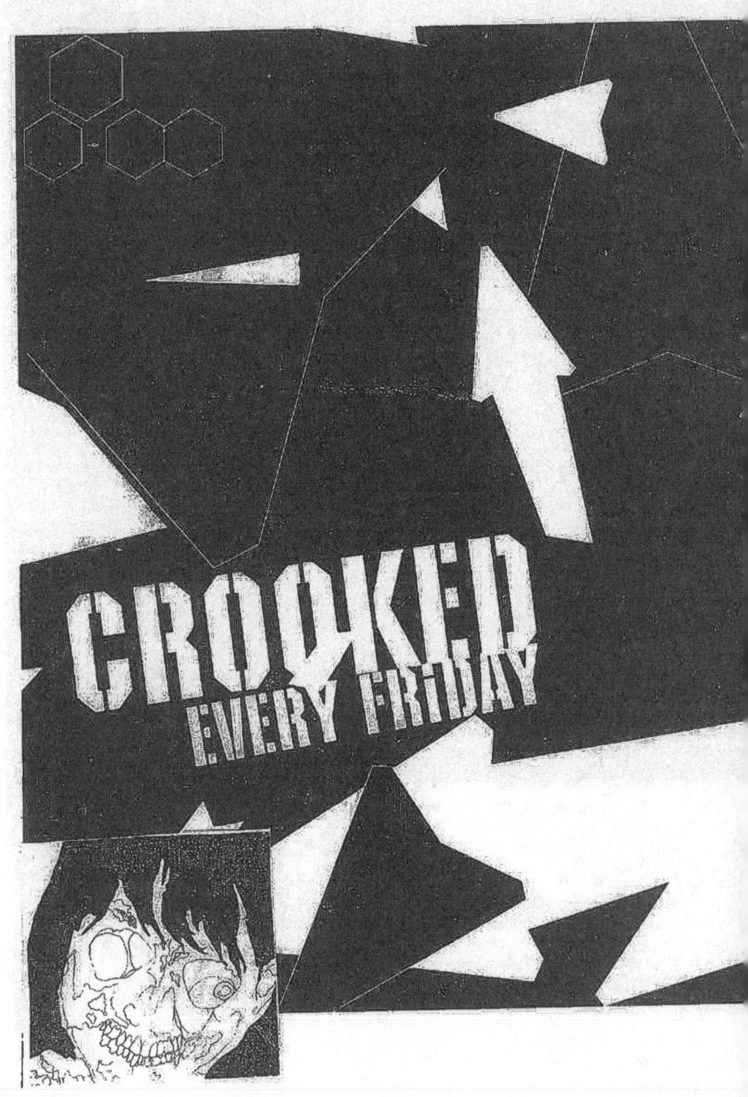
CROOKED
EVERY FRIDAY

STRICTLY
HIP HOP,
ROOTS
DRUM & BASS
THE CROFT
INSTITUTE
21-25
CROFT ALLEY
96714329
EXHIB
-ITION ST
RUSSELL
ST
LT BOW
-RKE
PAYNES PL
CROFT
AL

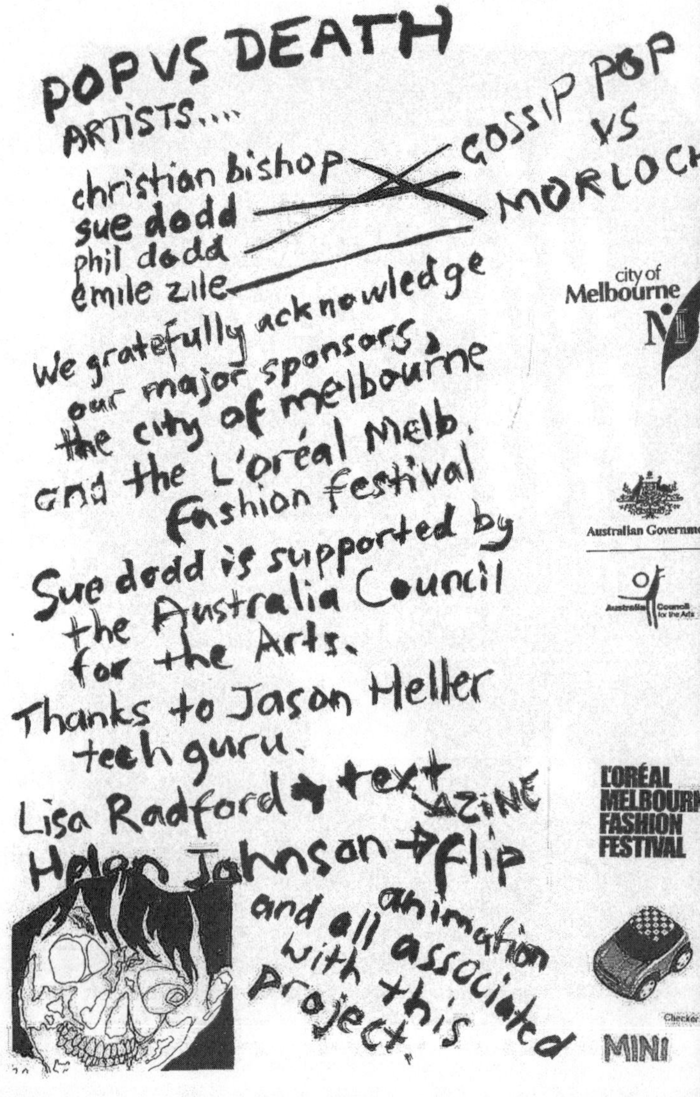
POP VS DEATH
ARTISTS....
christian bishop
sue dodd
phil dodd
emile zile
GOSSIP POP VS MORLOCK
We gratefully acknowledge our major sponsors, the city of melbourne and the L'oréal Melb. Fashion festival
Sue dodd is supported by the Australia Council for the Arts.
Thanks to Jason Heller tech guru.
Lisa Radford & text ZiNE
Helen Johnson & flip animation
and all associated with this project.
city of Melbourne
Australian Governme
Australia Council for the Arts
L'ORÉAL MELBOURN FASHION FESTIVAL
Checker
MINI

Punch drunk lovers

When there are so many voices trying to be heard and fighting for existence, it's interesting what fragments of experience, moments of glory and flights of fancy make the cut. Which fragments get replayed, resaid and circulated—who gets to tell the story and who is granted the get out of jail free card. Maybe it has something to do with desire and love, maybe it has to do with power and control—maybe they are one and the same. Lane Cormick makes stuff about things that he *kind of* knows about; he takes sound bites and images from movies and songs he might not be able to remember the name of. The specifics are there for you to find, but they're not force-fed to you like in a television commercial or like the banter of some smart-arse-know-it-all. Lane replays for us fragments of stereotypes that are dislocated from their original source and become the truth that might be worth remembering.

A friend said to me recently, 'Lisa, I read architecture magazines like you read a novel, like they're fiction'. The problem is, I read fiction like it's fact.

Lane, although assuming different roles, and often enacting various male stereotypes (the pimp, the cowboy, the rock star), doesn't hide behind a mask, disguised and askew. He is himself every time, trying out the roles, seeing if they fit, wearing them for a while and letting them fall apart when they don't, when he can't be bothered any more, and once he has had his turn. Like in *Being John Malkovich*, you try the portal and you'll probably get spat out at the New Jersey Turnpike, but you still want to go for another ride.

Peter Sellers once said: 'I'm a chameleon'.

Cunningham Antoinette Mahgninnuc is almost a nonsense title—Cunningham is a brand name that means nothing—it could be the name on a basketball singlet, like Jordan or Nike—maybe they mean nothing now—what's in a name? Antoinette—the name of the champagne flutes, we think it might be because the glasses were modeled on a goddess with the same name. No one is sure. Miscommunication, ill communication—The Tower of Babel?

I always hated these questions, and it wasn't until recently that I realised it was because the question is mere rhetoric. 'What do you want to be when you grow up?', 'What are you going to be when you grow up?', 'What do you want to do when you leave school?'. Once you do—finish school, that is—the question evolves and takes on a new twist 'What do you do?', as if the means by which you live defines you, and an answer as simple as, 'I'm an electrician' will then justify all your actions and delineate, for the interviewer, your past, present and future. As a kid, I had a different answer every week. This was not a deflecting strategy or a hand pass—I was only 12 or so. The facts of the matter were I just didn't know—accountant (boring, but I was good at maths), cartographer (apparent factual picture making), lawyer (favourite TV show: *LA Law*), psychologist (read a few novels about one—they seemed kinda cool)... all the time secretly wanting to be an actress! It was kinda like if I said it out loud, the desire would disappear, or it would mean nothing. If I made up my mind, would it mean I couldn't be one of the other things?

Lane picks a role or an image, maybe two or three, and then fucks with them a little. He takes what he wants from them, combines a few together, spits it out, tries it back on, and then finds something else. When you watch a film, you put yourself in the shoes of the different characters, draw comparisons with your own personal experience and then return it to the narrative of the film—you do it—even if it's only so you have something to talk about later.

Perfection obsessed—work hard, beef up your body—perpetually self-improving—self-help, self-conscious, self-obsessed—Tyler Durden gets punch drunk love while practicing some anger management.

The stacking of the champagne glasses is an all too familiar reference, perhaps from that movie you saw, you know, the one you can't remember the name of. The building of a champagne tower by a man in a pair of overalls—where is the tuxedo? He's a little bald and doesn't quite look like he should be doing it... the process of stacking is slow and almost painful to watch. Error deliberately inserted into the equation. The tower is going to fall, but when?

Mr Universe 1979 is Governor of California—the state that has the sixth largest debt in the world?

'Why the champagne glasses?', I asked Lane.

'Decadence', he replied, 'its all about decadence.... It's kind of like pulling the tablecloth from under the table setting.'

Do-it-yourself-kit construction then deconstruction—self made man, imperfection then self-annihilation—because the allen key doesn't always work, and because it's kind of fun to pull things apart. Jumping on the sandcastle is as fun as building it—especially when your older brother made it?

In the 1980 film *Being There*, Chancie says to Eve the first time he takes a ride in a car: 'this is just like television, except you can see much further'.

Some friends of mine call us the '70Ks'. Born in the '70s, we grew up in the decadent '80s. TV: a new drama every 30 minutes, a new character every hour, our heroes randomly picked from movies, cartoons, *Countdown* and MTV. We did our homework while watching TV, with the sound down and the radio on. We grew up skeptical of what was forced down our throats, perhaps realising early on that identity, rather than being constructed is perhaps instead continually negotiated, dependant on contexts, situations and an exchange among individuals in society. We don't want to purchase one identity anymore—but we will purchase the bits we want to, the fragments that are almost insignificant.

Lane seems to be preoccupied with personas and the items, objects, and languages that are associated with the Male Idol'. His snippets of generic male representations are re-framed in constructed environments and stage sets, with wanna be' glamour props and supporting actors. Suburban Cowboys in the local pub who ride on the back of a mechanical bull. A nervous blues singer belts out a tune in the set of a blackened room that is blazoned with huge flouro pink letters that read: BLUES MAMMA. In a sparse, beige, makeshift hotel room, a Dutch gigolo rambles about his surroundings to his uninterested female friend. In Cormick's videos, an array of white male stereotypes are stripped from their macho' roots and given new scripts, sets and props, so that, rather than remaining as objects for 'glorification', his characters become mundane, imperfect and self-conscious reflections of idols. Stuck in a 'what am I gonna be when I grow up' phase, Cormick seems to be searching for some sort of authentic identity, questioning whether it is trapped within the simplified generalisations we are so often presented with. Apparently identities are pre-programmed and formulated by the mass media and a culture obsessed with fame and stardom.

Someone once said to me 'Lane's an expressionist'—I suppose that's funny, 'cause it's kinda true. Lane takes that story you saw on television, read in the newspaper, heard from your friend. The story you can't quite remember, the one where you wished it was you, the one you where you were glad it wasn't you. He takes it and presents it, just as it is—as a story.

You didn't win *Australian Idol*, you didn't get *the girl*, you didn't make a million dollars and you won't be famous. You're just another John Doe—go make a video.

Previously unpublished, 2005.

Love 2005

Herman Day has been described as a maverick economist. In an interview I once read, he talks about a future in which economics moves away from being a self-centred academic discipline interested only in working out the consequences of its own assumptions. The approach is somewhat anthropological — to leave behind the idea of the isolated individual and move towards that of the person in community, not only with others but with the ecosystem. In my mind, art has always been somewhat anthropological in nature: the borrowing of cultural artifacts, experiences and motifs, rearranged to form another artifact — an analysis or reflection upon the culture within which the artist lives. If we can forget that, unlike economics, art has already sought to be cross-disciplinary and inclusive, perhaps we can be left with an idea that people collect stuff and arrange it to remember and to find out. Some of us put the little Buddha we bought in the Philippines on the mantle next to a photograph of our friend wearing a Jesus and Mary Chain T-shirt and every now and then we look at it and consider the humour. If we thought about it more, we might consider how going to the Philippines made us consider Christianity and Buddhism existing side by side — one informing the other — and how, in turn, the little installation on the mantlepiece was a reminder of this.

Blair Trethowan's exhibition *Love 2005* is somewhat like this. The six simple assemblages are like an investigation into what the artist knows and doesn't. How they intersect, and what they then become. The six works are more a remnant of an experience or a thought than solid, resolved, conceptual pieces. *The Queens Teeth*, a folded five-dollar note stuck carefully in the centre of a piece of Stringybark sourced from Injalak Art Centre in the Northern Territory. Looking closely, the way the fiver is folded creates an almost Rorschachian ink blot version of fellatio — Queen Elizabeth's pearl necklace becomes the teeth and her neck becomes a penis. A slip of the tongue, a party trick, a reference to republicanism or to the failure of colonisation. Or is it a gesture of humility — one that admits it doesn't know about the land on it which it lives—but wants to? One that signals an ally—dissent within the ranks of the privileged white man. *Fuck in the back seat* reiterates it. An old 1980s Road Transport Authority sticker that once said 'Buckle up in the back seat' is changed in an adolescent fit of rebellion, of humour. The fluorescent letters are vandalised, a black texta erasing the 'kle', and altering the 'B'. Subversion for the fun of it, because it's cool—or a juvenile act as precursor to a life of looking for something else.

Sweat skulls and love hearts is more personal in its approach. A series of photographs, stuck to the Stringybark, depict Trethowan's chest. In some, the sweat marks on his T-shirt make a shadowy skull, other times a jagged heart. They are a coincidence—or are they an experience with meaning? *Mutlu/Zeppelin* is a little more perplexing. It needs further thought, and perhaps a glance at the accompanying fanzine-style catalogue—an excellent text by Danae Mossman. It's a photograph of Trethowan's mother's house. Perhaps the kitchen. A pelican mural on the wall has been 'slashed' by a graphic from a Led Zeppelin cover—he did it because he had heard that Mutlu Çerkez had done the same when a teenager. Re-creating an art world urban myth—if you are out of the art world loop, you need the catalogue to explain it… but that's part of the point, I suspect. Engaging in more than one system of representation, another version of reality. In the case of *Love 2005*, thread strung from nails hammered into the bark forms the words 'Love 2005' in a 1970s, kitsch, *Home Beautiful*, folk-art style. This version learned from a book coincidentally published in the year Trethowan was conceived. Is that not the way we know 'love'? As Michael Hardt and Antonio Negri reflect, the modern concept of Love is almost exclusively limited to the bourgeois couple and the confines of the nuclear family. Love has become a strictly private affair.[1] With Trethowan, I suspect his version has more in common with what Negri and Hardt propose—that, as in the past, love is a political act.

Nick Cave had not been to the outback until asked by John Hillcoat to write the script for *The Proposition*—it enabled him to consider and research a history that until then he had not known. Trethowan's task is similar: a reflection on what he knows, his experiences, combined with an enquiry into what he doesn't. Germaine Greer, in *Whitefella Jump Up*, asks us to go back to the point where we went wrong and think about it. I guess Trethowan is taking us there with him, exploring culture as a learned experience—and one that *can be* learned. It's not too late, Ms Greer. Perhaps you are right: a hundred years from now, Australian children will be amazed to learn that Australia once considered itself a 'British' country. They will understand what a hunter-gatherer republic might be, and how the interests of hunter-gatherer minorities have to be reflected in international policy because they are fundamental to any notion of sustainable development—socially and ecologically.[2]

Sedition takes many forms. In this case, it takes the form of wanting to know more about what those in power would prefer we knew less about. The artwork in Trethowan's exhibition is not only in the bark pieces, it is in the accompanying text, in the exchanges between Trethowan and those in Arnhem Land, in one audience member explaining the Queen, fellatio, and colonisation to her Japanese friend, then in the friend's recognition of the joke and the failure of Australia to acknowledge wrongs of the past. Thomas McEvilley once wrote that the act of self-recognition can grow into an expanded self creation. We perhaps haven't yet had time to stop and think about Scott Parkin's deportation, the proposed new Industrial Relations laws or the recently implemented Terrorism Act—fear continues to blind our attempts at self-recognition. *Love 2005*, in its simple form, returned to us, for a brief time, that space to think.... It's true, we will not save what we do not love.

Previously unpublished, written as a review of *Love 2005*, Blair Trethowan, Studio 12, Gertrude Contemporary Art Spaces, 2 September – 1 October 2005.

Notes

1 Michael Hardt and Antonio Negri, *Multitude: War and Democracy in the Age of Empire* (London: Penguin, 2004), 351.

2 The 'hunter gatherer' label used to describe pre-colonial Aboriginal Australians has been recently challenged as understating the role of agricultural production in pre-colonial Australia. See: Bruce Pascoe, *Dark Emu* (Broome: Magabala Books, 2014).

2006

Getting Used to Yourself

I've been addicted to Wikipedia for a couple of months. Doing something like 'Googlewhacking', I type in random words and see what comes up and then follow, like an information junkie, the chain reaction and stream of facts. I'm particularly fond of the disambiguation pages, where lists of information relating to a particular word scroll before you, each piece of information linked, usually to another page, with further information. Some information isn't verified as being correct — it's there anyway, for you to peruse and use as you require, I guess. When I typed in 'degradation', I found this, it's about electronics, but seemed kind of poignant:

> *Graceful degradation* is the property that enables a system to continue operating properly in the event of the failure of some of its components.

Which led me to this…

> *Elegant degradation* is a term used in engineering to describe what occurs to machines that are subject to constant, repetitive stress. Externally, such a machine maintains the same appearance to the user, appearing to function properly. Internally, the machine slowly weakens over time. Eventually, unable to withstand the stress, it breaks down. Compared to graceful degradation, the operational quality does not decrease at all, but the breakdown may be just as sudden.

I was thinking about Kati's drawings and Miranda July popped into my head. I was thinking about her movie *Me and You and Everyone We Know* and how it acted as a gesture or representation of self and community. Miranda has spoken about the film in a kind of cathartic way — that the issues dealt with in the movie are pretty dark and that they came from a dark place within her. She talked about trying not to judge that dark part of herself, and I guess she did that by creating a whimsical comedy about people and their awkward moments, living with life and death, love and loneliness. Its awkwardness comes across as a form of honesty rather than truth, an acknowledgement that sometimes it's hard. In his review in *The Observer*, Sanjiv Bhattacharya writes that although July's characters are filled with doubt and appear fragile and bumbling, they remain undefeated and their efforts to reach out are brave, heart-wrenching and often hilarious. I guess it's a movie about getting used to yourself, by yourself and with others.

My feeling is that people don't really have any rituals of coming together now — other than during a disaster.

Miranda said that too.

Kati got other people to draw on her beautiful, delicate, photo-booth self-portraits — a kind of communal self-identikit.

There is an all-girl band from the '60s called The Shaggs. They were sisters and they recorded an album called *Philosophy of the World*. Self-taught musicians, the music reminds me of people clapping out of time to a pop song; a tinny-sounding, out-of-sync, slow rock. The lead singer deeply whines, her voice breaking and cracking with the odd, out-of-time tempo. The lyrics to the title track go something like:

The rich people want, what the poor people got
And the poor people want what the rich people got,
The fat people want, what the skinny people got
And the skinny people want what the fat people got.

It's obvious and kind of naïve but at the same time self-conscious and honest.

When I walked the streets of Milan, there was graffiti, up to arm's reach, on almost every wall. I felt like I was in a place that thought and questioned — the obvious blurring of public space with private desires seemed to bring home some kind of obvious truth — a personal ownership of a shared space.

At first, I thought of Kati's drawings like electronics and machines. I thought the drawings, perhaps like humans, were subject to a kind of elegant and graceful degradation. Her drawings are less fatalistic though.

When you carefully and meticulously copy an image,

you find every little discrepancy. You look closely at something you would otherwise not. When Kati was drawing herself over and over again and then getting others to draw over her, I wonder if she was getting used to herself and then letting someone redefine her. There is the risk of making a bumbling mess or an awkward arrangement of marks; of fragility disappearing; of a sentimental, heartfelt dedication or an act of vandalism. But, in the end, perhaps it's the most honest way of 'painting a portrait'—not just of Kati but of the rituals of identity and community.

First published as a catalogue essay for *There has got to be another way*, Kati Rule, TCB art inc., Melbourne, July 2006.

Tomorrow is Another Today

When I lived in Japan there was a museum exhibition in Tokyo of mythic animals called *youkai*. The *youkai* in Japan serve the purpose of telling moral and ethical tales—they embody a way of living, courtesies and cultural niceties. In Japan these symbolic mythic monsters could take a real form—for example, a taxidermied fish and small possum sewn together—as proof to children that these creatures did exist and should be heeded. *Youkai*, I guess, are like a form of control, an enforcement of a particular hegemony. But on the other hand perhaps they could be reminders, prompts or cue cards: a *genius seculi* of a certain time.

The sleep of reason breeds monsters, and Sharon Goodwin's exhibition at Uplands, *Tomorrow is Another Today*, is perhaps like Goya and the *youkai*: a pertinent reminder of our own apathy. The cyclic nature of the title perhaps pessimistically alludes to our present political climate and our own stumblings through life. Change can sometimes move slowly. The nightmare of the small but engulfing installation is a metaphor for our internal conflicts, or a vision of the rumblings in our bellies coming to the surface. Contrary to what we are led to believe, the personal and the political often intersect. Goodwin's exhibition, in its gothic beauty, succinct and poignant, rendered in the graphic starkness of black and white but eerily illuminated with a hellish red light, points us to an underground where many are one, and one is at war with everyone.

First published on *SPEECH* web magazine, for *Tomorrow is Another Today*, Sharon Goodwin, Uplands Gallery, May–June 2006.

2007

Thinks she can't, thinks she can

So, I've been thinking about Meg's exhibition… the idea of difference seems to linger.

Meg thinks she can't draw.[1] So she decides she will. She then decides that she will ask her friends to nominate what it is she might draw — however ridiculous, however sentimental, however personal.

An email is sent out. Meg's friends then trust her to represent their idea, she will draw whatever picture they propose to her.

A gesture for change. An acknowledgment of what she can't do becomes an understanding between many people of what she will attempt to do. A desire to learn something.

When I lived in Japan, I indulged in a sento every week. Bathing with the other women, they often commented on how my legs were longer, my nose pointier, my skin pinker. The differences were an acknowledgement of where we were, and became a point for understanding, and then the beginnings of further conversations.

Meg is out of her comfort zone. Naked. Exposing her inadequacies through the realisation of drawing what she thinks she can't. Revealing a part of herself through the gesture of representing another's idea of a drawing.

Naked. I think of Gabriele di Matteo's suite of over 140 paintings. Titled 'History Stripped Bare' (1999–), the paintings depict famous scenes from history: JFK's assassination; The Beatles playing on the rooftop; Stalin and Hitler. Rendered quite crudely, in oil on canvas, by a hired commercial painter, the images are somewhat accurate except that those depicted are naked. A reference to painting itself, to history and heroism, iconography and the media — the paintings are funny and critical; an image (or images) of the inadequacies of representation.

Meg begins with an inadequacy and starts a conversation. A little game of risk. Meg trusts our understanding of difference and encourages our ability to engage in an exchange that she has begun.

First published as a catalogue essay for *Drawing*, Meg Hale, TCB art inc., Melbourne, October 2007.

Notes

1 From a conversation with the artist, sometime in March 2007.

Relentless Optimism

ZIPPER

A scene appears that is at once grotesque and alluring—a siren calls you in, deeper… deeper. You drink in the sight with voyeuristic intensity. It unsettles, delights and makes you laugh, but there is a collision that can never coalesce. Like a weird dream that revisits you in fragments throughout the day—you search and try to recall the entire dream, but never really understand the visceral weight welling up. Seeking—never to reclaim and connect the wires that trigger a spark of familiarity, inextricably foreign. Ghastly and beautiful… horribly sublime.

Carny / `ka:ni/ n. *N. Amer. slang.* A carnival; a person who works at a carnival. (Shorter Oxford English Dictionary)

Watching

A trickle at first… then more… especially the kids, with their homemade Esky—blue-handled Tupperware filled with ice. Cans bob in a watery ice bath, the 'cheapest so we can get well and truly fucked up' alcohol peeps through the side of the clear plastic. Take another swig… swagger past the girls frozen in singlets and short shorts, being careful to cast just a brief glance. An atavistic dance of courtship and lust unfolds… hormones bouncing around like dodgem cars.

ZI ^
PP ^
ER ^

The ZIPPER clunks another rotation, thrusting into the dark, red yellow white neon flicks… on off on off on off.
A distorted Ferris wheel.
Twisting, upside down, arsy-versy.

The ticket booth attendant with a voice like a dirt road… a young girl asks, 'whadda yous want?' She peers out from her booth, eyes level to my crotch so I'm forced to squat or deeply bend to make eye contact. I watch as this odd height discrepancy forces people to perform this shrinking dance over and over. Are they just trying to be polite or does the fourteen-year-old girl's genital focus unsettle and topple even the most rigid suit into submission?

Little kids choo choo train through a mock Western scene and run rings around a polystyrene cactus blooming in gaffer tape petals, limp, toppled on the dirt. The foundations of a hastily erected teepee clutch at torn canvas… flapping. AstroTurf, dumped, discarded and rotting back into the earth and a rubbish heap that's punctuated by Coke cans and wisps of clit-pink fairy floss.

The families flock to the dodgem cars to act out their aggression. Even the dourest face leaves smiling. A speed-freak carny picks out the little kids and rams them when the parents aren't looking.
Whack…
Whack…

Erin Cresswell, January 2007.

Dress Sexy

A throbbing drumbeat punctuates the room and its unrecognisable rhythm provides an ominous sign. Authoritative masculinity resonates. The prohibited violence of caged men. Tribes, leaders, saints, martyrs, scoundrels, libertines, heroes, villains, saviours, knights and liberators. I don't know if the story the community has been telling itself makes sense; the characters are unrecognisable. The drumming starts again. There is a fit of rage and a meeting of those who might want to change, recompense, redeem, indemnify. Out of the confusion, a man appears. In a wheelchair he sits, and with a wry smile he professes:

> In Em City, the guards are with us 24 hours a day. There's no privacy. Everybody sees what everybody's doing. Eyes everywhere. McManus's eyes. See, in

> Em City, retribution gives way to redemption. Timmy boy believes he can save every one of us, from each other, from ourselves, from the system that dumped us in here. Only thing he don't get is, you gotta want to be saved.[1]

Emerald City. When you click your heels you go home… but you are home, there is no other. Reality is a spectacle of spit, semen and bloodletting; of symbolic and ritual suicide; of harsh concrete enclosures, played out fantasies of fatalities, desire and risk; of cruel and unusual punishments; of conniving patience and premeditated vexation. Accidents? Are there any? Psychological and excessive force, and games. No delineation between the two. There is no source of absolute power, it's a muddled mess of restrictive behaviours, objectified fear and disease-riddled emotions….

As a swastika is slowly, methodically and ritualistically being branded on your ass, the man in the wheelchair recites:

> They call this the penal system, but it's really the penis system. It's about how big, it's about how long, it's about how hard.[2]

Is the history of masculinity in labour and war? Is it? The man in the wheelchair comes into view and, while a silent movie is projected behind him, he spins around in a glass cage. With a sardonic smile and a hushed, sincere voice he informs us…

> We got these routines that are supposed to give our lives order and meaning. But I'm here to testify that I'm less afraid of getting shanked in my back than the routine. Cause the routine, man, the routine'll kill you.[3]

If taboo is about the sociology of danger for the protection of individuals, is fear a taboo hidden in the appearance of an equal' distribution of power? No water, solitary confinement, no car, no electricity, no oil, and no drugs—legal or otherwise. Invisible enemies and unknown allies.

You fall in love but you can't say it. If and when you do, you are led down a corridor by your rapist and your lover, accompanied by a guard. Snap… thud… crack. Your lover breaks your arms. Snap… thud… crack. Your rapist breaks your legs while your lover holds you down. You're on the floor of a basketball court wincing in pain while the guard looks on… No. No. Not a guardian angel.

There isn't one.

I'll have nightmares again… but I'll fall asleep because Bill is singing…

Dress sexy at my funeral my good wife,
For the first time in your life,
Also tell them about how I gave to charity,
And tried to love my fellow man as best I could,
But most of all don't forget about the time on the beach,
With fireworks above us.[4]

Co-authored by Erin Cresswell, first published as a catalogue essay for *Relentless Optimism*, Rob McHaffie, curated by Mark Feary, Carlton Club, Melbourne, January 2007.

Notes

1 Tom Fontana, 'The Routine', *Oz*, season 1, episode 1 (New York: Home Box Office, 1997), television broadcast.
2 ibid.
3 ibid.
4 Smog, 'Dress Sexy at My Funeral', from *Dongs of Sevotion*, Domino Recording Company, 2000.

I'm not there, like a ghost ship in a storm

I sat in Irene Hanenbergh's studio scrolling through images she had collected of wolves, cats, fantasy posters, spectral and astrological matter, churches, mosques, bridges, Caspar David Friedrich paintings and castles.[1] Her collection, devoid of hierarchy, sourced images from high art, pop culture, advertising and bad taste. Coming to an image of a small forest not overly dense with trees, I asked Irene to stop.

Spindly barren branches growing out of slender trunks of the most vivid green.

Had I seen this forest before? Was there a Faraway Tree here? If you walked through the forest would you eventually walk into a wardrobe lined with fur coats? Was this the forest of the Trumpalar, where you could climb into a tree and in fact dissolve into the trunk, disappearing into a cavernous tangle of tunnels that transported you back in time to the land of the Trumpalar? Patricia Bernard's *Riddle of the Trumpalar* (1981) was a novel I read when I was eight or nine years old. Instead of in a forest, the story was set in a park and the tree that you could 'enter' was a Moreton Bay Fig. As a 9-year-old growing up in Coburg, a Moreton Bay Fig could have been any tree, and parks sometimes seemed like forests.

The vivid green forest was *het Ericase bos*, not far from where Irene had grown up in the Netherlands. We talked about difference of experience and place, and of Irene never really thinking about the greenness of the trees. To her, the forest was a reality, while for me it was an anomaly and a representation of a mythic place. The image, like a portal, had transported my mind somewhere else. Then, quite briefly, Irene mentioned the *hunebedden*…

Hunebedden are megalithic burial tombs dating from the Neolithic period, some 6000 years ago. Of the 55 *hunebedden* that still exist in the Netherlands, 54 are found in the province of Drenthe, the home of *het Ericase bos* and Irene.

Found all over Europe, each tomb consists of a chamber

formed out of upright stones with large flat capstones laid across them to make a roof (picture a kind of enclosed, smaller version of a Stonehenge). This structure was then covered with a mound of earth. One translation refers to them as 'passage graves' probably deriving from the Spanish *tumbas de corridor*, like passages that enable movement through time and space, or portals for the dead.

In 1877, Dutch archaeologist D. Lubach speculated that there were more *hunebedden* than the 54 known in Drenthe. Lubach speculated that at one time, all of Drenthe was covered with *hunebedden*.[2] Following the introduction of Christianity in the late eighth century, the people of Drenthe began to destroy the passage graves that they previously regarded with awe and veneration. Lubach suggests that many of the churches in Drenthe were built with the materials gathered from the destroyed *hunebedden*, noting the similarity of the stone used in churchyard walls, dwelling foundations and marker stones. Is Drenthe itself a large passage grave? A site for many ghosts? Fredric Jameson speaks of 'spectrality making the present waver'.[3] The passage graves of Drenthe destroyed and reused, the ghosts of her dead creating a reality perpetually in flux.

D53 is a *hunebedden* in Havelterberg, Drenthe. In 1945, the occupying German Army ordered that it be dismantled for the construction of an airfield. The demolition took place, and the passage graves for those that existed some 5000 years ago were destroyed. The Dutch authorities dismantled D53 and stored the 50 or so boulders in a six-metre-deep pit covered with earth. In 1949, after the occupying German army was gone, the rebuilding began.[4] With the grave itself displaced and buried, perhaps forcibly repressed, I wondered how long you could hold onto its ghosts? Rebuilt, would the site still speak of identity, of place, and of unknown ancestors? Did Derrida say 'ghosts return of that which history has repressed traces of those who were not allowed to leave a trace'?[5]

Irene's paintings are not based on the *hunebedden* but, like them, they are landscapes alluding to the idea of passages through history and place. Her paintings are not paintings as such, but digital prints on aluminium. They are literally ghost paintings, and are not ghosts the embodiment of that which history has rendered invisible? Invisible painting? Invisible cultures? Wispy strokes of turquoise and white, coaxing and teasing, invite you in. The areas of unprinted aluminium, almost reflective, catch shadows of shape and blur—a wavering present. Unlike the *hunebedden*, Irene's portals do not reveal facts, but instead allow space for the existence of myths.

Were not myths originally an account of an event that happened? A way of recounting 'glimpses' of reality that shed light upon what it is to be human? I think of Borges and Calvino and their alternate universes. I think of Guillermo del Toro's fabulist films, *The Devil's Backbone* (2001) and *Pan's Labyrinth* (2006), his ghosts reminders of past wars and oppression. I think of William Blake and Henry Fuseli, their paintings of Shakespearian tales, parables and myths being reflections of the turbulent times in which they lived.

The French philosopher Jacques Rancière talks of good art being about 'a world in search of something'.[6] I imagine stepping through Irene's ghostly portal paintings into a world in search of something that was forgotten or not allowed to speak before. Perhaps it's like referencing 'low art', not to highlight the difference between high and low, not to subvert an 'idea' of hierarchy, but to give the unknown a voice again and let it expose some kind of truth… maybe.

Rancière calls it 'anarchic equality'.[7] I like that phrase.

First published as a catalogue essay for *Freedom Holidays in the Rudolphine*, Irene Hanenbergh, Gertrude Contemporary Art Spaces, Melbourne, April 2007.

Notes

1 The title of this essay is drawn from the lyrics of Jim O'Rourke's song 'Ghost ship in a storm', from Jim O'Rourke, *Eureka*, Drag City, 1999.

2 D. Lubach, 'On the hunebedden, or Cromlechs', *The Journal of the Anthropological Institute of Great Britain and Ireland*, vol. 6 (1877): 158–167.

3 Frederic Jameson, 'Marx's Purloined Letter', *New Left Review*, I/209, January–February 1995, https://newleftreview.org/I/209/fredric-jameson-marx-s-purloined-letter

4 Most of this information was found on 'Dolmens in the Netherlands', a brief English translation of a Dutch website, http://users.bart.nl/~jbmeijer/d53eng.htm

5 Jameson, 'Marx's Purloined Letter'.

6 Bettina Funcke, 'Displaced Struggles: On Rancière and the Art World', *Art Forum* (March 2007): 283.

7 Jaques Rancière in Funcke, 'Displaced Struggles'.

What's the Difference To You?

From: Lisa Radford <lisa█████@optusnet.com.au>
To: Masato Takasaka <██@hotmail.com>
Subject: What's the difference to you.
Date: Sat, 24 Feb 2007 17:14:50 +1100

Hi Masato,

At the moment I'm thinking about the difference between Steve Vai and John Fahey.... What's the difference to you?

In the Tim Bavington essay you were reading, by Dave Hickey, he writes about the difference between a rock palette and a folk palette. I think you've got rock colours, but with a folk-hand touch....

I saw Robert Hunter's exhibition today and thought about the time I met him when I was working at the Adelphi. He left his credit card behind the bar and I ran after him to return it. I asked him to write on a piece of paper saying... 'Dear Lane, white is better than red, love Robert...' (Remember when Lane used to use a lot of red in his work....) Robert looked at me in a perplexed way and said... 'But I like red too'.

And then there's that Record Cover Show curated by John Nixon...[1] it's like the in-between of his EPW[2] and a folk-tale or cultural history of sorts... if you think about it, the collection of pottery at TarraWarra, the record covers and his work are the same—made by the same people, who wanted to make something, because they felt like it, because they could.

I think your drawings are like ad-hoc market stalls and street sellers.... Regardless of how much order is imposed by architecture, humans always seem to subvert it and make use of it how they want.... Maybe that's why you could never figure out the maths to make those buildings. Maybe you're too human?

Your drawings aren't imposing, nor are they grandiose or attempting to pass on some profound knowledge to the worl They're Texta Domestic—little meanderings through time and life.

Sometimes I imagine you as a teenage boy in his room—trying to emulate Steve Vai and making posters for the musi I looked up his website and an image of his Ibanez JEM 2KDNA came up. It was uncanny, the similarity between the design on the guitar and your drawings—except Vai put some of his DNA in the paint... which is funny because it reminds me of conservators who have to try and prove that a painting is a Rembrandt. In 200 years what will Steve Vai's DNA prove? That he sold 300 really expensive guitars?

Michael Haneke is a filmmaker I really like. He makes these beautifully aesthetic films—perfect photography, drawn-out social narratives... But they are incredibly human because of their sentiment... Their ability to question the structures of social orders and the logic of film-making.... I guess it's like the guitar stuff—classical structures subverted by excessive electric guitar....

Maybe your drawings question the logic of picture making. They are like the folk version of *Miami Vice*, the TV show, not the movie. You might listen to Yngwie Malmsteen and Vai, but your drawings are more Sonic Youth... Same indulgent guitar noise, but less like a soundtrack to a soapie.

On that Steve Vai CD someone yells out between the songs—'Shut up! We know you can play!' That's kinda funny.

Remember when you got me to buy a T-shirt for the Sonic Youth gig you didn't go to. So you looked like you went, so you looked like a fan. Your drawings look like you're a fan of modernism, but maybe not a die-hard fan, more like you've got other things on your mind—a fan that wants to know what happens when it's not quite right.

Lisa x

First published as a catalogue essay for *Structural Jam: It's All Lead Guitar When Prog Rock Ruled the Earth*, Masato Takasaka, The Narrows, Melbourne, March 2007.

Notes

1 The 'Record Cover Show', titled *Ronald Clyne: Folkways Records Cover Design, 1951–1981*, was curated by John Nixon and Stephen Bram and showed during March 2007 at The Narrows, where Masato's work would soon be exhibited.

2 'EPW' or 'Experimental Painting Workshop' is a body of work that Nixon began in 1990, which continues to this day.

Never is forever

> The problem for those in power is how to get people to do the dirty work without turning them into monsters.

Sharon Goodwin's graphic depictions of familiar yet strange and ominous forms allude to conflicts, neither real nor entirely imagined, but which present a frightening vision. Sourced from an extensive collection of comics, illustrated mythologies and art history, Goodwin adapts and reconfigures images into new compositions that combine different narratives and genres. In *Never is forever*, a stockpile of skeletons, a knotted host of angels tumbling through space, and a conglomerate of gremlins, griffins and gargoyles, appear entangled in cyclic struggles. Having turned on themselves, hero and foe are one and the same, and any distinction of good versus evil is complicated by the metamorphosis of human and animal forms.

Goodwin's staunch linear renderings in acrylic and gouache refer to the drawings and prints of German artist Albrecht Dürer (1471–1528). His *Apocalypse* of 1498, a set of fifteen woodcuts illustrating the visions of horror and impending doom described in the Book of Revelation, reflected the artist's impression of the complexity of society and the breakdown of religious and political order. Goodwin's fantasies of internal upheaval and collective struggle, which manifest in unimaginable creatures and scenarios, could similarly be seen to embody menacing characteristics of contemporary social and cultural conditions. Her work refigures Dürer's allegories of power, beauty, morality and belief, issues that are as prevalent and contested today. Amidst the meticulous line work and the fusion of fantastical motifs, an underlying turmoil hints at the all-too-real existence of 'dirty work' and monsters.

Originally published as a catalogue essay in: *Never is forever: Sharon Goodwin*, Heide Museum of Modern Art, Melbourne, 2007.

Note

1 Slavoj Žižek, 'The Depraved Heroes of 24 are the Himmlers of Hollywood', *The Guardian*, 10 January 2006, https://www.theguardian.com/media/2006/jan/10/usnews.comment.

2008

Aesthetic nonsense makes commonsense

Sometime late last year, while I was experiencing a little case of self-indulgent introspection, I mentioned to a friend of mine that perhaps I should try writing for other people, other artists, ones I haven't known for a long time. He told me not to be stupid. At first I took offence—wasn't I good enough? When I thought about it, I realised perhaps he knew me better than I realised. What I liked about writing was the conversation. I liked talking about art in the world via experiences. Mine and theirs, and mine in relation to theirs, theirs to mine. I've always had a hard time separating one thing from another. The links between things always seem pertinent and writing is one way of connecting them and also sorting them out. I met Jon when I was studying at TAFE. He was the drawing teacher. He came from the suburbs like the six or so of us who were left in second year. He had the same $3.50 Sonic Youth T-shirt from Forges as four of us, and he seemed to make work that was part of his life and ours. I don't think any of us have the Sonic Youth T-shirts anymore, but we're all still friends.

It was probably about this time that Colleen and I started speculating about playing music instead of being artists. We wanted painting to make us feel like we felt when we listened to records. Maybe it was about the ability of some songs to make you feel like you wrote them, or that you owned them. I remember reading an essay by Laurent Goumarre. He writes about the viewer becoming the subject. I guess most music has this intrinsically—somehow existing outside, alongside and inside your life. So do Jon's paintings.

Music—straight up, a little bit honest, takes a risk at being cheesy, soft, wacky or catchy. Most times a song is aware that it's not the first, or, for that matter, the last—aesthetic nonsense makes commonsense.

$23,000,000 would buy a hell of a lot. Trillonario.com, a site that allows you to buy lottery tickets outside the country of your residence, had a jackpot for that amount last weekend. Trillonario's proclamation: 'a great service that allows lottery enthusiasts to make the most of their money and time!' Goethe's Faustian bargain takes another twist: global gold from local money / local gold from global money. Buy a paper ticket from the US to have my suburban dream and book an overseas holiday in Australia. Buy a ticket and you could build a ceramics plant in Vietnam, cover the administration costs of an NGO delivering aid to Burma or buy a house in Hollywood. Whatever tickles your fancy.

I don't know many people who would turn down $23,000,000. U2 did. They couldn't bear to part with the music to 'Where the Streets Have No Name'. Happy to work with Apple, not so content to work with a new ad suitor. It's a nice idea, to be able to take $23,000,000 home without the responsibility of spending it, or, on the other hand, having to reject it for a falsified integrity. $23,000,000 is an abstract concept to me. I can't picture it, count it, or accumulate it. If it's a neon sign, I can keep the dream without having to sell my soul or turn paper into gold.

Richard Prince started collecting signed cancelled cheques when he came across them accidentally while looking for signed portraits. I don't know how much Jack Kerouac's $10 bounced cheque would have cost him. Prince talks about choosing the cheques: he says it's all about who you choose. He wouldn't buy Richard Nixon's bounced cheque, he would much rather find one of Lee Harvey Oswald's. Assessment and accumulation of intangible value, the cost and worth of ethics and integrity. Jon's $23,000,000 is just a bright sign; he'd like you to take it home. A gesture and a concept to shift between lives. Aesthetic nonsense makes commonsense.

A friend of mine, Evelyn, has a solo music project called Pikelet. Before Pikelet, she was mainly a drummer in some hardcore bands. She still does that too. She started the solo project because her mum was sick and she wanted to make some music for her. Simple melodies—accordian, hand claps, a floor tom and electric acoustic guitar. When looped, her melodies and songs create a type of suburban backyard ethereal chant. A type of folk, I guess—or ambient pop. There is a song she has written called 'A Bunch'. Six lines of lyrics, looped and repeated like the music.

To all of those that I love so dear.
Thank you for surviving this far and making it here.
For making Now Now
You're so familiar it's clear.
You've been here before it's like you've always been here.
And you're here now now.[1]

It's addictive and repetitive. It's an everyday kinda song that's awkwardly sincere. It's about a tangible type of value, and the listener is the subject. Aesthetic nonsense makes common-sense.

She called her solo project Pikelet when recalling that her mother made them often when she was a child. She remembers loving them — sweet, warm comfort food. It was only later that her mother confessed to making them because there was no other food in the house, that pikelets were what she could afford to make. Food that was needed, music that was needed. Not to change the world, but so as to be in the world.

Wikipedia refers to pikelets as small, thick, colonial-style pancakes and states they were once part of traditional Welsh teas within the mining communities. A Scotch pancake. A drop scone. Perhaps the pikelet derives from the word piglet, or the Welsh *bara pyglyd* meaning 'pitchy bread'. Either way it's an ordinary, run-of-the-mill food and can be appropriated as a staple. Made by anyone, for anyone — any Tom, Dick or Harry'.

My brother the butcher talks in rhyming slang. Most of the time I can't understand him. I have to ask him what the fuck he is talking about, where it came from and what it means. Some of the phrases I recognise. My favourite is Stuart Diver', meaning 'survivor'. I like the remnants of meaning that exist in the slang. Most of the time it seems to run against meaning, perhaps in the way I remember Goumarre suggesting: not to prohibit meaning, but to prevent it from being the keystone. Rhyming slang is impermanent. Evolving and changing over time. What was once

'Jat Crackers' for 'knackers' may now be 'Kerry Packers'. No one really knows when it first appeared in Australia. It finds its roots as an underworld language that was eventually taken up by the street traders of London in the early to mid 1800s. Used primarily by men (there are 15 phrases for wife and only one for husband), rhyming slang was employed when other language was considered inappropriate or rude. It is learnt through experience, not taught *per se*—a language of dissidence, or a language formed for the sheer fun of spontaneously inventing and using a phrase where the meaning slips…

Aesthetic nonsense makes commonsense.
It's all square when it's round.[2]
You're talking bout nothing, I'm talking bout everything

First published as a catalogue essay for *$23,000,000*, Jon Campbell, Uplands Gallery, June 2008.

Notes

1 Pikelet, 'A Bunch', from her self-titled album, 2007.

2 A lyric from Eddie Current Suppression Ring, 'It's all Square', on *Eddy Current Suppression Ring*, Dropkick Records, 2006.

3 A lyric from 'I'm talking', on *Gloss Enamel*, 2006.

2009

From Memory

From memory, we arrived there later in the evening; it was dark and some four-and-a-half years ago. We had initially boarded the wrong train, but, after some preliminary panic, we transferred to our correct route of passage at a stop somewhere between another origin and one more destination. Neither of us had been there before, nor did we know what to expect. We only had three days to take in some three thousand years. He had hated it there, returning home with tales of gypsies and pickpockets, of indecipherable signs and an incommunicable reality — the symptoms, perhaps, of prolonged solitude and melancholy.

In the dark, we could see nothing, and caught a taxi to our hostel. Women up these stairs, men up those. Gendered dorms. Families divided, partners split, and wanderers waiting on the stairs. We searched for the bar and sat with a beer.

We were staying on the outskirts of the capital. Rising in the morning, we began walking, stopping briefly for coffee, slowly making our way in the direction of the large cathedral. The city within a city. Soft light, a temperate breeze, crisp air: a cold winter was surely approaching. We walked and walked: temples and memorials, thousands of years of history beneath our feet and before our eyes. Queues on entry and queues to follow. Mosaics made to resemble baroque paintings, large letters and scripts designed to deceive. Elaborate altars made from bronze taken from another building's roof, unrecognisable edifices, unbelievable domes, ceilings painted in narratives of ancient myths and tales, cast away stones and remnants of columns, arches and porticoes.

Marble.

Disembodied and headless, heroes and heroines. A weighted and almost visible history — one of wealth and war, of contested beliefs and hedonistic paganism.

A silent clowder of cats and a congregation of unidentified birds, sleeping in rubble and flying in flocks of cyclonic formation. Guardians and émigrés.

An abundance of ruins — some restored, some abandoned. A dark romanticism and forgotten symbols. Gateways closed, then opened and a substantial entry paid. Alternate lineages broken and restored, only to be broken again. A gentrified past.

Walking. Walking.

Theatres of the macabre, graves of thousands. Museum after museum, villa after villa, basilica after basilica. Coffee shops and tourist memorabilia, fountains and garrisons. Lupa and Bernini beside us.

Walking. Walking.

More ruins, more questions. Who decided not to repair them? When did *they* decide? If they build a new underground train line, it is abandoned — another layer of history found and in need of excavation. Archaeologists employed to carefully recreate the past. What has been erased? What has been built over? A malleable, rather than functional, record — a timeline obscured and obtuse. Was it Diderot who said, 'To make a place an object of interest, one must destroy it'?

The time has passed, we leave on a train, perhaps Hypermnestra is beside us, while both ahead and behind the fascination and spectacle of crumbling ruins, a contrived nostalgia and the possibility of an alternative historical present.

First published as a catalogue essay for *Guardians of the Departed*, Amanda Marburg, Uplands Gallery, Melbourne, March 2009.

Here it is...

..if it is too late, boring, condescending, ridiculous, outrageous, bland, sad, melancholy, dry, edible, flaccid, then scrap it and simply put in the attached image.

Later and luck to you.

Hi Greatest Hits

You asked me whatever you think will work? At the moment this is working for me (see below). It may, indeed, change between now and tomorrow, next week or next year. In some ways, it annoys me now. It has something to do with…, and something to do with utilising the natural cycle or production of things by people (notover production nor production for a market), shared spaces, tastes, dislikes and worlds.

Not at the moment, but always, I wish I was funny.

Lisa

> Reed: To propose or initiate something is vastly different than to author something. It's the first step in a process-obviously an important step, but one in a potentially long road. It's the launching of an idea—and a 'hosting' of that idea throughout a process. Crucial, however, to this notion of 'hosting' is equally the capacity to 'un-host'—for a conventional host assumes situational authority. What I mean by 'un-hosting' is not to relinquish authority completely within a group dynamic, but to view the process as a partiality-that is, both being and not being a 'host' simultaneously. Throughout the process of un-hosting a certain degree of control (not all) is dispersed…[1]
>
> Communication occurs in reciprocity: it must never be a one way flow from the teacher to the taught. The

teacher takes equally from the taught. So oscillates — at all times and everywhere, in any conceivable internal and external circumstance, between all degrees of ability, in the work place, institutions, the street, work circles, research groups, schools — the master/pupil, transmitter/receiver relationship. The ways of achieving this are manifold, corresponding to the varying gifts of individuals and groups.[2]

Can you add this into my submission *(Bluff your way in Art)* as part of mine from madeline Kidd?
i had been waiting on it, also think it works!

First published as artist pages / catalogue essay, for *Keep it together*, Greatest Hits, TCB art inc., Melbourne, September 2009.

Notes

1 David Goldenberg & Patricia Reed, 'What Is a Participatory Practice?', *Fillip* 8 (Autumn 2008).

2 Joseph Beuys, 'I Am Searching for Field Character' (1973), in *Energy Plan for the Western Man* (New York: Four Walls Eight Windows, 1990) 21–23.

Anarchists in the Academy

i

Christopher L.G. Hill's *Y2K Melbourne Biennial* offered a glimpse into how contemporary art practice can be presented properly. This may be a fairly large boast, but I am convinced that it is an appropriate statement for an artist-run-initiative show that titled itself a Biennial. In contrast to the often sterile and disappointing presentation of contemporary artwork that frequently greets us when we view the public staging of art, the *Y2K Biennial* gave us an alternative vision. It showed that art could be exhibited in a way that embraces and enhances the experimental, inquisitive, process-driven and open-ended nature of contemporary practice. It showed what happens when art isn't cleaned of its edges and what happens when it isn't orchestrated into something palatable and easy to digest. Not that the *Y2K Biennial* was unpalatable, far from it, it's just that it deliberately organised the works to—and chose artists that—maintain a speculative edge. It demonstrated the potential of bridging the gap between the interactions with art practice as they occur through the making of an artwork and how art can be received. After all, how many times have we heard the words 'the work looked better in the studio (or *in situ*)'? The *Y2K Biennial* successfully brought to the gallery the chaotic, difficult and rewarding practice of dealing with art in its raw state.

Nicholas Selenitsch

ii

The anarchist anthropologist David Graeber suggests that the difference between Marxism and Anarchism is that Marxism has tended to be a theoretical or analytical discourse about revolutionary strategy, while Anarchism is concerned with ethical discourse about revolutionary practice. In this sense, the exhibition posited as the 'second (fourth) biennial of Melbourne' offered a type of participatory democracy—multiple curators and diverse disciplines both acknowledging and disguising what markets have glorified as consumable authorship and collaboration. As we perhaps know, for democracy to work it needs many voices and visions—the *Y2K Biennial* collected and elevated the transient, fluid, subjective and at times schizophrenic approaches of contemporary artistic practice in Melbourne. This was perhaps evidenced on entry by Jon Campbell's flag *It's gonna take a lot of love* and Xin Cheng's knotted-sheet escape route; both works symbiotically confident, welcoming and self-doubting. Funnily enough, in a rather humble and local way, the *Y2K Biennial* not only extended what has been cited as the 'complex and humanist legacy of the first biennial, *Signs of Life*; it deliberately questioned the economic and hierarchical structures that have since prevented another Melbourne International Biennial from being staged'.[1] In addition, by being held in this branded and acronymic economic climate, the *Y2K Biennial* further questioned the structure and 'all-star casts' of the international biennial and triennial circuit. Ignored by the mainstream media and art press, the *Y2K Biennial* has perhaps highlighted that the local establishment is still, unfortunately, not ready for artistic practice to be generative of social knowledge without a clearly defined (and marketable) figurehead and product.

Lisa Radford

iii

'When Will I ... Will I ... Be ... Famous?!' (I Kant answer ... he can't answer that). So I'm trying to remember what the *Melbourne International Biennial* (the first one) back in the late 90s was like ... oh yeah, I remember now ... I was in my Honours year at the VCA and I was an installation volunteer for Ricky [Swallow], not actually making the work (my blades weren't sharp enough to cut the cardboard to make the sculptures ... I'm good but not *that* good!) but just doing menial labour work ... well, to be more exact, cleaning the windows for Ricky, where his record player works were going to go. Anyway the thing is I remember cleaning, cleaning, I'm not really good at cleaning ... especially windows ... 'Hey! I'm not a window cleaner! I AM AN ARTIST!' *I thought* ... but I guess it's like when you start out as a kitchen hand you can eventually become the head chef… then a celebrity chef? Gordon Ramsay?! Anyway, I remember the Biennial being a big deal at the time… it was going to be the first one and as it turned out the last one… I remember Callum [Morton] saying 'If we don't have another one, it's going to be known as the Melbourne One-ennial!' at a forum at Gertrude Contemporary Art Spaces about a year after the Biennial.

Fast forward, back to the future. Now it's no longer the 'One-ennial', thanks to Chris [L.G. Hill], my installation was part of the second (fourth) one? I built myself my own pavilion (well, I guess it's probably going to be the only biennale I'll ever be in, so I might as well make the most of it!) and named it the *STUDIO MASATOTECTURES PAVILLION*. Actually it wasn't really a pavilion, I just crammed (almost) all the stuff I had amassed over the years, my old work… because I like *my old stuff better than my new stuff…* (remember that Regurgitator song?). I also included some of the TCB art inc. furniture, the other artist's stuff I liked I had hanging around in the studio, plus two special guests: a painting by Lisa [Radford]—the cast in Dawson's Creek… (you remember that TV show? 'I don't wanna wait'…), and an abstract painting (kinda like a blurry version of a Tomma Abts) that Madeline gave to me for my birthday.

You know, 'If you build it… they will come!', and they did!
Masato Takasaka

iv

The (self initiated, artist-funded) second (fourth) Y2K Melbourne Biennial of Art (& Design)'s existence and positioning in an artist-run space such as TCB art inc. seemed to be the natural outcome for a generation of practitioners who, whilst collectively disillusioned and disconnected from traditional mainstream hierarchies and avenues operating in the Melbourne art world, function as both self-sufficient and networked artists with a do-it-yourself, 'taking care of business' attitude.

Y2K, organised by and centrally welded around the interconnections of Christopher L.G. Hill, became the physical manifestation for an alternate model or structure of production and presentation that exists and is based in networks, in cyberspace, on blogs, YouTube, online groups and group discussions. With shared knowledge and shared resolve to make things, and to make things happen regardless of isolation, location, and capital, the networked generation are taking control of their own destiny.

Y2K could be read as a critique on the lack of opportunity and support for an alternate space within a largely monosyllabic artistic culture. For some reason I continue to think how great it would have been to see the *Y2K* project exhibited in the smaller galleries at ACCA, or even overseas in an external context, to showcase the breadth of such a creative 'zeitgeist'.

Danny Lacy

Co-authored by Danny Lacy, Nicholas Selenitsch and Masato Takasaka, first published as 'Anarchists in the Academy: Four perspectives (from inside and outside) on *The (self-initiated, artist-funded) second (fourth) Y2K Melbourne Biennial of Art (& Design)*, TCB art inc (Level 1/12 Waratah Place, Melbourne), and other locations', in *un Magazine*, issue 3.1, June 2009, pp. 44–47.

Notes

1 Felicity Fenner, 'New Life in Melbourne — first Melbourne International Biennial, 1999', *Art in America* (January 2000).

Not Helminithic Therapy

There is a parasite called *Dicrocoelium dendriticum*. Some call it 'liver fluke'.[1] Its life begins in the bile duct of cattle, where adult parasitic flatworms or flukes lay their eggs. Bile, which is produced in the liver, travels along the bile duct to the intestine to aid digestion of dietary fats. In infected cattle, the liver fluke spawn goes along for the ride. Not long afterwards, the larvae are expelled with the cows' faeces, and then consumed by passing snails. It is in these snails that the eggs then hatch.

Cercaria — the free-swimming larval stage in which a parasitic fluke passes from one intermediate host to another.

The cercaria migrate to the respiratory system of the snail where 'snail slime' is created. As the snails move across land, excreting their slime to move, the cercaria are also expelled. The slime, now hosting the cercaria, is then consumed by ants.

Inside the ants, most of the cercaria embed themselves in the walls of the abdomen, but some migrate to the head of the ant and make a home in the subesophageal ganglion part of the brain. This part of the brain controls the mouthparts, the salivary glands and certain muscles of the ant. Here, the cercaria become metacercaria and although not infective like those in the abdomen, these metacercaria colonise the ant's brain, causing a type of temporary but recurring insanity. Each day, as the temperature drops and evening approaches, ants infected with liver fluke climb to the top of local grasses and cling to the blades. Clamped on by their mandibles, the ants remain there, paralyzed, till the sun rises.

The temporary insanity lasts only as long as the sun is down. The ant returns to its colony in the morning. If subjected to the heat of the direct sun, the ant would be at risk of death, along with the parasite. Night after night, the infected ant repeats its blade-clinging-ritual-trance, until the grass is consumed by a passing grazer.

The ant is ingested, the fluke has a new host and the cycle begins again.

First published as a catalogue essay for *Pissing in the Infinity Pool*, Rob McLeish, Ocular Lab, October 2009.

Note

1 Much of the information about parasites in this essay is informed by: David Fisher, 'Parasites', *RadioLab*, season 6, episode 3, first broadcast 7 September 2009 (New York: WNYC Studios, 2009).

Peripatetic Priapism: an un-illustrated dictionary of exhibited wandering cocks

Cock-head. *n : fool, idiot.*

In Ancient Greece and Rome, depictions of the penis were almost commonplace—a symbol of fertility, punishment, beauty and humour. Priapus was a minor god with a large appendage that was permanently erect and thus rendered useless—a punishment for his attempt at raping a goddess. In fact, rather than a fertility god, he was more akin to a scarecrow and was hence a protector of livestock, vineyards and gardens. If we think about Michelangelo's *David*, his privates are more modest in size—an example of quantitative beauty, perhaps. In Ancient Greece, spring *phallophoria* festivals were held—phallic processions in honour of Dionysius. Large phalluses were carried through the streets, and people dressed as satyrs (a gang of male companions to Pan and Dionysius who roamed the woods and are often associated with sex drive) while exchanging crude jests and insults. The revellers were called *komasts* and their songs called *komodeia*. Komodeia—the etymological root of the word 'comedy'.

Cock-up. *v : mistake, error, blunder.*

Sometime last year, hidden between the bananas stocked at a hypermarket in the small town of Bolsward in the Netherlands, a Brazilian wandering spider was discovered. It was only in 2007 that this species had appeared in the Guinness Book of Records as the world's most venomous spider. Also called 'armed spiders', from the Portuguese *Arans Armadeiras*, they are a considered an extremely aggressive spider and are found only in tropical South and Central America. No one was hurt at the hypermarket. After travelling many thousands of miles in a banana box, the spider was carefully trapped in a jar by an employee who later showed it off on the supermarket counter. Had the employee not been so lucky, and had he been bitten, the venom would cause intense pain and would possibly lead to death. Between the pain and possible death, the venom of the spider can cause priapism—an uncomfortable erection that can last for hours, which then leads to impotence. At present, Brazilian and US scientists are looking into using the Brazilian wandering spider's venom as a possible natural alternative to Viagara—the emasculating spider would come good.

> **Cock-off.** *n: SLANG description of a competitive cocktail party, where guests vie to make the best drink.*

Apparently, the practise of removing the human penis was popular amongst some ancient civilisations. The lopped penis was probably considered both a trophy and a means of counting the number of enemy combatants killed—primarily, though, the removal of the penis was considered to be the ultimate demonstration of superiority. Before Lorena Bobbitt there was Sada Abe, a geisha, prostitute, maid and author, who, on 18 May 1936, killed her lover, Kichizo Ishida, and then removed his genitalia with a kitchen knife, wrapped them in a magazine and stored them in her handbag until her arrest three days later. Apparently, Abe practised necrophilia with her 'trophy', explaining to her interrogators: 'I loved him so much, I had to have him all to myself'. Soon after WWII, Ishida's penis and testicles were put on display in the Tokyo University Medical Museum, however they have since disappeared.

Ishida's once-exhibited-and-now-missing penis is perhaps no anomaly. There are several other examples of apparent penile-pinching-for-public-presentation. An object thought to be Napoleon Bonaparte's penis (apart indeed), has circulated among auctioneers and collectors for sometime. Napoleon died in exile in 1821, and an autopsy that was conducted on the island of St Helens by the emperor's doctor, Francesco Antommarchi, in front of 17 witnesses, concluded that Napoleon had died of stomach cancer. His heart was removed and given to his estranged wife Marie-Louise, as requested by the deceased. According to most accounts, Napoleon was sewn up, dressed, and remained unattended while laying in state. It is rumoured and claimed by Napoleon's manservant Ali that, at this time, he and a priest named Vignali removed several body parts, including the penis. In 1916, Vignali's decedents sold his collection to a British rare book firm, who in turn sold the artefacts to a Philadelphian bibliophile in 1924 for approximately $2,000. The buyer, A.S. Rosenbach, exhibited the presumed penis at the Museum of French Art in New York. The Vignali collection was sold and re-sold a couple more times before being put on the block at Christie's in 1969. Eight years later, the penis was put up for sale separately at a Paris Auction house and bought for $3,000 by John K. Lattimer, a professor emeritus and former chairman of urology at Colombia University. The story finally penetrated my consciousness via online TV and a recent episode of *Law & Order SVU*.

Grigori Rasputin, *Mad Monk* and advisor to the Romanov family of pre-revolutionary Russia, was also rumoured to have posthumously flashed his crown jewels. On 29 December 1916, a conservative nobleman who feared the influence of the mystic monk on the Tsar's wife, murdered him and, some accounts claim, castrated him. According to legend, a maid then discovered the detached penis at the murder site and kept it until sometime in the 1920s when a group of Russian women living in Paris acquired it and worshipped the organ as a type of fertility charm. Rasputin's daughter caught wind of the story and demanded that it be returned to her along with other personal artefacts once belonging to her father. It is thought the penis stayed with her until her death in California in 1977, when it then turned up at a flea market and was purchased, along with some of her other possessions, by Michael Augustine. Said penis was then consigned to Bonhams auction house, where it was realised that the artefact was in fact not a penis, but rather a sea cucumber. It has since been speculated to be a Geoduck (a type of large, edible saltwater clam, incidentally pronounced 'gooeyduck'). It is also thought that the specimen may have been a horse or bovine penis—its 30cm length perhaps a clue and an explanation as to why it was used as a fertility charm, although, if we have learnt anything from the Romans, perhaps it should have been considered a curse. The story seemingly ended in 1994, but, ten years later, Igor Knyazkin, director of the Russian Museum of Erotica, claimed he had purchased Rasputin's pecker from a French antiquarian for $8,000—he also claimed that merely viewing it would cure men of impotency.

> **Cock-teased.** *v past-tense: to tease provocatively via dress with the promise of sex that never eventuates.*

Cynthia Plaster Caster, otherwise known as Cynthia P. Caster or Cynthia Albritton, is a self-professed artist, groupie and fan. Her artistic practice began in 1968 with the casting (not castration) of her friend's penis, in preparation for a larger project where she has cast, or has at least attempted to cast, the penises of many rock musicians whose music she admires. Under the banner of The Chicago Plaster Casters of Hampton Wick, and with various assistants and associates over the years, who have provided the needed stimulation, Cynthia, quite clinically and rudimentarily procures the cast following a verbal contract and via a simple process involving alginate, circular containers and Plaster of Paris. More recently, she is inclined to work by herself, while partners of the subjects 'assist' as required. Cynthia has managed to amass a collection of cocks which she refers to as her babies, including but not limited to those of Jimi Hendrix, Noel Redding, Jello Biafra, David Yow, Jeff Beck, Pete Shelley, Eric Burden, Chris Connelly and Ian Svenonious. Erect at the beginning, often flaccid by the final cast, the penises range in length, girth and states of arousal. If one of Hendrix's headbands, of which he had many, can fetch $30,000, how much would his prized one-off penis fetch? Gene Simmons and Paul Stanley, having not been asked, wrote a song about Cynthia, alluding to an alternate history. Gene was apparently getting around town claiming a cast had been made, when it simply had not. The song, titled 'Plaster Caster' (1977), opens with the following lines:

Baby's getting anxious, the hour's getting late
The night is almost over, she can't wait
Oh, things are complicating, my love is in her hands
And there's no more waiting, she understands
The plaster's gettin' harder and my love is perfection
A token of my love for her collection, her collection

Cynthia was offended and in her presence, Gene and Paul retract their claim on public radio. Noel Redding, at a time when he was low on cash, sold his own penis to an English auction house — only to regret the act and ultimately request another copy, which, upon receiving, as documented in *Plaster Caster* (2001), he simply says to Cynthia, 'Thank you for my penis'. The casts are white, chalky souvenirs of a mannered and simulated emasculation — *civilised* trophies. Perhaps they are the artefacts that Rasputin and Napoleon's penises could only ever hope to be — playful death masks of (cock) rock (music) heroes exhibited for all and sundry in a white-cube downtown New York commercial gallery.

First published as a catalogue essay for *COCK & BULL*, John Beagles and Graham Ramsay, Jon Campbell, Tony Garifalakis and Matthew Griffin, VCA Margaret Lawrence Gallery, Melbourne, March 2009.

Subprime Galleries

>sorry to let you down -
>
>From an email conversation October 1, 2008
>
>>Subprime Galleries
>>
>>To access this increasing market, exhibitors often take on risks associated with
>>showing artists with poor exhibiting ratings or limited exhibiting histories.
>>Subprime exhibitions are considered to carry a far greater risk for the artist due to
>>the aforementioned exhibition risk characteristic of the typical subprime artist.
>>Galleries use a variety of methods to off set these risks. In the case of many
>>subprime exhibitions, this risk is off set with a higher exhibition rate or various
>>exhibition enhancements, such as private viewings). In the case of subprime
>>exhibition, a subprime artist may be charged higher late fees, gallery bond fees,
>>catalogue fees, or up-front fees for the exhibition. Late fees are charged to the
>>resulting in over-the-limit fees. These higher fees compensate the gallery for the
>>increased costs associated with servicing and exhibiting such artists, as well as for
>>the higher default rate.

First published in: Matthew Griffin (ed.), *Reader #8*, Gambia Castle, Auckland, March 2009.

Not About Slayer (Lyrical Wax Museum)

Hey Lisa,

Can you edit my text for Shazza's show? Do you still want the *Dawson's Creek* painting and *Simpsons* painting for your show at Hell?

I had this crazy idea that I (or wii?) could write about both yourself and Shazza's work, the space of knowing and not knowing (?!) (re: about alchemy) because I don't know how this essay will turn out and also the work (Shazza's) relates to the idea of alchemy as 'South of Now', which I understand to be *South of Heaven* which points to hell? (sort of) and your work is going to be shown at Hell?

(…is this what they mean by relational aesthetics?)

I am thinking about getting Griffo to write something about how he listens to 'South of Heaven' by Slayer and what that means? I want Geoff to write about the time he went to see Slayer live at Rod Laver… also there was an email from Madeline's cousin Dave, who used to work at Madame Tussauds in London that Shazza would find hilarious… I'm not really sure if it's going to work but…

Anyway, I was going to write about Whitesnake album covers, the cover art and how the Whitesnake logo looked like Shazza's work, but Shazza didn't want them to look like album cover art or tattoos, so maybe not a good idea…which reminded me of the time when Blair told me he always imagined Stieg Persson looking like a big biker dude with long hair and a beard because Stieg painted tattoos and skulls (remember when he was doing those?) anyway turns out it was Tony Clark…(who doesn't paint tattoos or skulls but anyway…) which also reminds me when Blair introduced me to Jarrod and told me that Jarrod was Shazza's brother who was a black belt in the art of Karate (this was back in the late nineties at the old TCB which used to be Grey Area) at ar opening in Port Phillip arcade (hadn't met Jarrod before at this stage)…anyway I guess I fell for it because they kind of looked the same, I believed them and everyone thought that was so hilarious.

I guess you had to be there.

Anyway, what I think I want to say is maybe things look the same but it doesn't mean they can't be different which reminds me of some lyrics by Ozzy Osbourne: 'it's the same old desire…nothing's the same…nothing has changed… everything stays the same…'

This reminded me of Shazza's work and how she hasn't really changed …using the same medium of gouache ink on foam-core…'old school' kind of like how Griffo told me he has *South of Heaven* by Slayer still on tape instead of on cd.

Anyway a couple of years ago after seeing her work in 'Relentless Optimism', I gave Shazza a cover of the copy of my copy of Whitesnake's *Greatest Hits* so she could do a copy of the Whitesnake band cover logo and give it to me for my birthday…

(remember at Madeline's surprise birthday we said we were going to write about ourselves instead of Shazza or her work so I guess that is what Shazza's going to get!)

I was also going to write about the new Tom Hanks movie, th sequel to Dan Arps…I mean, Dan Brown's *The Da Vinci Code* (…Alchemy!) starring Tom Hanks called *Angels and Demons* (even more Alchemy?!+ Heaven and/or Hell?!)…

I thought about not even seeing the movie and reviewing it… kind of like when Marco told me about a writer called Richard Meltzer from Rolling Stone magazine that used to review Led Zeppelin gigs by not going to the gig and instead staying in his hotel room and taking acid and writing like he was at the gig…not that I need to take acid…I am still getting flashbacks from the time I took half a tab of acid in my first year of art school which is another story…

Anyway, less about me and more about Shazza's work…

I know Tom hanks has got nothing to do with Shazza's work although that he (Tom Hanks) starred in *Big* and that was about how a magic arcade machine transforms the young adolescent boy (played by Tom Hanks) into an older version via some magic process of alchemy which is never really explained.

Maybe that is why it's alchemy?

Shazza's tells me the new work is about this (alchemy).

I guess this whole Tom Hanks thing is inspired in part by this essay I have just finished reading by Richard Flood called Not About Mel Gibson'…which basically blames Mel's choice of movie roles and films he made like *Apocalypto* and how America would be free of human sacrifice and ritual cannibalism if he hadn't dreamt it up.

Apparently according to Flood, 'things wouldn't be out of control in the Middle East if he (Mel Gibson) hadn't started flinging the guilt and violence around in *The Passion of the Christ*. Think about it…'

I am thinking…Pop (but not pop) will eat itself? Popular culture as a form of entertainment, kind of like alchemy: folding in on itself' to disguise and conceal a hidden message: hidden, inexplicable, something which goes beyond explanation?

When thinking about alchemy, the Brett Whitley painting which is on the cover of the Dire Strait's album of the same name 'Alchemy' also came to mind.

Not that Shazza's work has anything to do with Dire Straits or Brett Whiteley so it's not going to make it in the essay (probably also because Shazza doesn't want to me to mention Brett Whiteley or Dire Straits and maybe because it actually hasn't got anything to do with her work...)

Also I thought about mentioning 'Enter Sandman' from the *Black Album* and how Metallica goes stadium rock, with James Hetfield singing 'exit light...enter night...take my hand... off to never never land', but that really has nothing to do with Shazza's work either, apart from having a snake graphic on the cover, and also one of Shazza's previous shows was called 'Neverlands'.

As for 'South of Heaven', I was excited because it was the title of a Slayer album from 1987...(Shazza was going to use this as the title of her show which lasted for about five seconds)... I said (to Shazza), Griffo would probably get pissed off because he was doing that stuff ten years ago...then I suggested *Powerslave* by Iron Maiden but then I knew Ry would get pissed off 'cos he already did that ten years ago...

Can anyone do anything anymore? And over and over, again?

Anyway, on Shazza's blackberry we surfed the net for more heavy metal album covers with skull imagery and *Seasons in the Abyss* and *South of Heaven* by Slayer popped up! It's kind of like Shazza does 'cover versions' of them via 'Coles Funny Picture' books crossed with 'Mad' magazine fold ins and the guy that did Sonic Youth's *Goo* album cover...what was his name again? ...maybe I will title the essay everyone loves Raymond? (not)...or everyone loves Slayer? (not)...anyway, what do you think? By the way, this may end up in the essay.

Best, Masato

From: ████████@optusnet.com.au
To: ██@hotmail.com
Subject: Re: not knowing
Date: Thu, 11 Jun 2009 19:04:29 +1000

I wonder what the wonder is? Do you use known signs and symbols to elicit or reveal something unknown or rather, do you do it to demand a set of responses that probably fall within a specified or expected zone? Alchemy uses the known to disguise/fool. The album cover uses known signs to appeal to an aesthetic and to suggest rebellion but not create it and indicate the anti-social within a social context. It's a kind of maze or like building on buildings.

On 11/06/2009, at 6:47 PM, Masato Takasaka wrote:

Yes i was thinking the exact same thing! To quote Hal Foster 'signs taken for wonders'…I guess it's like a magic show… a simulacra of alchemy…i guess that's what alchemy is…is it real but not real..huh?..Slayer's magic show being about black magic?…which is coincidentally also a song by Slayer: 'Black Magic' off Slayer's 1983 album *Show No Mercy*, which shazza also liked (the cover art and lettering of) not the music…

> 4 min 3 sec – 19 Aug 2007
> *Slayer black magic 1983*
> *www.youtube.com/watch?v=FtmNOaG1KBA*

From: ████████@optusnet.com.au
To: ██@hotmail.com
Subject: Re: not knowing
Date: Thu, 11 Jun 2009 18:09:56 +1000

It's funny, that Geoff text has nothing and everything to with Sharon's work…The upside down crosses, skulls, tattoos and terms bandied round like they are almost objects 'the guys in Iraq'—a whole heap of mixed up signs and symbols drawn from, mashed up, projected, looked at, sung too. Ya know I wonder whether they fold-in on each other and almost dissappear… The slayer gig kind of sounds like alchemy.

Magic. Sorcery. I dunno

Slayer at Rod Laver

Stu and I got loaded up on Super Bourbons (a thing that *Reggae* from the Rock Ape used to do for five bucks) and pushed our way through the crowd of sweaty tattoos and Auschwitz skulls. There was a palpable excitement that hung in the air, something like BO and beer and feet. We took our seats up in the Z stall and waited for the band to come out. A skinhead next to us was bouncing around in his seat in anticipation, all cagey and fierce like. When the band started playing we all started a kind of spasmodic rock / sway/ mosh in our seats as though a charge of electricity pulsed through our bones, grinning and screaming parts of the song. I noticed a big guy in the pit take his oversized ice hockey jersey off and throw it at another guy who wiped his head with it then try to set it alight. I had to take a piss and when I came back everyone was heavily applauding the drum solo. The singer introduced the next song with 'This song was for the true heroes in Iraq….' We looked at each other in our seats before the answer came: 'The American Armed Forces'. Was it irony? During that song we were treated to a load of 911 images and Arabic script flashing against a backdrop of bloodied corpses. Before the next song they projected a bunch of white crosses turning slowly on the back wall, then as a guitar broke into another song, the crosses turned upsid down. It was truly evil. A guy screamed like a woman. I think the skinhead wet his pants. A few songs later we stumbled out, pissed and broke. G

Geoff Newton

To: ███@hotmail.com
Subject: RE: south of heaven
Date: Tue, 26 May 2009 01:41:30 +0000

Hey Masato,

I don't want to write about how listening to Slayer on Tape is

Old School'. I think that being 'Old School' is lame. It seems to me that folks that call themselves that have given up trying to keep up with the world. Not keeping up with the world is fine, but wearing it as a badge of pride, as if you have some secret information, as if you are above everyone else's interests is retarded. Riding a penny-farthing may indeed have its own sort of quality to it, but it seems foolish to try and convince somebody that everyone else has got it wrong with there new fandangle 10-speeds. I have a copy of *South of Heaven* in the car because I long ago gave up on trying to keep up with music. The 50 cents it cost me was less of a loss than the time I would have to invest in learning about Lamb of God or Mastodon or what not. So me spruiking on about how that modern metal is rubbish is like my grandfather claiming *My Fair Lady* was the high water mark of pop culture. Who cares? Wondering about Sharon using the same method to make art for the last 10 years is a like looking at a finger pointing to the moon.

matt

[No Subject]

..Anyway I am still at Madame Tussauds, and enjoying every minute! My original contract was only for three months, but they extended it for another three months, which was welcome news to yours truly. The extension also meant that I'm not running around with blood all over my face scaring the living daylights out of as many nationalities as I can anymore. No, now I'm upstairs dressed as a pirate, saying things like, ahoy, me hearties! Welcome aboard!', working with Johnny Depp. Yep, the Johnny Depp. He's a lazy bugger to work with but. He just stands there like a wax figure and leaves me to run around sweating it out. haha..

I must reverse for a second : Whilst I was working as a psychopath down in the chamber scaring people, I had a bit of an accident with one of the many wax figures that live in the building. I was in mid-scaring people mode, on this day feeling particularly energetic, so I scared someone then ran down to the back of the chamber to scare the next group of people. I must point out that this is a very dark environment to work in, just flashes of light here and there. Anyway, on the way there there was a swinging wax figure hanging from the ceiling.

Because it was so dark I didn't see it swinging towards me and inevitably smashed right into my face, quite close to my left eye, forcing it to bleed. The initial shock hit me for 6, then when the reality of how bad it hurt reached my brain I immediately knew I had to get to any form of first aid, or at least to a sink. Here's where it get's quite comic. On the way out I had to pass the group of people I initially wanted to scare. Ironically, I was trying to get out of this environment as fast as I could, with blood streaming from my eye, but it was mixed with the copious amounts of fake blood and make-up that was all over my face for the character, and upon passing the group on the way out they thought I was in character and in pain and they screamed their bloody heads off. How's that for method acting? Anyway, upon inspection, it was bad, but it could have been worse. Like, it could have pierced my eyeball type of worse, ending many dreams in the process, but as luck would have it that didn't occur. Ya gotta look at the glass as half full at times like this, yeah? So I grab a taxi and head to the nearest hospital. On the way there I quietly realise this is my first time in a London taxi. I get to the hospital, and join the queue. It's long. I finally reach the receptionist and upon asking me my name the next question she asks me is to describe what happened. Now, because this is my job, and everyday I put on make-up and run around scaring people, this is normal to me by now. But I forgot that in this scenario and as I casually (within reason) explained to her that, "well, I work at Madame Tussauds and I was running around when all of a sudden a wax figure came out of nowhere and smashed me in the face", the receptionist lowered her head and started shaking uncontrollably.

I paused, not knowing what to do, or what was wrong with her. I then realised she was laughing at the explanation I was giving her!

Realising the bizarre nature of the situation, I didn't blame her! Anyway, it's healed well and there is no scar, so no worries (and no compo, haha). I'm sure there's more to write about but I want to go and buy some chocolate. Simple. I hope you are all really well and I look forward to the day I have the pleasure of seeing you again,

that's my rant!!
Let me know the goss from your end,
Dave.

Co-authored by Masato Takasaka, Geoff Newton, Matthew Griffin and David Souter Loney, first published as a catalogue essay for *South of Now*, Sharon Goodwin, Uplands Gallery, Melbourne, 2009.

Notes

1 Richard Flood, 'Not About Mel Gibson', in *Unmonumental: The Object in the 21st Century* (London: Phaidon Press, 2007), 10.
2 ibid.

Convenient and contrived

Two weeks ago, my partner and I headed to Kinglake to visit his friend who had survived what is now known as 'Black Saturday' or simply 'the Victorian Bushfires'. With a camera packed, we naïvely thought we would take some pictures for future reference. After hesitantly gaining permission to pass through the police road block at Mittons Bridge, the intensity of what had occurred only a month prior hit. I drove, tears streaming, at only 40km/h. Slowly, on windy roads, once disguised by dense forest but now clearly laid out before us. We talked. No photos, we decided. It didn't seem right. Army trucks slowly passed us, SES workers tended to their work, people camped on what remained of their land, hand-painted signs warned off looters — we are part of your community too one said. Australian Flags attached to remaining gate post after gate post. I wondered who the flags were for — were they symbols of a contrived community or an actual community? I wondered about the convenience of nationalism. The need to feel a part of something bigger than yourself, bigger than the event you had just experienced. The need for that thing to be broad and loosely defined. The friend who had survived was sceptical of the flags too. But, at the same time, she wondered if the support she had received from the people she didn't know would have happened elsewhere in the world. Surely it would. Are we that unique? Who is 'we'?

There was a picture of Pauline Hanson today in the paper, holding a beer and wearing an Australian Flag T-shirt, following her defeat in the Queensland seat of Beaudeser. I wondered if it was the same Australian Flag as those in Kinglake or on the jumper my friend owns, the same as the one flying at Government House and on my packet of cereal, or flying above the mosques and catholic churches? I reflected on the classifying terms and symbols of disparate communities and then the possibility of other ways of representing a unified populace. Should it be national and bound by borders, when expressions of togetherness, bipartisanship and community are fluid (culture/lifestyle) and at times intangible (the internet)? At other times, it is convenient, contrived, transmissible and proximate. Or, in this instance, were the flags like the sign asking others not to loot, a simple gesture expressing 'we are part of your community too'?

Previously unpublished, 2009.

2010

A Mined Atoll For Upward

Carefree your way of life may be
And though you roll in wealth
Just spare a thought your home will soon be gone
Time will soon be here that we
All would find nowhere to live
Oh there, there I don't know what to do.
— *A Handbook of Nauruan Crafts, Songs & Recipes*

I would go there alone, not knowing I would never be lonely. A tiny island, twenty-one kilometres square. That speck in the atlas our mother had pointed out to us nearly thirty years before. Her home for the beginning of her being. An intermittent island home. On the map, almost invisible, perhaps also in our consciousness. Twelve hours of day, twelve hours of night. Consistent temperatures, some rain, some wind. No shoes, no windows, no blankets for sleeping, few rules, much swimming. Demarcating a year, any year seems arbitrary. Sixty kilometres south of the equator in the empty pacific. The middle of nowhere to her, and to them the centre of everything.

When we're in mid-air, the hostesses do their narrated and well-rehearsed dance. Facts, figments, a sci-fi novella. Going there alone, not ever being lonely. From memory, a year ago, the friend had returned. In conversation, a question: have you heard of a place, this place called Nauru?

Nauru or utopia, once called Pleasant Isle. Those that live there, it is said, have been there for a while. So long, it is said, that they have no traditions of ever having arrived. Individual, collective, amalgamation of memory. Silence, subsistence and accidental discovery. Visitors, beachcombers, protectorates, custodianship. Exploited natural resources, sovereignty, then dependency. Landowners, land invaders, independence, self-determination. Mined for the reserves that others were lacking. The smallest but richest. *Naoero Ituga*—someone's promised land.

Hello world! Welcome to capitalism and the cash

economy! Sorry, it is time. We really must be going. Farewell, *Tarawong ka* and good luck with your journey.

In the air, we have three seats to ourselves. Forty on board, a faux-private jet. The intention to sleep, but mostly we read. Our histories divergent, our reasons disparate. Timing interchangeable and also coinciding. The tall strong man, once ousted in a coup. His team, a woman and five serious men assigned to survey progress, profit and growth. A land once of wealth, where billions have been squandered. Feeble laws and incentive to preserve future. Mismanagement, dishonesty and predatory merchants. Economic, political, perhaps social collapse. The end of a world, before that of the one we all know?

The quiet economist and statistician from Mali hands you his card, some conversation and an invitation to drink. Aeroplane engines and an infinite darkness. Are we halfway to nowhere? A short time and soon an invisible landing. A smile, then a smoke, and a bus to the Menen.

Do we ever really see where we are going or from where we have come?

Alone, not lonely, the humidity feels thick. The sun rises. The land you are on could be swallowed by the sea. Your vision, the ocean, 360 degrees. From here, can we see the weather of the world? The explosives expert, the dynamite jockey, your company at breakfast and first friend on the island. 'I broke it, you fix it', he says to his daughter. To you, 'Let's swim. Shall we eat? A ride to topside? I hope you find what it is that you did not know was your search'. Six tourists, you're the seventh. Is it possible invisibility is zero? Òbùrùbûr—white skin.

Alone, not lonely with your albums and photos. You never knew him, just his wife and his daughters and one is your mother. Guilt, ghosts and pictures. Past lovers, new friends, you give her a rainbow. The moonscape disappearing the pinnacles between jungle. What has vanished? What will follow? What might then grow?

When asked 'where is home?', Diogenes replies 'the world'.

A melancholy island for melancholy travellers. Qfwfq was here? You saw him, saw her? Indeterminate experience reduced to silent memory? An abyss of understanding. A cavity, a depression, a controlled excavation. A mined atoll for Upward.

This essay was commissioned by the Art Gallery of South Australia for *Before and After Science: 2010 Adelaide Biennial of Australian Art*, curated by Charlotte Day and Sarah Tutton.

Halfway to a threeway

Halfway to a threeway.[1]
I don't suppose it matters which way we go.[2]

The First and Last Hotel is on the corner of Boundary Road and where Sydney Road almost becomes the Hume. It is a Tatts pokies pub, now, neither first nor last. It appears as an American Western saloon, its exterior painted, faux-cracked, faux-saloon-doored and -windowed. Located on its own small wedge of land bordered by a police station and train tracks, it enters your consciousness a kilometre past Pentridge Prison and just before the vast flat expanse of what seems to be the largest of all cemeteries.

A pub between destinations both first and last.

Peter Dupas used to drink at the First and Last. In 1997, he murdered Mersina Halvagis in the Greek Orthodox section of that large cemetery—The Fawkner Crematorium and Memorial Park. His grandfather's grave was a mere 128 metres away.

Malevolence, benevolence, death and three life sentences. Carrots and boots and nothing to be done.

Madam, just because I drive a truck does not make me a truck driver.[3]

The First and Last Hotel was once a marker between here and there, a link between somewhere and nowhere. A halfway point to everywhere. Highways—vast tracks that enable you to speed through landscapes of plenty that appear to be nothing. Grasslands, forests, plantations, farms, protected and logged, perhaps first, perhaps last.

Marked distance, marked time, sales, secrets and folklore. Far from and far to. Eight songs, 43 minutes, the intro repeated exponentially. Insignificance. Eureka. Bad Timing. O'Rourke to Roeg. Long conversations over kilometers of silence. Change omnipresent yet seemingly invisible.

Nikki: Ah, look, K.F.C.
Alan: What?
Nikki: Ka-Fucking-Ching![4]

First published as a catalogue essay for *Jewel of the Newell*, Colleen Ahern and Tully Moore, Firstdraft, Sydney, 2010.

Notes

1 This is the title of an EP released by Jim O'Rourke in 1999. It is also the title of the fourth track on the EP; the song is dark, kind of humorous and a little bit disturbing.

2 Si Litvinoff, *Walkabout*, directed by Nicolas Roeg (Los Angeles: Twentieth Century Fox, 1971).

3 Richard Franklin, *Roadgames*, directed by Richard Franklin (Embassy Pictures, 1981).

4 Bill Bennett, *Kiss or Kill*, directed by Bill Bennett (New Vision Films, 1997).

Head Under Ground (Yekaterinburg's Plots)

Yekaterinburg is a major city in central Russia. Founded in 1723, it was named after Tsar Peter the Great's wife, and Empress Yekaterina's namesake, Saint Catherine.

After the Russian Revolution, on 17 July 1918, Tsar Nicholas, his wife Alexandra, five of their children, a doctor and two servants were executed by the Bolshevik Secret Police at Ipatiev House—a merchant's home in Yekaterinburg where they were imprisoned for several months. Apparently the execution squad was comprised of four Russian Bolsheviks and seven soldiers who were Hungarian prisoners-of-war. The Hungarians spoke little if any Russian and were chosen because the commanding officer (the Cheka) didn't think a Russian soldier could kill the Tsar or his daughters. It is alleged that one of the Hungarian soldiers was Imre Nagy. When ordered to shoot the Romanovs, Nagy laid down his weapon and said he refused to kill innocent people and children.

Nagy later became a national hero and Prime Minister of Hungry (for a second time), following his role in the anti-Soviet revolution of 1956.

Between 1924 and 1991, Yekaterinburg was known as Sverdlovsk, named after the Bolshevik party leader Yakov Sverdlov. Sverdlovsk was Boris Yeltsin's home town. Yeltsin, before becoming the first President of the Russian Federation ordered the destruction of Ipatiev House. It was 1977 and Yeltsin was following orders from Moscow. The destruction was carried out in order to prevent the Ipatiev House from becoming a shrine to the Ramanovs.

In 1998, 80 years to the day after their execution in the cellar of the house, Yeltsin represented 'the people' at the funeral of the Tsar and his family when they were reburied in St Petersburg.

During the 1991 coup attempt, Yeltsin selected Sverdlovsk as the 'back-up' capital of the Russian Federation.

After the failure of the coup and the dissolution of the USSR, the city returned to its historical name: Yekaterinburg.

In October 1991, Yeltsin declared 'shock therapy' on the country in the form of sweeping, market-oriented reform. The privatisation that resulted meant control shifted from the state to a selection of groups and individuals, many of whom were reported to have had with links to both the government and the mafia. In the following years there was a substantial rise in criminal gangs and crime. It is around this time that Yekaterinburg became one of Russia's most violent gangster zones. Home not only to Yeltsin, but many of the Russian mafia bosses, the early- and mid-nineties in Yekaterinburg were notorious for their gang wars. In one 10-month period, 1,142 people died in gang-related crime. Many of these were gang leaders, Russian mafia bosses who died in wars primarily fought over the control of the precious stone and metal industries of Yekaterinburg.

You can find the local cemetery in the industrial Uralmarsh area of Yekaterinburg, which was once the centre of the USSR's military manufacturing. It is home to many of the Russian mafia's fallen comrades. The markers of their graves are monolithic, black marble tombstones. Often life-size, many of them have photographic images of the deceased meticulously etched into them.

Effigies of the deceased, these imposing black and white death portraits depict men posing at tables laden with signifiers of their wealth. Some stand in front of their lavish mansions, others beside their expensive yet ultimately generic cars. The headstones, mostly of men, reproduce their mafioso garb — designer suits, leather jackets and tassled leather shoes. Thick (I assume gold) chains and bracelets, their hands hold cigarettes, vodka or perhaps the keys to their prized Mercedes. If you were not in Yekaterinburg, you may be mistaken for having come across a shrine to Al Capone, or perhaps a monument to his Hollywood versions: Robert De Niro or William Forsythe. Distinguished memorials, tributes or mere characterisations. Lonely portraits in a necropolis.

If *memento mori* works are to remind us of our own mortality and the punishments we face if we 'break the rules of our religion', these Russian mafia headstones are more like cinema posters laying claim to the narrative of a gang, its members and the power they command. Embellishments of underworld chronicles, another grand historical narrative is proposed, sitting beside those plots of the apparently ordinary and less influential. Markers of the death of one cold war and the continuity of another. Hierarchies of memorial in cemeteries of ambiguity.

First published as a catalogue essay for *Head Under Ground*, Tully Moore, John Buckley Project Space, April 2010.

The Outback Denier

This interview first appeared in the Summer 1976 issue of the journal South by Southwest *published in the Department of English and History at the University of Melbourne. At times brutal, the interview is a stark reminder of white Australia's obsession with cultural ownership of the outback, and a timely example of the prodigious nature of Dr. David Loeb's once-controversial theory of outback denial. With permission from the original publishers, we re-present sections of that infamous interview between Dr. Loeb and his colleague Dr. Katharina Graw, which was conducted in the West Tower of the John Medley Building at the University of Melbourne, Parkville campus, in 1975. Given white culture's sustained interest in depictions and representations of the outback, we believe it is time to revisit this little-known but significant moment in Australian academia.*

Katharina Graw: David, you recently presented a paper at the *Ruptured World: History of Land Clearing* conference, where you argued that there is no outback in Australia, that even as a construct it is deceptive to use the outback as a metaphor for non-indigenous spiritual or cultural rituals. You went so far as to completely deny the existence of the outback, which is of course absurd, but I am intrigued at the genesis of this idea. Do you still stand by this claim?

David Loeb: There is no outback, Katharina. I have already stated this. What there is, is a short history of land clearing slapped on the back of identity issues that can only apply to indigenous inhabitants. What I am referring to is representation. Anglo artists and authors are not capable of making a meaningful contribution to Australian identity because it will always be a case of narcissism combined with aesthetics disguised as understanding. In the end, it's meaningless. If I were to pursue this goal, this goal of constructing a discourse for Australianness, I would need to avoid the mythical history of the landscape, at least the ones Anglo inhabitants constructed in the nineteenth century. Obviously Australia is a construct, it's a colony. It must always be considered that we are not at one with this land. Perhaps this can be called post-colonialism, a theory of something that comes after the colonial mentality has collapsed. But this post-colonialism will probably never occur if artists and authors continue to reinforce myths of the outback. When you consider examples such as *Jedda* or *Wake in Fright*... let's think about *Wake in Fright*. How can that be considered in terms of identity and the outback, what do you think?

Katharina Graw: Are you questioning whether these films are simply metaphors for psychological isolation? Or do you see something more sinister going on, where, perhaps, a myth is perpetuated and Aboriginality is denied? In *Wake in Fright*, the protagonist John Grant finds himself in a comparable position, having made a pact with the devil, so to speak, where in exchange for his education he must teach in a small, arid, perhaps imagined outback. Seemingly trapped in a drug-induced, alcohol-fueled, hunt-or-be-hunted terrain, Grant attempts suicide and then escape, but the truck he leaves on delivers him back to the town from which he is trying to escape. The portrayal is that the town is 'outside of culture' and the parable is perhaps not too far removed from the original settlement of Australia—white, apparently cultured and educated man attempts to conquer the 'wild frontier'. I'm wondering what you were thinking, David? Is there some sort of fissure in terms of the narrative and representation?

David Loeb: Fissure is polite, Katharina. In fact, there is a lot you are saying that is polite, but what you were getting at in terms of the parallel between history and representations of the outback, such as that in *Wake in Fright*, is correct. There is a cultural problem, both in imagining and actually experiencing this idea of the outback or frontier in Australia, if not in all settler and colonised societies—myths and stories generated to justify the chain reaction of arrival, occupation, dispossession and then the continued domination of indigenous peoples and their land. Australia is not an isolated case — we can also consider the United States and Canada in this issue. *Wake in Fright* is an excellent example of how representations in culture perpetuate the occupation, dispossession and continued domination of land in the ongoing construction of 'our' official history and national identity, where the outback is something to be conquered rather than known. The outback is not a place of life, or rather of any life that is worth 'knowing'. This is the representation, Katharina, and it is disturbing, not only in its dystopic rendering but also in its negation of the other.

Katharina Graw: It's a big place, David; not everything can be 'known'. Maybe there is a relationship between an inability to comprehend an expansive landscape with an average of 0.02 inhabitants per square metre, and an inability to unravel 60,000 years of history that predates white settlement?

David Loeb: That's the point, Katharina, it's the illusion of 'knowing' that's the problem, that combined with worth and an imposed value system. Most depictions of the landscape present a digestible version of history — barren spaces and a romanticised landscape at times inhabited by 'strong' pastoralists and patronising visions of noble savages. They are renditions of a filtered experience that suggest a 'nice' history, or a dramatised notion as discussed previously, one that alleges or alludes to an honorable conquest of land and distance, rather than a conquest by extravagant violence and violations of man and landscape. I could suggest that these representations are like those of Holocaust deniers — opportunistic appropriations colluding with a desire for home, place and identity. Representations such as these can only lead to the corrosion of public memory and thus a failure to reconcile with a past. This failure, this corrosion, is exemplified in policy, such as the recently ended 70-year White Australia Policy. It's a type of repression that will lead to abnormality. In the primary phase, which I am going to suggest is invasion to federation (1778–1901), we learn that some aspects of reality aren't pleasant. We learn that both the pleasant and unpleasant are sometimes controllable and sometimes not. The natural assumption that all things are equal is repressed. Self and other and fear and desire are determined and distinguished — an analogy for white settlers and indigenous peoples. In psychology, the second stage of repression, which might indeed be federation to dissolution of the White Australia Policy (1901–1975), sees the child learn that acting on desires causes anxiety leading to the repression of the desire. We are in, or heading towards, an abnormal cultural repression, or even a complex, culturally neurotic behavior where this internalised anxiety will lead to a potentially illogical, self-destructive and anti-social society — evident in forms of extreme nationalism and patriotism that are enforced and justified by the representations we are talking about that justify a desire or rather intervene on a desire to 'conquer' and own without any identifiable threat. I'm describing this in a linear way, but it is a complicated, interlocking and concomitant process. Specificity in terms of time and space are essential, revealing, and reintroducing the repressed aspects of Australian history is pertinent for a conscious awareness of place and identity.

Katharina Graw: Well, David, that is a lot for us to swallow. If I were to take your position of the outback denier and run with it, how would I then account for the history of colonial representation of the landscape — I'm thinking of Australian pastoral painting ending with Sydney Nolan's *Inland Australia* series? These works have come to represent what is considered to be a greater Australianness than the representations made by the original inhabitants. When you think about the avant-garde we saw in the exhibition *The Field* a few years back at the opening of the new National Gallery of Victoria, it is clear that representing the 'outback', or the mythologised Australia, is obviously not of concern to Anglo-Australian artists, with the exception of those continuing the traditions of the sentimental pastoralists — the colonials, if you will. And when I think about the artifacts that are being made up north in Papunya, where that school teacher has started things, when you think about how they are being mythologised by the institution, there emerges a potential for the apologists to follow your lead. My point being, if you are making a claim to be the first outback denier, what is the future for the Australian myth?

David Loeb: I am no apologist, Katharina, please don't go there. The outback is a right-wing conservative myth stemming from an ideology impairment. Think of it as a conceptual and moral disability. Imagine someone presenting the idea that the conflict between Aboriginal Australians and white settlers had been fabricated, that the numbers of Aboriginals killed and displaced by white Australians was a politically motivated fraud… you just wouldn't do it, it's an absurd proposition. Considering that, my position—denying the existence of the outback—is nothing more than a furphy constructed to upset the moralistic right who continue to maintain this immoral and unethical myth of the Australian outback. They are denying the Aboriginal Australian, they are maintaining a landscape that is not lived. It is simply unreal, and its continuation is irresponsible. It will eventually be of great social and cultural detriment.

Katharina Graw: So by claiming to be an outback denier you are suggesting that any depiction of a mythogised outback is a condition unique to a far-right-wing racist attitude?

David Loeb: Yes.

Katharina Graw: So, it is the clearing of land for agricultural profit that has perpetuated the outback myth by making previously vegetated areas of land appear barren. Western Victoria is a great example, north of Horsham, past Managatang, the areas south of the Mallee Cliffs National Park… these are great examples of areas cleared for agriculture that can be romanticised in terms of being part of the harsh, barren, remote Australian outback.

David Loeb: This is where my denial originates because it is hardly ever acknowledged in creative practices, or documentary for that matter, that the Australian outback is a cultural construction. Almost 75 per cent of the population lives on the eastern littoral. There's a psychological escape, a sea route out. What can we find in this 'accidental' location? If there is no outback, is there no need for escape? No outback, no violent delineation of the other? You know Katharina, I doubt there is an 'outback' or 'frontier' if you are indigenous. The outback only exists when in someone else's place. You arrive and deem the place and its inhabitants in need of conquering. When the outback ceases to exist, so too does the desire to possess it. The need to dispossess its inhabitants is emasculated and what is repressed can be freed. After that, inclusive and fluid ideas can be explored and more interesting representations of actual, lived culture will result.

Co-authored by Jarrod Rawlins, first published in *Art & Australia*, vol. 48, no. 1, Spring 2010.

2011

The Dans

Set: A tiny island surrounded by circular walls with a threshold at the rear of the island. The island is bare except for a somewhat pathetic palm tree at its centre. To its right is some water, but this depends on the direction you are facing. Inconsequentially, the island is temporarily located at 37 degrees, 49 minutes and 36 seconds south of the equator, while it is 144 degrees, 58 minutes and one second east of the meridian passing through Greenwich, England. The audience is generally located in close vicinity to this. The audience enters the set via an L-shaped corridor and a locker located in a cleaning cupboard. They are intermittently close to the performance. This cupboard is simultaneously a utility, a refuge and a cell. Its air is thick with the fumes of ammonia-based cleaning products.

> [*No curtain rises, nor is there semi-darkness. DAN is sitting with his back resting on the palm tree. In one hand he fiddles with a CD Walkman, with the other he sifts slowly through the sand. DANNER's head is poking through the threshold mentioned above. DAN and DANNER are wearing knee-length shorts, black caps and Rambo T-shirts on which Rambo's face has been replaced with their own.*]

DAN: Call me Dan.

DANNER: [*looks towards the centre of the island, questioning*] No coconuts on that palm?

DAN: Is this where I'm meant to be? Is this all there is?

DANNER: [*voice mimics that of a documentary narrator, perhaps David Attenborough or Benedict Cumberpatch*] Perched on a tiny island in a watery desert, the lone specimen stares vacantly into a void, slowly mustering the courage to speak…

DAN: [*disgruntled*] Yeah, right… and before the BBC, you joined the Navy in order to travel. Dude! Listen! I'm being serious.

DANNER: Did you really choose where you wanted to be or did you just end up here?

DAN: [*dreamily, far away*] Not sure… I'm not sure where the story begins. I was a carpenter once. I can build things. Building is like choosing.

DANNER: [*walks on to the island, squats and lets the white sand run through his fingers*] Like choosing what? You're not as funny as you think you are, Dan.

DAN: [*ignoring Danner and almost talking to himself*] I built a canon once—an impossible canon. A fake escape… don't know why or where to though…

DANNER: [*looking to the audience, winking and tipping his cap*] Sometimes, making something leads to nothing.

DAN: [*looks at Dan*] I'm not fond of your soliloquy, Danner! Do you think I got here via the canon?

DANNER: Why would you build a canon if you've been trained to build boats? The best way to get to an island is by boat, isn't it?

DANNER: [*looks out across the small stretch of water*] Hey! Is that… Is that a white whale out there?

DAN: White elephant, more like it. I'd buy a boat, before I built one.

DANNER: Do you have to be so friggin' quixotic?

DAN: Exotic? An island's supposed to be, don't you think? Hey… you know what I heard? I heard that England is deserted.

DANNER: Trifle! How can England be deserted?

DAN: [*frantic*] No-one bought it. You know… where they're building the world… the world in islands. Instead of the millennia it takes for an island to naturally emerge, they just build them… plonk them in the sea and then put them up for sale. They're man-made islands. A paradise-island-world for sale — but it's sinking. Paradise lost! Easter Island means nothing.

DANNER: [*starting to sing*] Islands in the Gulf Stream… that is what we are…

DAN: [*annoyed with Danner for not listening, Dan drops the CD Walkman*] The Irishman committed suicide.

DANNER: What do you mean?

DAN: His Irish home in the sun began sinking… or the sands started eroding… or he went broke. I think.

DANNER: [*still crouching and picking up handfuls of sand*] The Irishman bought Ireland? Lucky perhaps, not like that Dutch dude who got sent to an island for sodomy in 1725. Ascension Island right… halfway between Africa and South America, which, I guess, is like the middle of nowhere then… maybe it's the middle of nowhere now, too. Marooned and castaway, with only a tent and some water. Pretty tough. When Ascension Island was initially discovered it was pretty dry and barren, and uninhabited except for sea birds and turtles.

DANNER: [*starts frantically scanning around*] Any sea birds and turtles here? You know… I'm rather fond of the booby. In Spanish…

DAN: Yeah, yeah… in Spanish *bubi* means dunce. What happened to the Dutch guy?

DANNER: Leendert Hasenbosch was his name. Well, he kept

this diary, for about six months. He lived on turtle and boobies, wrote about devils and demons and then, six month later, he died. A captain on a passing ship found his sitting skeleton, the diary beside it.

DAN: Island dumping, dunking islands, sinking islands, island building.

DANNER: Hey… on that floating-global-island-map thing you were talking about, did they include Ascension Island? What about the 20,000 or so other islands in the Pacific… I mean… how do you choose which countries become an island and which ones don't? Are they scaled? Or is scale irrelevant? I mean, if they are all sinking and merging like you said…

DAN: [*irritated*] You're rubbing my head.

DANNER: And then, if you get to buy one, right… then what's that about? Are there rules? I mean, let's take Binyamin Netanyahu… can Netanyahu buy Palestine?

DAN: [*rubbing his head*] I got so much trouble on my mind…

DAN: [*puts his hands down and stares at the large shell in front of him*] You know… I'm just thinking… is building an island like pretending to be God?

DANNER: Dunno… maybe buying an island is like false free choice… You have enough money to buy an island, so you better buy an island. So maybe buying an island is being like a god, but building one is like being an atheist.

DAN: This is almost theatrical, isn't it?

DANNER: Exile as punishment, exile as pleasure.

DAN: What would Wilson say?

DANNER: [*ignoring Dan*]: You know what I'm thinking? I'm thinking that you might have a little bit of 'islomania'.

DAN: Islowhat?

DANNER: Islomania. You're obsessed with islands and varying island forms… workrooms… cupboards. You know, perceived isolated spaces. It's like you are escaping yourself to find yourself and then escape yourself again.

DAN: Well, that's a bit serious. George Berkley said, 'to be is to be perceived'… or something like that.

DANNER: I've never read any English philosophy! If you buy an island you are asking to be perceived?

DAN: It is funny to think that the world is sinking. They haven't even started building the universe yet.

DANNER: [*wistfully*] All these other worlds…

DANNER: [*breaks from a dreamlike state*] Hey! What's that beyond the rainbow walls?

DAN: [*rolls his eyes*] You know… there is a program called Desert Island Discs'. It's been on BBC Radio for 80-plus years. They ask people, important cultural people, 'If you were marooned on an island, what eight pieces of recorded music would you need, and what book and useless item would you take with you?'

DANNER: Your point?

DAN: I dunno… It's like even in the hypothetical, being on an island is a way of talking about your life. And that's kinda odd because, well, doesn't the saying go, 'No man is an island'… or something like that? You know what?

DANNER: What?

DAN: Tracey Emin said she would take the Beach Boys' 'Good Vibrations'.

DANNER: [*bored*] Of course she would.

DAN: That wouldn't be for Vexation Island, would it?

DANNER: I guess not. So, maybe you need an island if you can't be an island. Maybe that's the attraction of buying one. Real or fake, though?

DAN: [*quickly stands, and in a loud, definitive voice*] I want out. There is nothing here… not even coconuts. I'd rather be a cleaner.

DANNER: But everything is here. Everything we need.

DAN: [*picks up a large shell*] I'm not sure a CD Walkman is really a very good diary.

[*Faint sounds of laughter, snickering and coughs come from the shell, growing louder. Lights dim.*]

Originally commissioned by the Australian Centre for Contemporary Art for *New11*, curated by Hannah Mathews, Australian Centre for Contemporary Art, Melbourne, 2011, pp. 42–44.

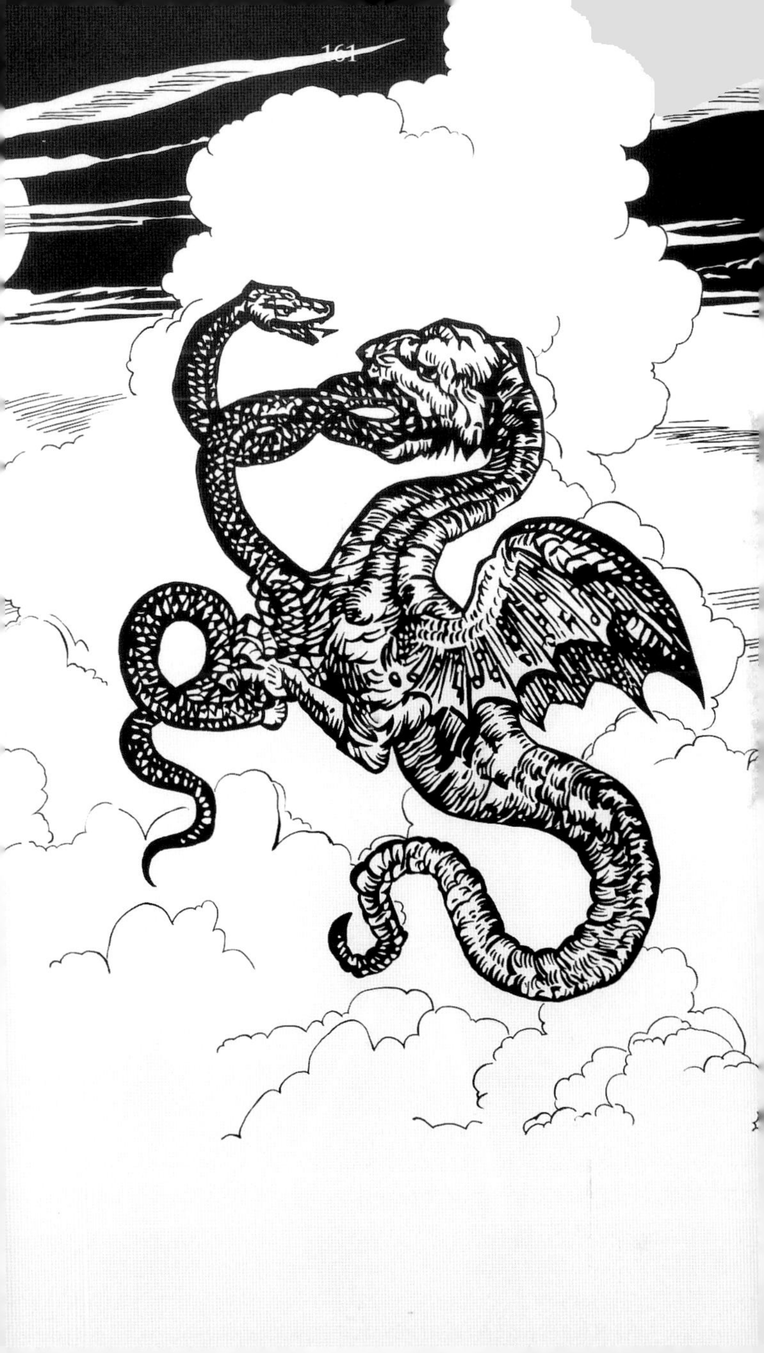

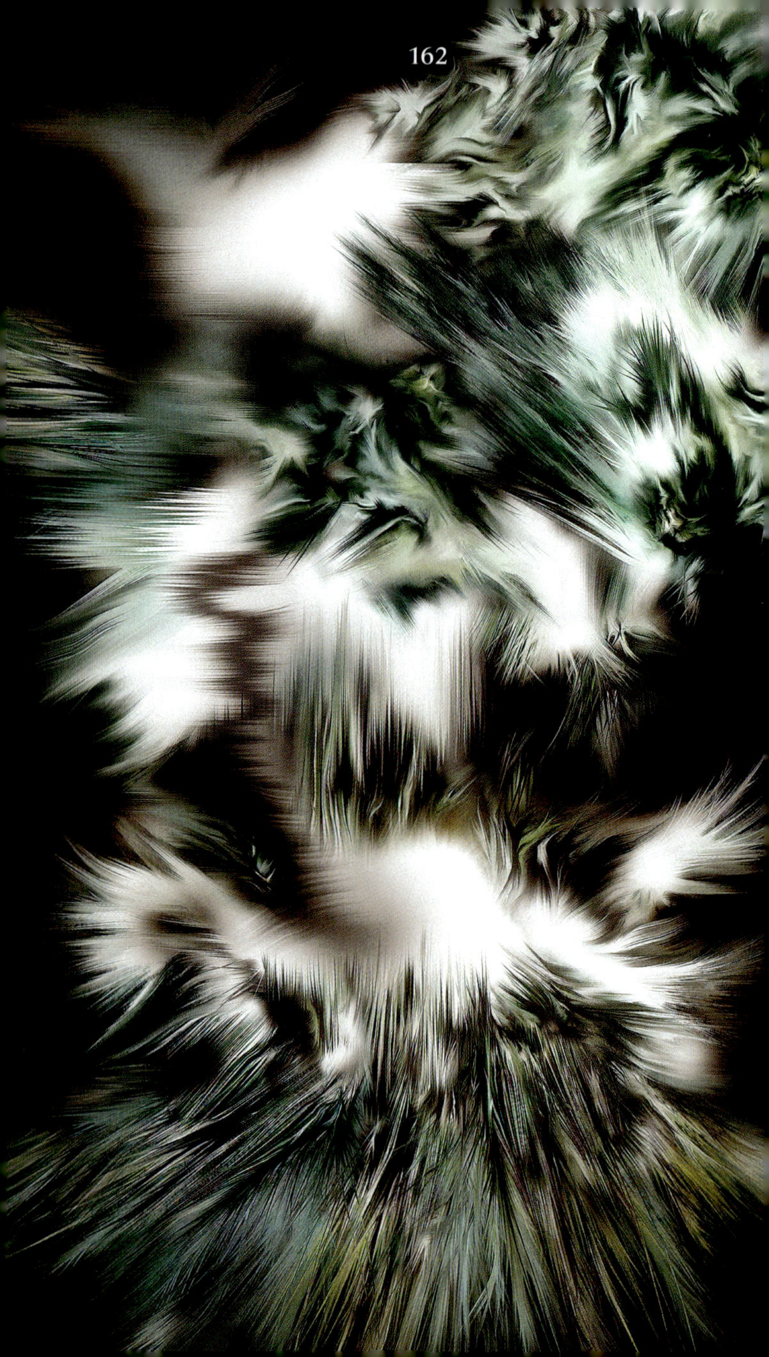

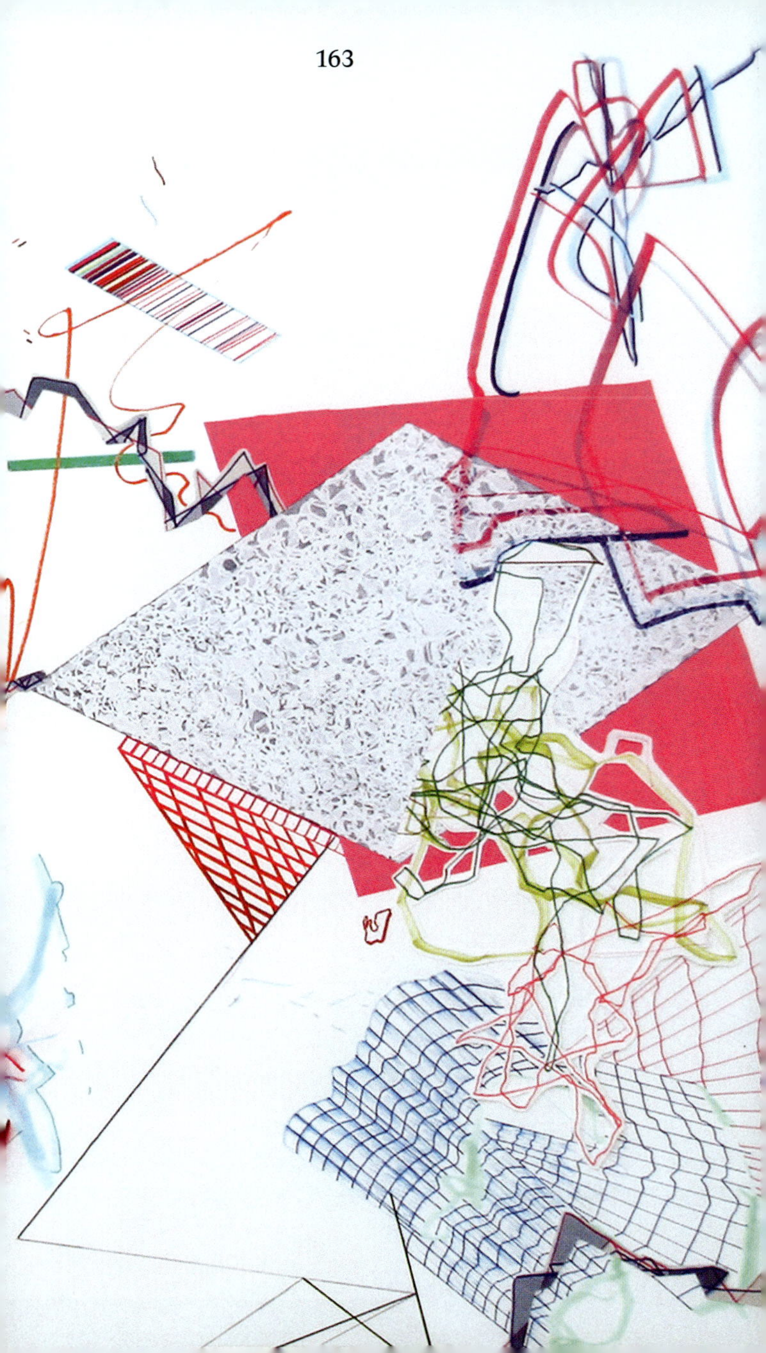

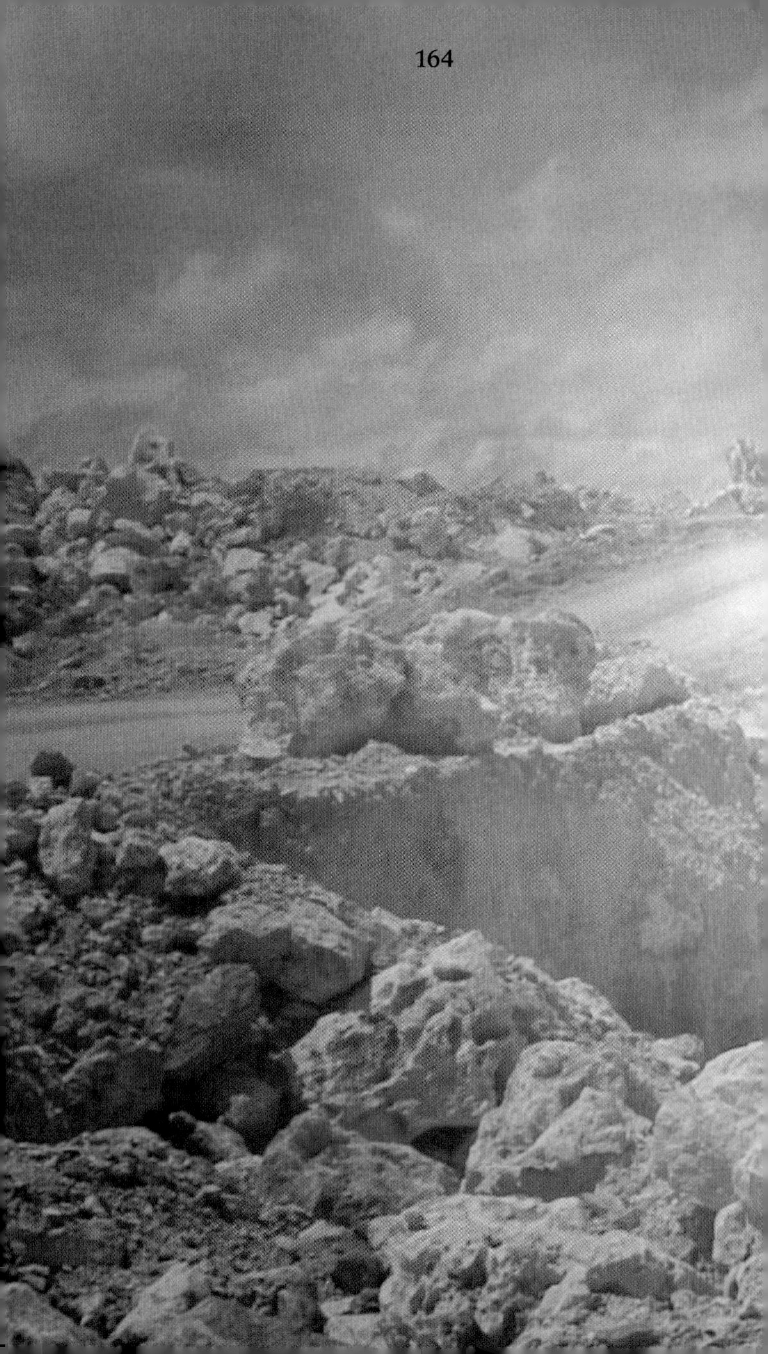

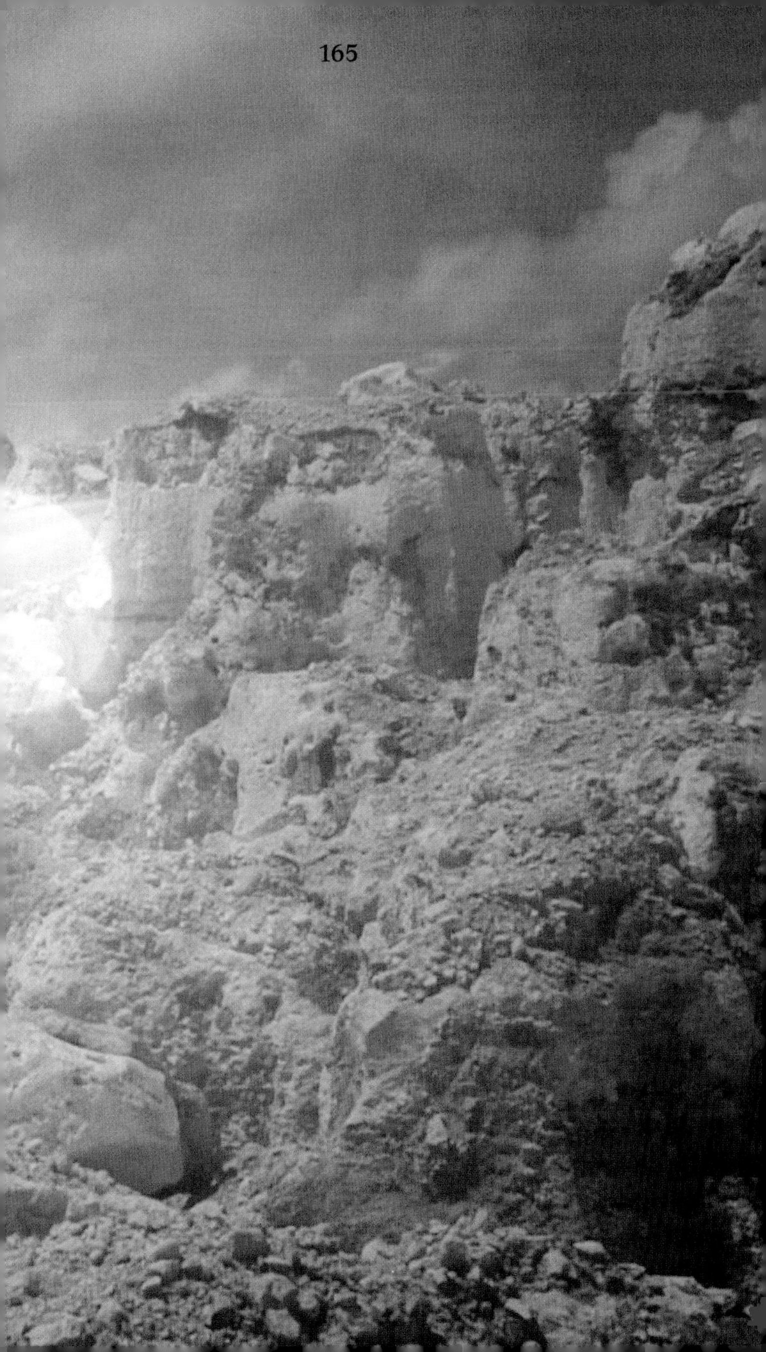

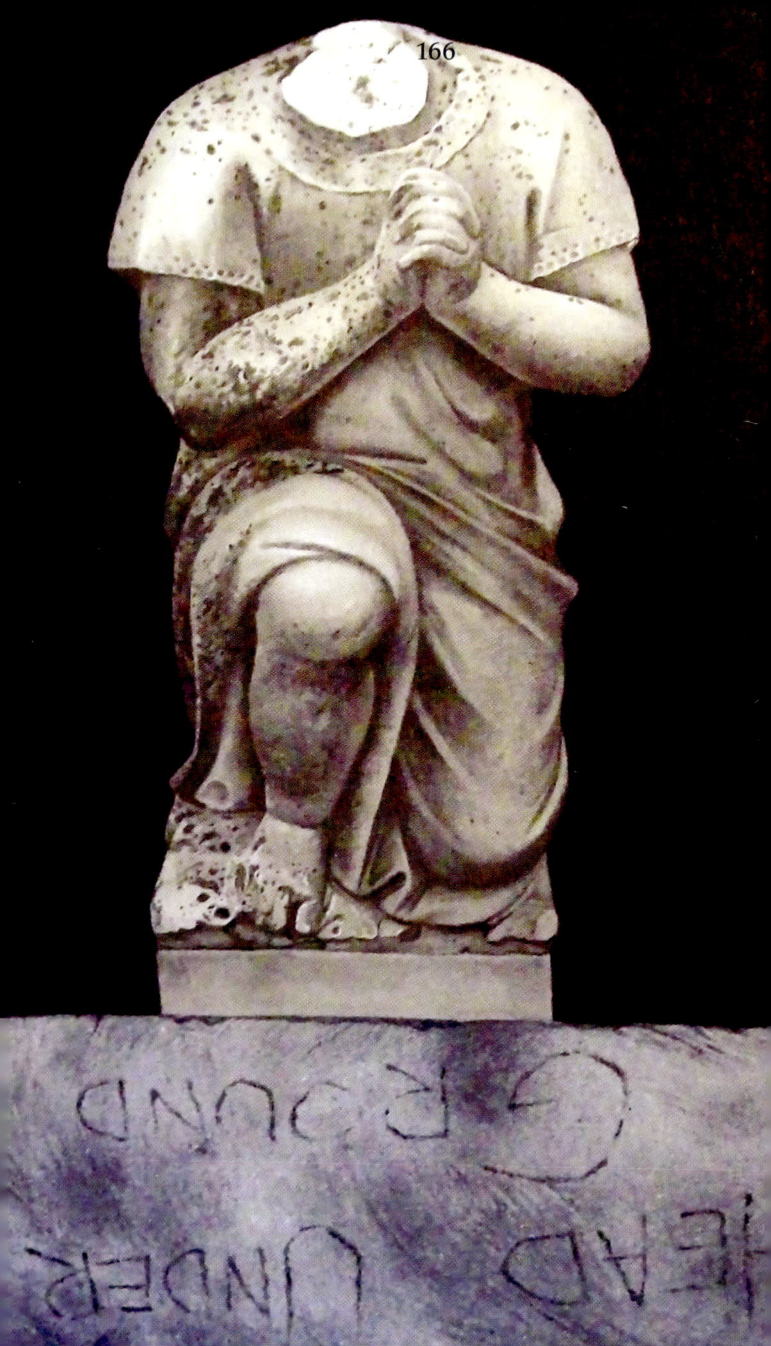
UNDER
GROUND

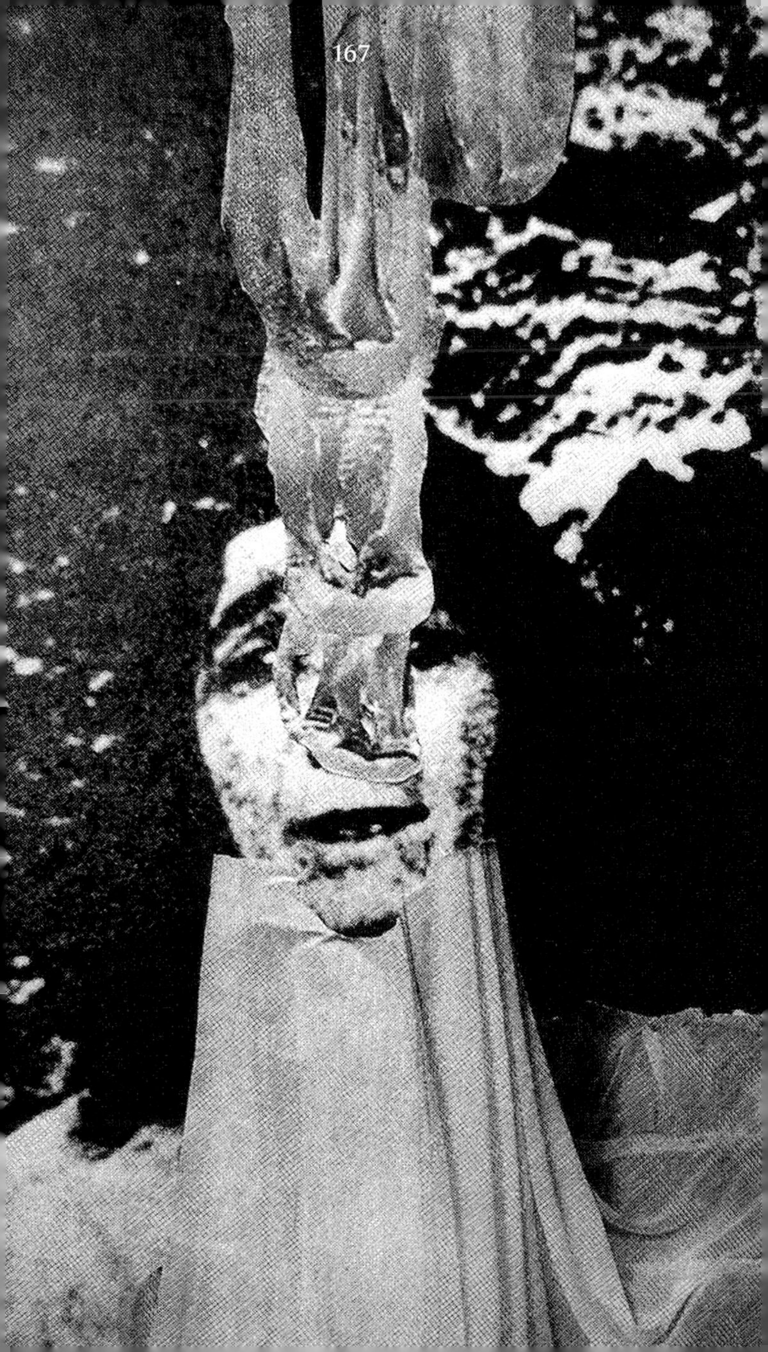

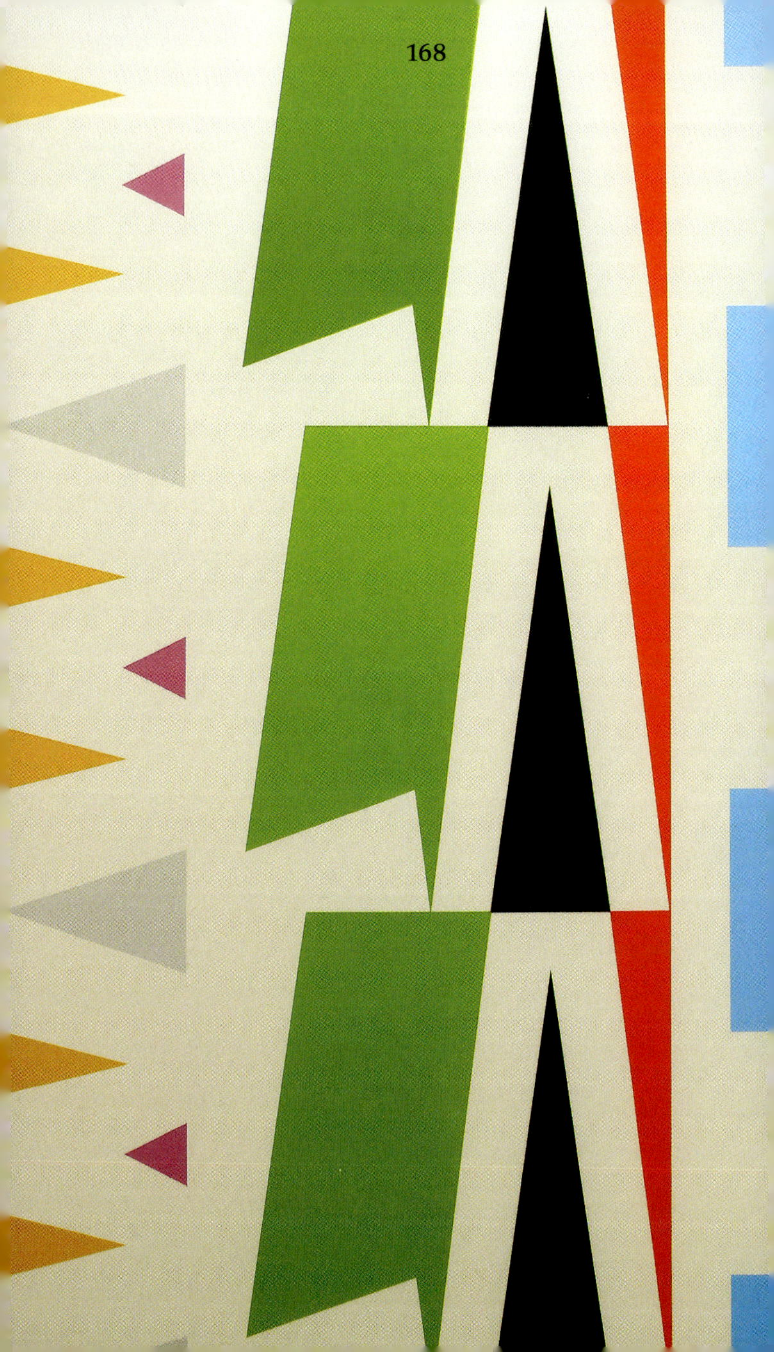

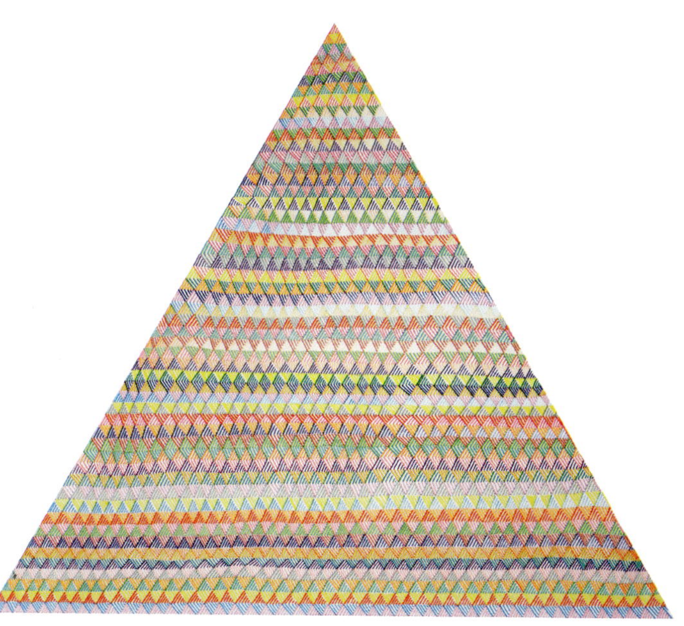

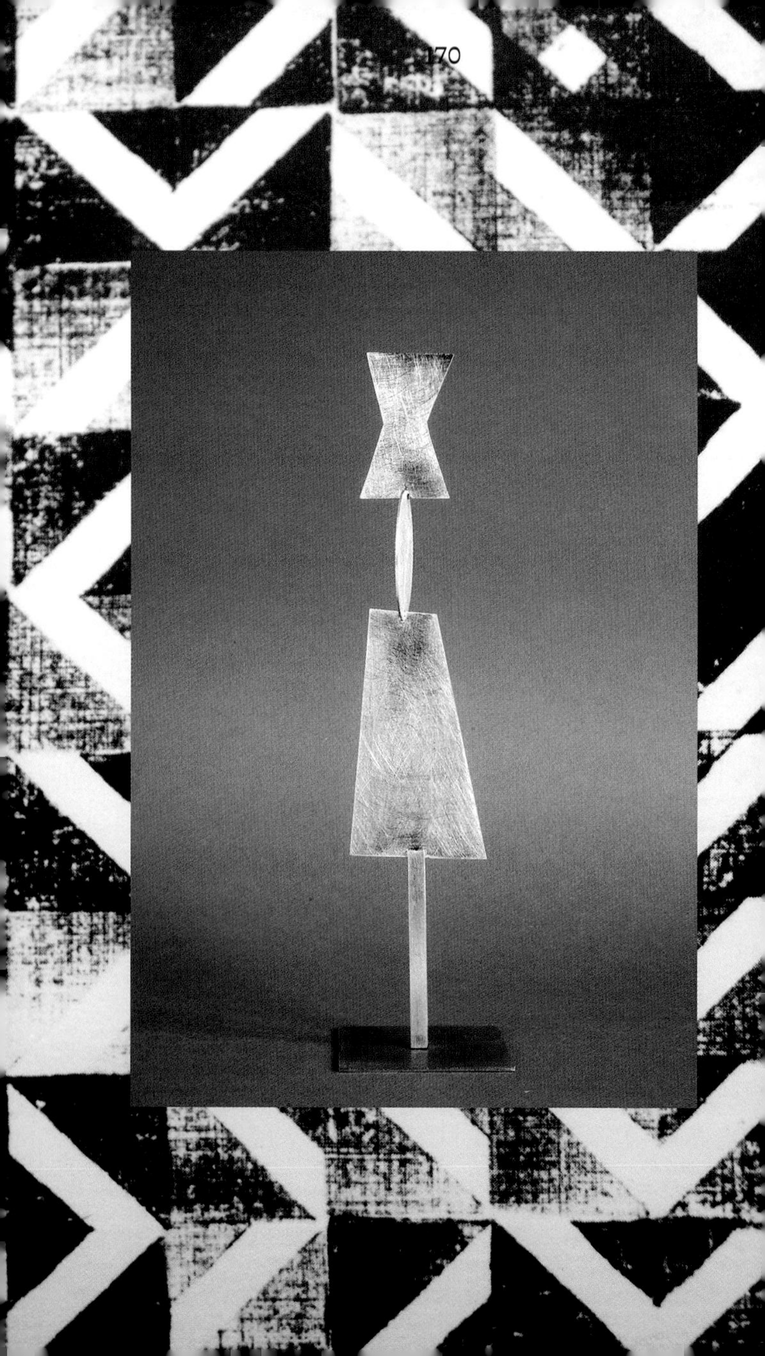

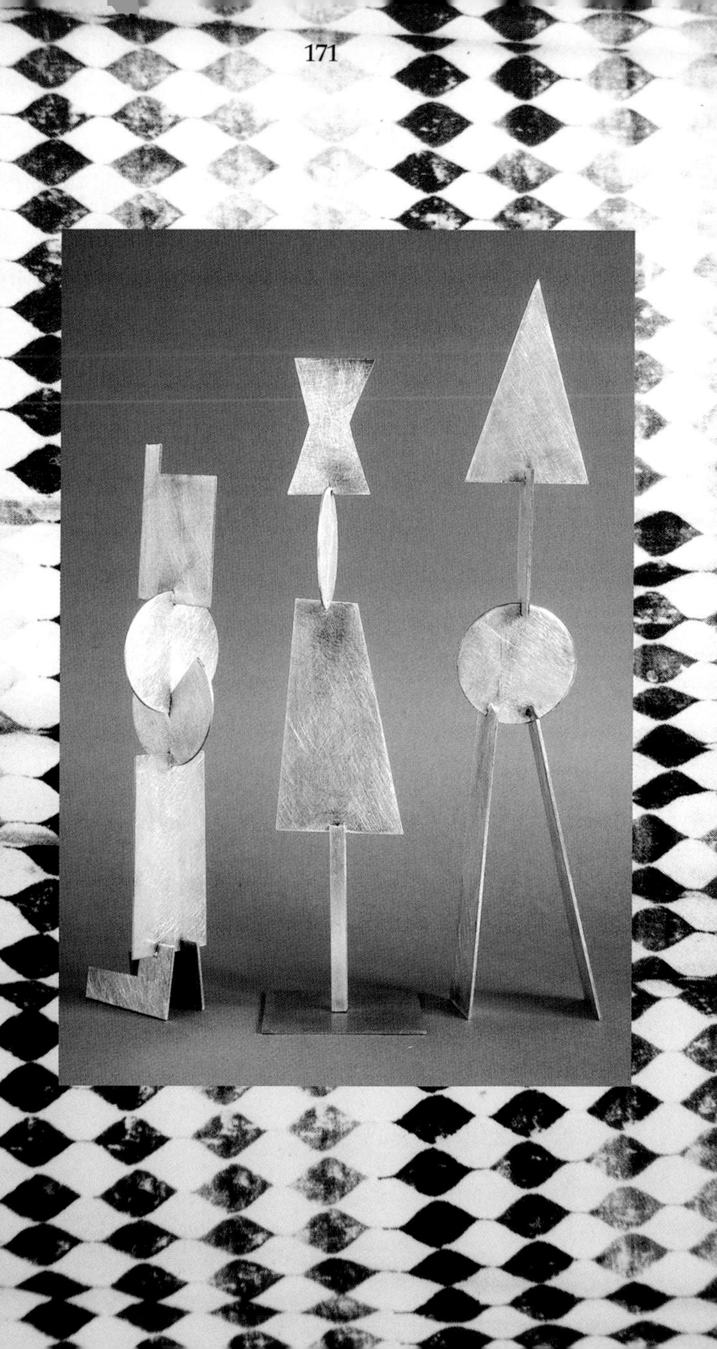

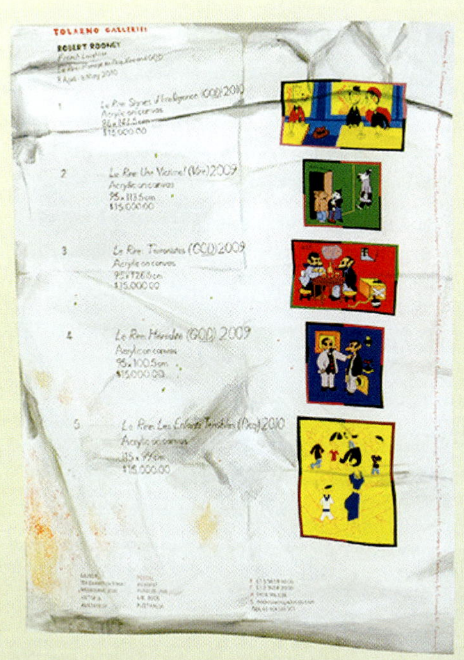
TOLARNO GALLERIES
ROBERT ROONEY
1
Acrylic on canvas
$15,000.00
2
Acrylic on canvas
95 x 113.5 cm
$15,000.00
3
Le Rire: Terroristes (GOD) 2009
Acrylic on canvas
$15,000.00
4
Le Rire: Héredite (GOD) 2009
Acrylic on canvas
95 x 100.5 cm
$15,000.00
5
Le Rire: Les Enfants Terribles (Pico) 2010
$15,000.00

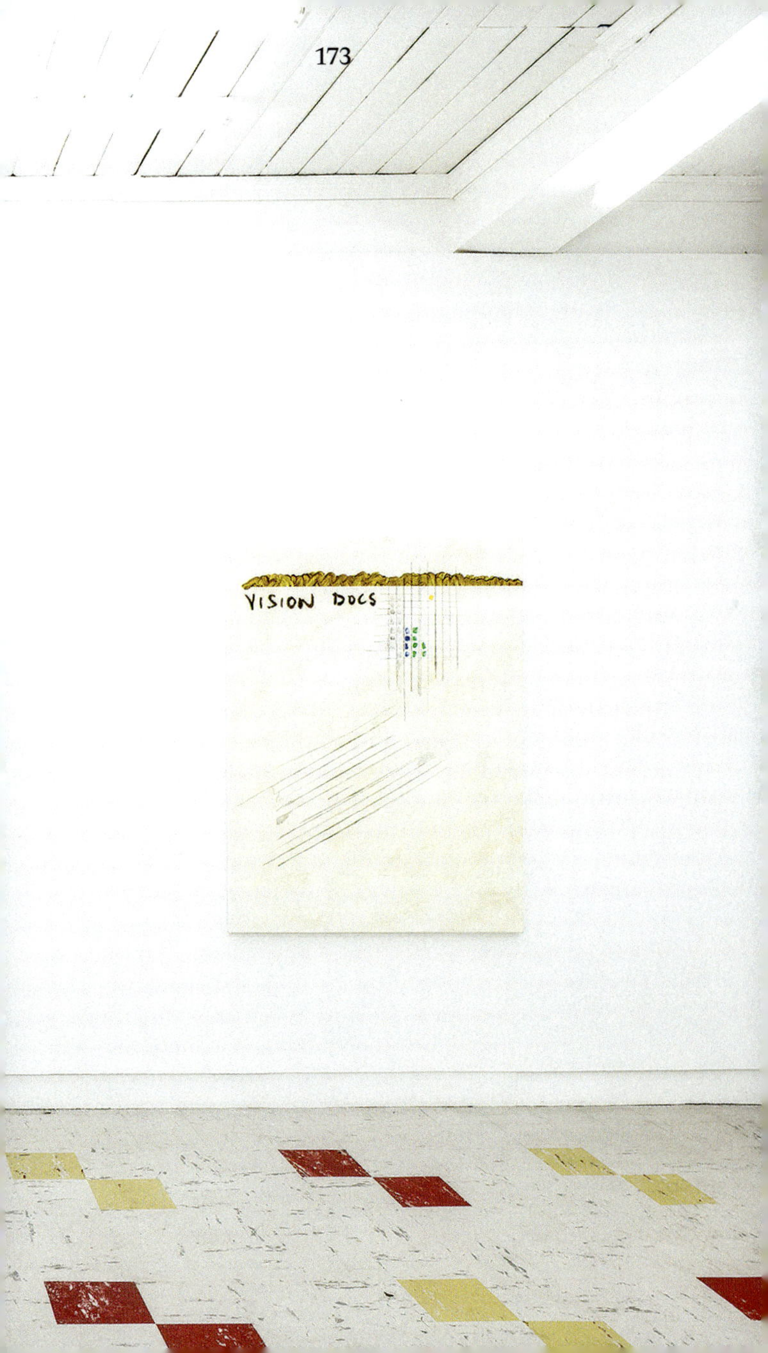
VISION DOCS

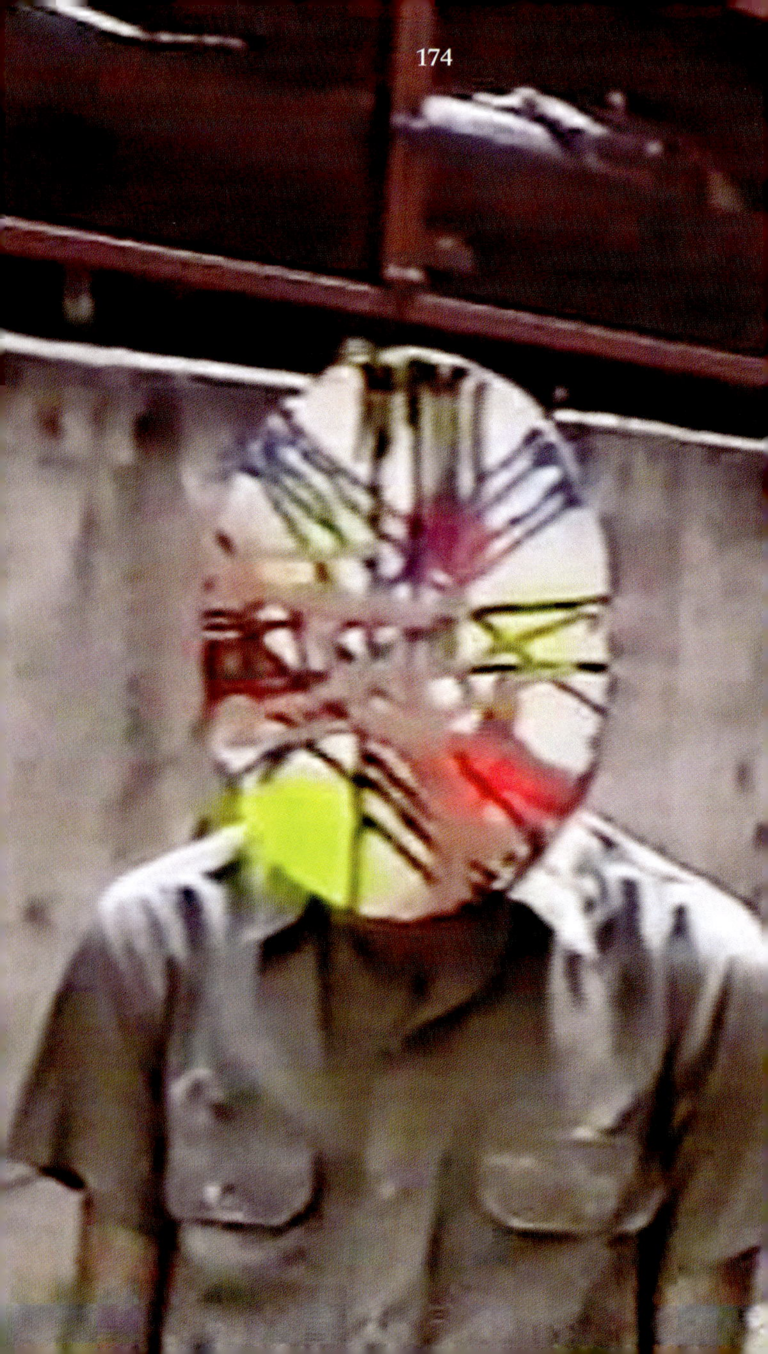

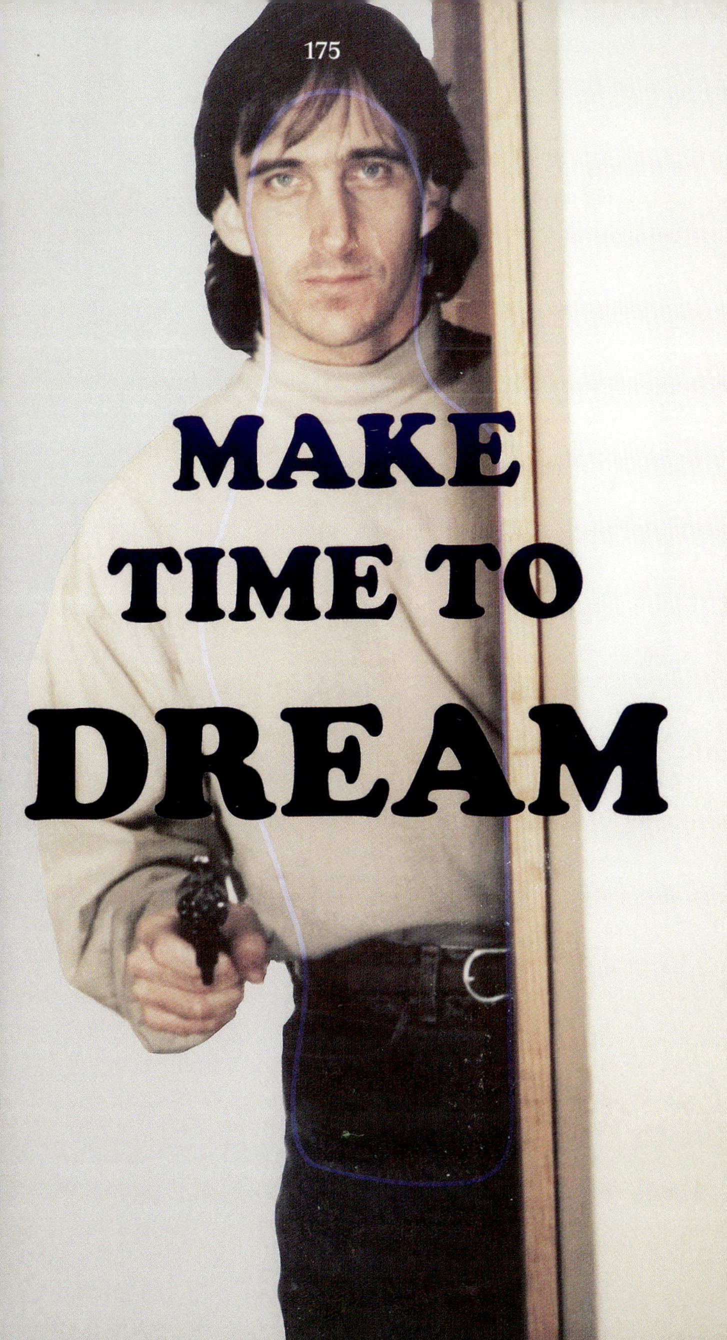
MAKE
TIME TO
DREAM

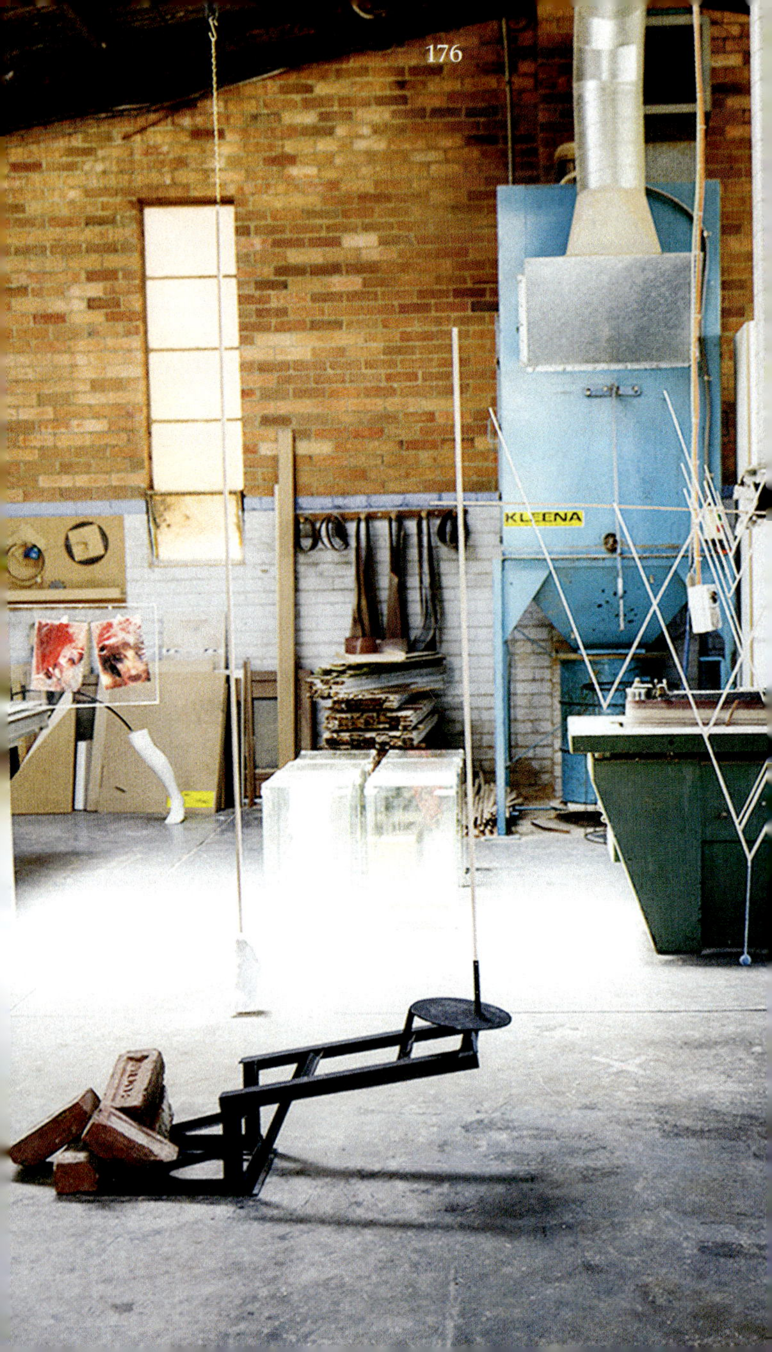
KLEENA

Iterative pratfalls

Some principles of Statistical Pattern Theory:

Use real world signals rather than constructed ones to infer the hidden states of interest.

Are offerings at temples in a secular society like gifts without a purpose? Without a purpose differs to being useless. Without a purpose implies that potential exists. Whoever the intended recipient of the gift is, and if they exist, determines the possibility of the offering having use.

Francis Bonami remembers Gabriel Orozco's *Empty Shoe Box* (1993), an open cardboard box left on the floor to be kicked about:

> I remember him rolling this ball of plasticine through the Corderie building and placing it in the space allotted to him between two gigantic brick pillars. Then, with a very humble gesture, he opened a knapsack and pulled out in front of a small group of friends his shoe box, and placed it in the middle of the proportionally immense space. The idea that such an uneventful object was taking up so much real estate caused quite a commotion among many artists. Space in a Venice Biennale exhibition is rare. Artists fight to defend every square inch for their work. Curators are threatened, people cry, voices are raised. When he saw the territory occupied by that shoe box, the American artist Charles Ray was up in arms. He and his assistants had been trying to place his 71/2-ton painted white steel cube.[1]

Discarded or unused packaging shared or found at work. Film liners from envelopes — the smooth paper backing you remove when ready to mail — arrive in the mail. The roll that remains when the receipt paper ends. An insert that protects another. Order via collection, collection via arbitrary order —

shape or dimension, stacked end-to-end like totems of discarded use.

Such signals contain too much complexity and too many artefacts to succumb to a purely deterministic analysis, so employ stochastic methods too.

The moment you become aware of a word, an idea or a thing, is simultaneously the moment it seems its existence is repeated—a word just read is uttered on the radio, yelled in the street, printed on a billboard. Random repetition. Synchronous stochasticity.

When formalist mathematician Ulf Grenander was in the tenth grade, he read an article by Ehrenfest and Ehrenfest. The article presented what Grenander has referred to as:

> the first rigorous treatment of statistical mechanics. It gave a very abstract treatment of gas particles consisting of small squares moving in a plane, simply going up or down and nothing else, with a uniform velocity but colliding! Starting with a very abstract formulation, Ehrenfest and Ehrenfest derived the laws of thermodynamics. I thought that it was wonderful. It was remarkable how statistical mechanics could be founded on just few general principles.[2]

Systems allowing for chance. Predetermined boundaries—one packet of markers, used till they don't work. A rule to be broken and an action repeated. Controlled immediacy and hand-drawn geometry.

Respect the natural structure of the signal, including any symmetries, independence of parts, marginals on key statistics.

Pattern and aesthetics.

The internet is filled with lists of fails and the fabulous. The list is itself almost an iterative process. The catchphrase of

Oh No They Didn't states: 'The celebrities are disposable. The gossip is priceless.' Cameron Diaz, they claim, repeats the roles she plays. Hollywood Groundhog Day. She plays the hot girl who is hot then makes herself look ugly/stupid and acts a fool to play down her hotness. This is usually done by wearing a ridiculous outfit or the over usage of slapstick comedy.'[3] The site gives examples: *My Best Friend's Wedding*, *There's Something About Mary*, *The Mask*, the *Charlie's Angels* movies, etc. The argument seems correct, but *Being John Malkovich* and *Shrek* are missing.

I think Deleuze made mention that repetition is not generality and that sense is found in problems.

Across all modalities, a limited family of deformations distort the pure patterns into real-world signals.

David Mumford is a mathematical formalist who, along with Ulf Grenander, has made significant advances in Pattern Theory—his principles form the structure of this essay. Mumford teaches at Brown University. The Pattern Theory Group's website states:

> The Brown University pattern theory group is working with the belief that the world is complex, and to understand it, or a part of it, requires realistic representations of knowledge about it. We create such representations using a mathematical formalism, pattern theory, that is compositional in that the representations are built from simple primitives, combined into (often) complicated structures according to rules that can be deterministic or random.[4]

David Mumford is colour-blind.

Texta entropy. When the markers start to stop working, the colours become faded. Their use also generates sound—a felt-tip beat. The colour may go, but the sound remains. Consistently inconsistent.

Stochastic factors affecting an observation show strong conditional independence.

Colour and pattern both deceive and authenticate. By ordering apparent randomness, they allude to surfaces of comfort or refrain, camouflage or warning. The safeness of white, made transparent or invisible by decoration.

Michael Taussig reflects:

> Love, money, and colour. Are these therefore untouchable subjects because they are foolish-making subjects about which the less said the better because there is something about them which actively resists language not by honest confrontation but by subtle ambush and deceptions? ... Nietzsche pointed to the magical power of rhythm in ancient times, not only in prayer as a magical snare to make the gods pliable, but in mundane activities as well, such as rowing, bailing water from a boat...[5]

Making marks on a toilet roll,
Making pantone pom poms
Collecting chads from a hole puncher......

First published as a catalogue essay for *Draw the line*, Anita Cummins, Bus Gallery, Melbourne, 16 August – 3 September, 2011

Notes

1 Francesco Bonami, 'The Early Adventures of The Zoro of Mexican Art', *TATEetc* issue 21 (April 2011).
2 Nitis Mukhopadhyay, 'A Conversation with Ulf Grenander', *Statistical Science* vol. 21, no. 3 (2006): 404–426.
3 '10 Actors Who Play the Same Role Over and Over', originally appeared on ohnotheydidnt.livejournal.com, https://www.buzzfeed.com/empressmaruja/10-actors-who-play-the-same-role-over-and-over-1fox
4 'Pattern Theory', *The Division of Applied Mathematics*, Brown University, https://www.brown.edu/academics/applied-mathematics/
5 Michael Taussig, *What Colour is the Sacred?* (Chicago: University of Chicago Press, 2009), 253.

2012

A letter from the editor, who is an artist, to the designer, who is also an artist

Brad,

If you recall, when Jennifer Allen wrote the article 'Divine Disorder', she reminded us of Kant's distinction between the beautiful and the agreeable, between beautiful decoration and agreeable use, and thus between art and design.[1] As such, for a long time, perhaps there has been an uneasy divide between the two: between what we have considered to be design and that which is art. Having said that, we all know, as Allen does, that this distinction was not always the case—that these sometimes hierarchical separations and classifications, explicit in twentieth-century manifestoes, are drawn for a multiplicity of intentions and reasons—capital, cultural, personal and material, technological and also in response to the desires of institutions and states. Boris Groys talks about this best in his article 'The Obligation to Self-Design' in reference to the Russian Constructivists, where it was assumed art should rather be placed entirely at the service of the design of utilitarian objects, making Constructivism a total project that wanted to design life as a whole.[2]

To be honest, the approach taken in devising a thematic approach to this edition of *un Magazine* came from seeing one work and thinking about it in relation to the *Impossible Objects* exhibitions curated by Helen Hughes and Melissa Loughnan at Utopian Slumps, and works exhibited during the two-year Y3K project led by Christopher L.G. Hill and James Deutsher. In 2011, Berlin-based Vassiliea Stylianidou exhibited a work at the VCA Margaret Lawrence Gallery, titled *PlaceLineLack*, in the exhibition *Future Possible*. The work, originally exhibited in 2007, consisted of a concrete-rendered model of an unfinished house and a video that documented a family dinner. In the context of the global financial crisis and, in particular, the austerity measures that many European countries were facing at the time, especially Greece Stylianidou's representation of a half-finished house presented as relic from the passing of Modernism's utopic future stood in stark contrast to Deutsher's cast feet wearing £300+ Maison Martin Margiela trainers in the exhibition *...beauty is something you have never seen before, but have always wanted to see* at Kalimanrawlins later that same year. Was I looking at Groys' design in a political context—the presentation of individuals as both artist and as self-produced works of art in re-organised social space?[3]

You and I have spent a while talking, wrongly or rightly, about the existence of an *artdesign* undercurrent that seems pervasive today. We imagined presenting our discussion in a form that echoed philosophical-texts-cum-manifestoes: five numeric (but unordered) titled dot points—*Phenomenology of the hyper modern*, *Use Value/Art Value*, *Luxury Goods*, *Arranging*, and the *Social Life of Objects*—but my inability to speak through a kind of 'historical knowing' prevented an attempt at that task. *un Magazine* issue 6.1 pitched a question about our relationship with design and art; the responses we received complicate the question and also answer it in a way that is both more and less. The relevance of the question is hopefully curious in the context of a 'two-speed economy' framed by political torpidity—once alert and alarmed, perhaps now subsidised and safe?

We continue to question our aesthetic relationship and responsibility to politics and space, regardless of what may be a safe distance, albeit merely an assumed one. At one stage, we tried to represent what we saw as the complexity of *artdesign* in a type of looped equation—conceptual art > service / experience < conceptual art. Although perhaps still wrong, I wonder if it is the closest in articulating a present. You are aware of Masato Takasaka's anti-aesthetic aesthetic (re)arrangements and planned used-but-packaged networks, towers and chaotic flat-packed venn(zen)-diagrams, which are both personified and commodity-fetishised, as well as art historical and design-present.[4] And Ash Kilmartin's spatial and rhetorical gifts—painted floors that clean, memorialise and ghost the spaces within which they exist, her invitation to us is through a gesture of material experience that puns, plays and nods to the realities and contradictions of (economic) life via titles such as *stop work* (2010). Kilmartin's *The Travelling Mime II* (2011) made of harlequined leather and silk, takes its cue from the designed-by-necessity altered blankets used by recent European migrants and refugees peddling cheap tourist mementos at sites of significance. In May, Greatest Hits' exhibition *De Facto Standard* at West Space gestured to our inability (and need) to coherently articulate our shared experience with objects and immediacy – a fake but flung printed piece of pickle, buy-two-get-one free (so three) Avatar DVDs and a sleek, stainless steel, cylindrical object dispensing *eau de MacBook*. By commissioning scent maker Air Aroma to distill a fragrance reminiscent of newly opened Macbook Air packaging, and exhibiting the scent alongside other constructions of frivolity and fun (the pickle), and James Cameron's multi-million-dollar ode to saving the world, Greatest Hits might have quietly placed us in the awkward and shifting space between ideal-desire and ideal-ethics.

I guess, for me, our complex relationship with *artdesign* is informed by tacit experience and knowledge, and, in a way, the collapsing of categories as a way of exploring the always-ongoing, social, personal and political transformation of aesthetic and material value in relation to our environment.

All my best,
Lisa

* * *

Lisa,

Thank you for the thoughtful letter, which prompted me to look again at Allen's article. I did something of a double take when re-reading it. In her suggestion that every designer since Kant has 'tried to put the parts back together again', I thought, for a second, that Allen may have overlooked an important historical moment, namely Viennese architect Adolf Loos's equation of ornament with crime.[5] As you know,

Loos fervently called for the abolition of ornament from modern design, an argument that apparently demanded a thoroughgoing divorce of beautiful decoration from agreeable use, i.e., precisely *not* their reunification. But this is not the whole story.

Loos's thesis is an aesthetic argument with an ethical foundation: he decries the extra (unnecessary) labour involved in the production of ornamentation, a labour that is doubly wasted because ornamented goods go out of fashion in a way that an austere modernism ostensibly would not. Thinking back via Deutsher's exhibition at Kalimanrawlins, I'm sure Loos would have liked the work of the Maison Martin Margiela very much, particularly the earlier stuff. This comparison is revealing: just as Margiela ennobled found and everyday garments, Loos's argument is, at base, a redefinition of beauty, but one that champions austerity over decoration. In this way, Loos did indeed try to 'put the parts back together again'—it's simply the case that one of those parts, beauty, looked different in his formulation.

From Austria to Russia, this essentialist aesthetic found expression also in Constructivism, but the latter presented an added political task, namely the education of the populace in the appreciation of the industrial products of the socialist state. There is an approximate process at work in Takasaka's use of found objects as material, and in Greatest Hits' vaporised MacBook. Such anti-aesthetic practices sensitise us to the aesthetic qualities of the everyday. Arranging, re-use and the relocation of materials and meanings figure strongly in these examples; in this way, they draw out those social relations between things that Marx recognised, but to which he never duly attended.[6] The works of Takasaka and Greatest Hits are acts of making something from something else, shifts in and of value. Already in Marx we find the recognition that every act of production is also an act of consumption, and vice versa,[7] but it was the Duchampian ready-made which really revealed to us that this productive potential of consumption is true not only in a material analysis, but also in a cultural one. And Bourriard's figure of the artist as DJ—as a *user of pre-existing forms*—reminded us of this in contemporary terms, in case we'd forgotten.[8] Yet, as Groys tells us elsewhere, the end of aesthetic trajectory in art, of which the anti-aesthetic is but a moment, is its own obsolescence.[9] For example, this trajectory meets its hypothetical end when the Soviet socialist populace recognises the beauty in the otherwise inaesthetic products of its collective labour. In Constructivism, however, art adopts the form of design for the state for another reason, namely its own survival: the quest for the new that finds a profound expression in modernist art elsewhere has no place in a political environment that is prefaced upon the end of history. Like the Constructivists, Christopher L.G. Hill sought to erase himself in *Problem Poem* (2012), his recent exhibition at Conical. Yet, it is ultimately not self-erasure but rather, for me, the kernel of critique that is more significant here: the practices we've been talking about do not face a political climate so inimical as Soviet socialism, but the example of Constructivism helps us to recognise an important tendency, namely a drive to interrogation that, however subtle, distinguishes these practices from anti-aesthetic aestheticism alone.

With regard to the matter of critique, Loos again rears his head, for we might understand his diatribe against ornamentation as a call for *design against design*. Whilst the thrust of Loos's polemic properly belongs to a very particular historical moment, design against design is alive and well today—as is *design against design against design*, for that matter, in residual postmodernisms. Of course, we also find art that is against design, as well as art that is *for* design. In fact, we find art that is either for or against (or both) design that is against design—I'm being deliberately obfuscatory here, but perhaps only such an oblique proposition can sum up the complexity of the practices we've been looking at and talking about. In other words, we can say that we can say a lot about objects, but also not very much at all. You'll recall that Ian Bogost's recent *Alien Phenomenology* attracted our attention promptly upon its publication:[10] in sum, taking a cue from Bogost's object-oriented ontology, which would place objects and humans on the same plane of philosophical analysis, we should perhaps be concerned less with what we can say with certainty about objects, and more with what they might be saying about us.

kind regards,
Brad

Co-authored by Brad Haylock, first published as an editorial in *un Magazine*, issue 6.1, June 2012.

Notes

1 Jennifer Allen, 'Divine Disorder', *Frieze* 138 (April 2011): 21.

2 Boris Groys, 'The Obligation to Self-Design', *e-flux journal* #0 (November 2008), http://www.eflux.com/journal/the-obligation-to-self-design/, accessed 28 May 2012.

3 ibid.

4 Masato Takasaka, *Almost Everything All at Once, Twice, Three Times (in Four Parts…)*, Gertrude Contemporary Art Spaces, 3 February – 10 March 2012, see: http://www.gertrude.org.au/exhibitions/gallery-11 past-14/masato-takasaka-1116.phps.

5 Adolf Loos, 'Ornament and Crime', in *Ornament and Crime: Selected Essays*, trans. Michael Mitchell (Riverside: Ariadne Press, 1998).

6 Karl Marx, *Capital: a critique of political economy* (Harmondsworth: Penguin Books, 1976), 165.

7 Karl Marx, *Grundrisse: foundations of the critique of political economy* (London: Penguin Books and New Left Review, 1973), 90.

8 Nicholas Bourriard, *Postproduction: culture as screenplay: how art reprograms the world*, trans. Jeanine Herman (New York: Lukas & Sternberg, 2002).

9 Boris Groys, 'Introduction: poetics vs. aesthetics', in *Going Public* (Berlin & New York: Sternberg Press, 2010), 9–19.

10 Ian Bogost, *Alien phenomenology, or, what it's like to be a thing* (Minneapolis: University of Minnesota Press, 2012).

Are we in a cone of silence?: A letter between two artists, who are editors (for now)

Hi Liang,

Let's make the most of this letter-as-trope-for-talking thing that we started. The irony of pitching an issue on work and unprofessionalism hasn't been lost on us, especially considering that we ambitiously wanted more content, we wanted to know what others thought and if there was something actually to be said. This is why desire is important to consider, because, really, the money just ain't that good!

As usual, not everything goes to plan…

In Hal Hartley's much-hated film *The Girl from Monday* (2005), set in an over-monopolised, global dystopic future, a girl from another planet arrives on Earth as the film's main character pitches an idea that sees people, as active consumers, register their sexual encounters with the government in the form of a mutually agreeable economic transaction. Spontaneous sexual intercourse is illegal. This somewhat handy-cam and minimally acted film attempts to present a satirical account of an apathetic-everything-commodified future. Described by some as a profoundly unnecessary film, I am left wondering why the hell this film seems to have resonated and stayed with me all these months since my first viewing. It's not, in the film at least, that sexual intercourse has become a credit rating, nor that teaching in a high school is a mode of punishment enforced by the state. Consumerism is law. Rather, it was that the exchange needed to be agreed upon as mutually beneficial so as to count. The room for error was marginal: you can't take a risk, you can't change your mind, desire for place and the other, sublimated.

Charlie Brooker's first episode of the satirical sci-fi television series *Black Mirror* is also set in the near future. A ransom note is sent to the Prime Minister of Britain demanding he fuck a pig live on TV before a global audience, in exchange for the safe return of the recently kidnapped princess. While the populace is fixated on the tube, waiting for the 'act', the princess is released early and the kidnapper is revealed as the recent winner of the Turner Prize, artist Carlton Bloom. The Prime Minister is praised for his act of sacrifice, his popularity rating rises while the public is kept unaware that the princess was released early—meanwhile, Bloom commits suicide (perhaps the only unmediated choice left?). In *Black Mirror*, the slippage between keeping-up-appearances, the ultimate artistic act and the desire to retain power are called into question. The spectacle and the lie both win, while the artist dies.

Brooker and Hartley's visions of the future feel like now. Paul McCarthy's excessive-decadent and motorised sculpture of (the?) two George Bushes fucking pigs, *Train, Mechanical* (2009), may or may not have been sold for a sum that we can't imagine, but this hauntingly hilarious after-image of a president some still hope will be taken to task, remains. Sue Dodd has recently made a series of videos titled *Significant Others* (2012) that animate the busts of the last twenty-seven Australian prime ministers. Each slowly mouths the name of his respective wife, as if in the act of cumming. A kind of vocal 'human centipede' with Dodd voicing the audio—Therese, Janette, Anita, Hazel, et al. Jules' bust, which is yet to be made has a stand-in modeled from clay, spray-painted gold and covered in shoe polish. Unbronzed like her lover, Tim is the only male referred to by name rather than in monument and is also the only lover not 'legitimised' by the apparent state sanctity of marriage—a simple shift of power, pleasure and representation through name. With the recent return to off-shore processing and the even more recent defeat of Penny Wong in the Senate, I am left with the question: will it take another twenty-six prime ministers before there is a change in the simplicity of how we are represented?

Recently, artist Lane Cormick and I have been talking about the importance of doubt in an artwork. After the 1800 or so emails, with approximately sixty writers and thirty odd artists mentioned in order to meander through content leading to stupid 3-a.m.-text-message puns, more questions and a few dead ends, I am left thinking doubt is our modus operandi. If Freud were around today, would he speculate that perhaps obsessional neurotics self-medicate with doubt? Doubt is proactive—with no conclusion from the two or perhaps three or four conflicting thoughts, we've gotta keep looking, don't we? I kind of hope our two editions of the magazine have tried to look towards, and into, this space.

There is a work by the artist James Lynch that I often think about. *Doubleday* (2008) was presented in Charlotte Day's TarraWarra Biennale 2008, *Lost and Found: An Archeology of the Present*. The installation appeared as an aestheticised ad-hoc post-house-party on a stage, complete with plastic chairs and fairy lights. It is accompanied by a projection onto an upturned table of a short, four-minute-looped, hand-drawn animation of TarraWarra's in-house cleaner, silently going about his daily duties accompanied by a soundtrack composed by Evelyn Morris. A collaboration in multiple parts, the work of the artist is inextricably linked to the work of its participants—the cleaner, the probably-mass-produced-in-China plastic chair, the museum and the viewer –the labour of the world.

In a recent essay on oil, climate change and the French refinery blockades, the anarchist-anthropologist David Graeber deliberates on the problems of precarity and the demobilisation of labour:

> there's no better way to ensure people are not thinking about alternative ways to organize society, or fighting to bring them about, than to keep them working all the time. As a result, we are left in the bizarre situation where almost no one believes that capitalism is really a viable system any more, but neither can they even begin to imagine a different one. The war against the imagination is the only one the capitalists seem to have definitively won.[1]

If we consider the Guy-Fawke-mask-wearing one per cent, the city of Bristol launching its own currency in September, the march of 30,000 people down Sydney Road, our own Prime Minister's globally recognised speech, not to mention the number of applications we received to write for this edition, it feels less like a death, and a little more like a whole lotta thought.

Editing this magazine has made visible the desire for the possibility to explore, to share, and to continue to engage in open discussions about materiality and its relationship to the world. These discussions are always, and must be, opposing, contradictory and in conflict with each other (managing a war without weapons?). It is this that is inherently political within art—that it bothers to negotiate an anarchic terrain, inclusive of multiple voices, institutions and capital. My persistent optimism, however annoying, injected with a healthy dose of cynicism, means I hope, even if there isn't any, that the artist doesn't have to die.

Now, tell me about your show!

With love, Lisa x

PS: I just received this text from my film-making friend musing about a recent Masters colloquium she participated in:

> The best thing on Friday was this odd eccentric genius who was into interpreting what possums say; he suggested that if you want a different perspective, ask a goth, because no one ever asks them for answers.

* * *

Dear Lisa,

It is 12:31 a.m. and I can't sleep, as I need to write my letter to you—at this time of night I fear Liam Gillick was right when he wrote:

> The accusation is that artists are at best the ultimate freelance knowledge workers and at worst barely capable of distinguishing themselves from the consuming desire to work at all times, neurotic people who deploy series of practices that coincide quite neatly

> with the requirements of neo-liberal, predatory, continually mutating capitalism of the every moment.[2]

When I first read this text, I felt like Gillick was writing directly to me—being a workaholic probably doesn't help me here. Whilst not emphatically suggesting that all aspects of artistic practice have been completely subsumed by capitalism, this text does capture a tension within the arts which has been perpetuated in a number of recent texts on the subject, as seen in *e-flux*, Sternberg Press and *Frieze*. Beyond the relevance of these publications, I think our reasons for pursuing the subject of 'work' is deeply embedded in our own experience of labour within the arts.

Whilst working towards the publication of this issue of *un*, Patrice Sharkey and I curated the exhibition *No reasonable offer refused* at West Space, Melbourne.[3] The exhibition hoped to interrogate acts of commerce and circled a number of ideas similar to this edition of *un*. Yet, as the exhibition drew closer, Patrice and I came to the realisation that by asking artists to re-imagine acts of commerce, we had perhaps created an impossible challenge—when writing the catalogue essay and speaking with the artists I had great difficulty in the articulation of these aims. Was this because we just couldn't imagine ways to nudge our current capitalist system? My gut feeling is no, but it seemed that our inability to articulate the workings of these systems and this negotiation in relation to the art object had became the crux of the exhibition. Agatha Gothe-Snape addressed this beautifully with her work for the exhibition *Emotional Wall* (2012), in which she paid Dan Moynihan to build a wall that blocked out the space in which a viewer would commonly view an artwork. By negating this material exchange between viewer and art object, Gothe-Snape instead highlighted the workings of this symbolic exchange and the anxiety (and possible aversion) toward putting an art object out into the world.

I remember when we first tossed about ideas for this issue, the subject of 'work' was key, but, more specifically, we were interested in artists' other practices—the aspect of their practice that gets sidelined because it is less cohesive to include multiple forms of production when characterising an artist's work. The work of Vivienne Binns and Dale Frank comes to mind. Beyond their painting practices, Binns held numerous craft workshops in rural NSW in the 1970s and Dale Frank facilitated a number of discos and performances in the 1980s and 1990s. One such work, *Bowie* (1994), saw five David Bowie CDs played continuously from speakers installed in the outside entrance of the National Gallery of Australia. By the time I went to art school in Canberra, that work must have been removed—what a difference Bowie would have made to my 9-a.m. starts, waiting in the cold outside the NGA for my art theory classes! Being a fan of both these artists' paintings, I'm interested in how their paintings have been informed by their 'social' forms of production. Immediately, one can see the cheeky pop culture connections between the lush, wet pours of varnish that make up Frank's paintings titled *Ryan Gosling* (2008) or *Daniel Radcliffe* (2008) and the intrusion of Bowie's pop hits upon the brutalist building of the NGA. As a painter myself, I feel a bit guilty for producing paintings—alone in the studio, painting is an unsociable activity (see Helen Johnson's 'It seems like everyone knows everyone already so let's get to work') and I think this is why I attempt to make my practice more sociable (the production of magazines is an inherently social structure). I wonder if Binns and Frank have a similar feeling?

lxl.

Co-authored by Liang Luscombe, first published as an editorial in *un Magazine*, issue 6.2, December 2012.

Notes

1 David Graeber, 'Against Kamikaze Capitalism: Oil, Climate Change and the French Refinery Blockades', *Shift* (November 2010), http://shiftmag.co.uk/?p=389, accessed 20 October 2012.

2 Liam Gillick, *Why Work?* (Auckland: Art Space, 2010), 3.

3 Agatha Gothe-Snape, George Egerton-Warburton, Kelly Doley, Christopher Sciuto and Juilet Rowe, *No reasonable offer refused*, West Space, 21 September – 13 October 2012.

Change Settings: Beiiing

Anthropologist Michael D. Jackson has described his fascination with the migratory and connectedness as located in the paradox of the social, where behaviors described by science become problematic, complicated by miscommunication and misunderstanding. Being able to mediate intersubjectivity within a mobile culture that has shifting limits, borders and ideologies, whilst maintaining a sincere and generous openness, is perhaps an always ongoing task.

The exhibition *Change Settings* at Techno Park Studios in Williamstown, Melbourne, presents seven works made by British-born, Birmingham/Berlin-based artist Elly Clarke. The exhibiton is a type of unfinished, potted survey of (or introduction to) Clarke's video and photographic practice dating between 2003 and the present.

Our first encounter is with the 11-minute projection *Cars & Cowboys*. Shot from a walkway between two hostels in Creel (a small town in the Mexican state of Chihuahua), *Cars & Cowboys* documents what may or may not be a choreographed event. The in-camera-on-site Latin music soundtrack frames a laneway flanked by unidentified, run-down, semi-industrial buildings while a parade of 4WDs and utilities enter and leave the frame. Five minutes in, marked by police sirens, the participants of the parade change from unseen drivers to an anonymous collective of cowboys on horses; the event passes and the inconsistent stream of utility vehicles return. This surprising change in events points toward unknown narratives, the distance between participant and passerby and the potential for future chance encounters.

Our framing as accidental observer is further reiterated in *Some Places I have Never Been To*, a collection of 81 slides taken by her father and projected onto a plinth; the timed images depict sites that are both familiar and estranged. The slides were discovered in a garage three years after her father's death; the work refers to the chance discovery of an unfinished archive that perhaps documents our subjective relationship to change and loss within moments of mobility. The missing people in the images call us to question the document and its history, and the implied but unarticulated story they depict.

This problem of accurately representing stasis, movement and the multiple narratives that result from intertwining perspectives is further documented in *Moscow to Beijing*. The three-screen video installation in the once pedagogical, occasionally administrative, now carpeted and glass-walled gallery is the most complex work in the exhibition. In September of 2005, Clarke, partly funded by the pre-sale of photographs she was going to take, travelled from Moscow to Beijing on the Trans-Siberian Railway whilst participating in a conference on mobility. Armed with questions translated into Russian, Mongolian and Chinese, Clarke documented her somewhat intimate encounters with fellow travellers. At one point in the video, the subtitles read, '…they change trains in Beiiing'. The simple misspelling of the destination is poignant. This visual slip of the tongue locates the work in the difficult to translate spaces that occupy our inter-subjective relationship to economy, experience, narrative and documentation. This work is expanded further with footage that documents the reactions of the translators as well as photographs taken by the participants. Already located in an area politically and geographically complex, Clarke's document in three parts—'Conversations', 'Translations' and 'Trans-Siberia'—attempts to explore the limitations and boundaries of travel and its effects.

In *Change Settings*, the synchronous relations between what Elly Clarke calls her 'moving photographs' and the site of their current installation is hard to avoid. Techno Park Studios was once a purpose-built kindergarten for the children of recent immigrants and displaced families from WWII, temporarily housed in the nearby brown brick units of Wiltona Hostel (prior to that Nissen huts) where now the semi-industrial landscape meets the sea, suburbia and an oil refinery. The historical transience imposed by the economy and conflict of those that once inhabited these spaces meets a different type of traveller that quietly presents questions about the complexity of being.

First published by *This is Tomorrow*, as a review of *Change Settings*, Elly Clarke, Techno Park Studios, Melbourne, 12–22 May 2012.

Obsolete Currencies

Dear Anonymous Pilot,

I've been trying to find someone who flew money out of that country. I have been thinking about it for a while, having heard about it nearly three years ago when I first travelled to one of the 20,000 or so islands in the South Pacific.

In my head, you are one of thousands of pilots in the air at any one time. As you know, at peak times, 5,000 or more commercial planes could be flying in US airspace. It's safe to assume that, at any one time, there might be 10,000 pilots in the air (equivalent to the population of the island I visited) and perhaps 1.5 million people (the population of Geelong). Persky Bunkermeister cites Flighttracker.com stating that by the end of the day on 23 January 2008, 46,118 flights had been completed.[1]

Potentially 13.8 million people flying around, steered by 92,000 pilots.

Counting is such a silly activity.

I imagine the 46,000 or so planes are filled with cash instead of passengers. Perhaps one is like the plane you flew. Chaperoned dollars fleeing a fledgling economy and impossible to tally—flying, rather than floating, currencies.

If you were the one, or perhaps one of many that flew cash out—an airborne march of zeros—for whom you did it, and why you did it, is important, I guess. I'm not sure why I see it as somewhat irrelevant. You're just the delivery boy, but one that gets quite a big tip. Jan says: these are difficult times for artists, writers and lovers alike. Perhaps for delivery boys also. Jan asks: how can we pretend to ourselves that we are still giving what we give freely when we know we'd be much better off charging a decent price for it?[2]

What's the price for all that cash moving around in the daylit night? Crossing borders and walls, thresholds and time zones.

Planes flying over walls whilst inside a bubble.

I recently heard the economist Richard Duncan refer to

capitalism as *creditism*. He mentioned that a shift had occurred. The current global modus operandi being credit creation and consumption subsidised by the state. Bubble making. Contrary to Japan's method of repairing its burst bubble in the '90s — by building bridges to nowhere via investing in what is now redundant technologies — Duncan is calling for sustainable investments.

Credit was born of the Latin *creditum*. Believe. I wondered if Duncan was asking us to believe in believing?

In Detroit, a decade or so after the Depression ended, a wall was built. The US Government had imagined a property-owning-democracy. The Fanny May reforms saw Savings and Loans (building societies) developing lending agreements guaranteed by the State. Building homes and owning houses. It eventuated that some were considered more loanworthy than others. Prior to WWII, African Americans were deemed uncreditworthy. In order to facilitate loans, developers built a six-foot-high wall dividing the city into zones of development based on credit ratings. Red and white. Those in the white were approved for borrowing; those in red were also approved, but at much higher interest rates. An apartheid system supported by a credit wall. Prime and sub-prime. Exclusion from the dominant economy erupted in riots on 23 July 1967. In five days of rioting and following a visit from the National Guard and federal airborne troops, 43 people died and 3000 properties were looted and burned. Real estate agents changed their practices, slightly.

Quantitative easing — of sorts.

More recently, quantitative easing has been called 'printing money'.

I've tried several ways to find you — via family and friends, newspapers and pilots' associations. The closest I came was in the pages of a pilots' rumor network. Upon posting my question and being promptly de-posted, I was informed by the moderator that no pilot would fly money out of a country. There was apparently no financial benefit to be gained in flying currency in or out of Australia, New Zealand or any Pacific nation. Delivery boy, doesn't one find systems of value and exchange everywhere?

I've no idea what 'a roll of carpet' is code for, but I no

longer think of 46,000-plus planes around with flying wads of cash. I found you, eventually—well, several of you really. Trophy listing under a thread titled 'Strange Freight'. The reality of what is and has been shipped is far more interesting—silver ingots in sacks going from the Gulf to Italy; white buffaloes traveling from Lahore to Varna; armoured Cadillacs flying to north Africa; an entire 747 sawn up into bits en route to Benghazi; 26 tonnes of toilet paper and beer mugs for Idi Amin; a satellite; 15,000 copies of Lara Croft; 14 pallets of Rod Stewart's band gear (the posty mentioned hating him); medical cocaine; three boxes of monkeys from Indonesia; one heavily sedated grizzly bear from the zoo; one human brain being sent for autopsy; 16 kilos of cryogenically frozen dog semen; human veins shipped in a mushroom shaped container the size of a 30 gallon garbage can; umbilical cords assumed harvested for stem-cell research; currency printed in the UK for Pol Pot in Cambodia, and 30 pairs of human eyes.

I realised that I don't really need to find you. Everything is circulated, whether for monetary and/or symbolic value and, as someone has said, with pure materiality manifesting, at best, through private consumption.[3] Those artists, writers and lovers Jan spoke of have a way of figuring out how to demonstrate the materiality of the things beyond their exchange value, whilst existing in a bubble and scaling walls.[4]

First published as a catalogue essay for *No Reasonable Offer Refused*, curated by Liang Luscombe and Patrice Sharkey, West Space, 21 September – 13 October 2012

Notes

1 See: http://www.answerbag.com/gview/S63606, accessed 30 July 2012.

2 Jan Verwoert, 'You make me feel/mighty real: On the art and risk of bearing witness', in *I'm Not Here: An exhibition without Francis Alys* (Amsterdam: Idea Books, 2010), 31–43.

3 Boris Groys, Art and Money, *e-flux journal* 24 (April 2011), http://www.e-flux.com/journal/art-and-monev-2/, accessed 30 July 2012.

4 ibid.

2013

A letter to Meredith

Lisa Radford
T 61 [redacted]
[redacted]@gmail.com
30 January 2013 – 06 February 2013
Meredith Turnbull
c/o The Other Side

Dear Meredith,

I am sitting at a picnic bench with castors resting on AstroTurf in the open-air centre of QV. To my left is the Queen Victoria Women's Centre. Built in Queen Anne style by J.J. Clark, it is what remains of the old Queen Vic Hospital building. Behind me, in front and to my right, students, city residents and tourists decide on whether they will consume something from Max Brenner's Chocolate Bar with its Kangaroo Cups and Hug Mugs designed by Iris Zohar, a burger from the literally named Grilled, or Japanese fine food from Hanaichi. Some, like me, simply choose to exploit what looks like public space. I've always thought the design of the Hanaichi franchise stores rather odd—something about the exterior resembling a chemist contrasting with the interior that reads as a Red Rooster—minus the chicken and microphone. The space I am sitting in is something of a threshold, albeit a threshold within a space—a $600-million space at that, 1.8 hectares in size and home to apartments and the BHP Billiton headquarters. It is a windy square inside a square formed via an arrangement of faux laneways—the Las Vegas version of those small squares you come across nestled in a labyrinth of smaller streets, such as in Barcelona, perhaps all of Europe, minus the complacency and the bling of the multi-national trimmings.[1]

The threshold. I guess this is what I have been thinking about in reference to your exhibition at The Other Side. Spaces that we move through to get somewhere else. I am thinking about this with particular reference to your statement, which declares that you explore the 'territory between the intimate, interior and large-scales'. Sitting at my laptop writing you a letter in a pre-fab pro forma called 'Classic Letter' whilst in this massive 'faux-but-po-mo-public' space while wafts of pre-fab-Japanese curry permeate the air, it is hard not to question this space that is a terrain for consuming or to be consumed by.

The space you are making work for is a type of threshold to an office—do you remember the MIR11 project run by our friend Masato, Jan van Schaick and Anton Marin, then Danny Lacy and Justin Andrews jumped on board? The aesthetics and politics of this space were challenged when the architects that owned the space decided that that which inhabited this threshold gallery space was unworthy of the visiting important clients. An 'appropriate' painting was hung in its place. Within the history of design and art, the space between adornment, decoration and political subjectivity is sometimes defined by those that play no role in its production.

I am at home now, and I am wearing your necklace, a necklace you made. Actually, I am always wearing one of your necklaces, this one is the wooden one that everyone thinks is made from Cuisenaire blocks—an assumption that we wear what was once utilitarian, and not wear what is? And I am still thinking about this space of production. In a small catalogue that documents Christoph Weber's work *The First Minutes of October* (2007), Ekatrina Degot discusses when artists from the Bauhaus were first shown in Moscow and no one really liked them. Degot quotes critic Alexei Sidorov: the products of German constructivism all had an air of prosperity; everything was so impeccable and precisely fitted, straightened out, hammered together, and lit by electric lamps; everything looked like a neat little toy. As Degot denotes and Groys acknowledges,[2] this is a move away from fetishisation, where the figure formerly known as painter or sculptor under capitalism is now set the task of designing murals and leaflets or writing theoretical texts—the dematerialisation of the object via the process of utility, with the aim of evading reification.[3]

When I think about your sourced patterns and self-referenced images of recent-but-previously-made DIY craft sources, and your own sculptures previously exhibited and documented and now presented as archival-cum-nostalgic black-and-white photos, I am reminded of images such as Alexandra Khokhlova modeling a dress designed by Nadezhda Lamanova in 1924. Lamanova's dress, which we might read as origami-like in form, is woven with a strong linear pattern design, which, when cut on the bias, creates an intersection of diagonals, horizontals and verticals. Khokhlova poses as if in angular 'little-teapot' mode — a strong image. Khokhlova is elegant and proud, presenting, it seems, herself more than the dress. In an artist's statement in the catalogue of exhibition *5 × 5 = 25* (1921), Varvara Stepanova writes: 'technology and industry have confronted art with the problem of CONSTRUCTION as a dynamic action and as contemplative visuality'. The sacred value of the work as something singular and unique has been eliminated. As the depository of this 'unicum', the museum turns into an archive.[4] There is a predetermined sense of loss in Stepanova's statement, where the operative of the work has already been consumed and distorted. I wonder if it is this that you touch on in your sampling and remaking of the patterns made, perhaps by our contemporary equivalents of Stepanova and Liubov Popova. Stepanova and Popova: women who started designing for the First State Textile Factory following a call to artists to work with industry, turning their functional non-objective patterns from *objets d'art* into national attire. Just after the Bolshevik revolution in 1917, the Second Modern Decorative Arts Exhibition opened at the Mikhailova Salon in the centre of Moscow, exhibiting 400 works by sixteen artists including Popova and, one assumes, Stepanova. The exhibition was visited by an American theatre critic, Oliver M. Sayler, who was researching Russia for forthcoming plays. Since 1917, all that remains of the exhibition are the 17 photographs he took. Most of the actual fabric and other articles have been lost or destroyed.[5] Which brings me back to your works as contemporary archive.

Following the revolution, the links between the fashion houses in Paris, and the textile industry in Russia were broken. When I think of Stepanova and Popova's appointment at the First State Textile Factory, I imagine them along with Alexandra Exter, Natalia Goncharova, Olga Rozanova, and Nadezhda Udaltsova in round-table conversation with Sophie Taeuber-Arp, Claude Cahun, Sonia Delaunay, Germaine Dulac, Florence Henri, Hannah Höch, Katarzyna Kobro and Dora Maar. A round table of women makers sharing camaraderie and independence, because as Art History has finally recognised, they were always liberated in conversation from their male partners, discussing painting and utilitarian design, the material elements of everyday life and the infinite permutations of the organisation of the object. Perhaps they would discuss being a woman artist at the beginning of the twentieth century—being post-object and freed from the representation as nude passive object, or perhaps they would chat about Malevich's embroidery designs (a skill he learnt from his mother), or the handbags Puni designed, Cubism v Suprematism v subject v content, and between abstraction and representation. Rumor has it, for all of Popova's pro-industrial comments, she loved to hand-sew Rodchenko's overalls for the people. Perhaps they would discuss the elimination of natural form, the necessity of concrete tasks and the intimacy of the individual versus the large scale of the state, and all the insecurities, complexities and contradictions that come along with living such things.

In a letter, Goncharova questions Boris Anrep:

> why do you write about the distance separating the artist and his work like that? Is it really so important that an artist remain completely bound together with his work? Man is a complex machine, perpetually moving and changing, and a work, once completed, becomes a static thing with its own individual life, a life that lasts longer than that of the individual who created it: the difference between the two has always existed and always will.[6]

The space Goncharova is perhaps talking about is an intimate shared space, an interior social defined by a collective of individuals—'Nonetheless, the material of the work and beyond that, its creative spirit, lies not in the individual, but in the people, in the nation to which the individual belongs…'.[7] No longer national, one would think—a certain amount of homogeneity contained perhaps within our experiences and production, I wonder, are our co-workers many?

Sincerely,
Lisa

PS: I have just had a thought—perhaps Gonchoarova and Popova are both talking about a threshold that is beyond them, the work being the threshold to spaces other than physical? When discussing a shift between periods of work Popova says: 'Spatial Force Constructions, which succeeds the Painterly Architectonics, produce the impression of consonance and stability thanks to the interactive energy of difference, forms, directions and forces. Now, movement unfolds, not in real space, but in new unearthly dimensions…'.[8] Perhaps these movements go beyond the confines of the wall or the body they are presented in and on.

First published as a catalogue essay for *Co-Workers, Interior World*, Meredith Turnbull, The Other Side, Melbourne, 2013.

Notes

1 Norman Day kind of summed up a type of design complacency when he described the development as 'architecture for generation X, once stereotyped (in *The Washington Post*) as a group, of slackers, cynics, whiners, drifters and malcontents, but also as ambitious, savvy, independent, pragmatic and self-sufficient, go-getters who are just doing it—but their way… By inspection, these architects got it right.' See: http://theage.com.au/articles/2004/03/09/1078594345810.html, accessed 2 February 2013.

2 Boris Groys, 'The Obligation to Self-Design', *e-flux journal* #00 (November 2008), http://www.e-flux.com/journal/the-obligation-to-self-design/, accessed 2 February 2013.

3 Alexei Sidorov in Ekatrina Degot, 'The Inevitability of Stardom', catalogue essay for Christopher Weber, *The First Minutes of October* (Vienna: Verlag für moderne Kunst Nürnberg, 2009), 115.

4 Varvara Stepnova artist's statement in the catalogue of exhibition *5 × 5 = 25* (1921), in John E. Bowlt and Matthew Drutt, eds, *Amazons of the Avant-Garde: Alexandra Exter, Natalia Goncharova, Liubov Popova, Olga Rozanova, Varvara Stepanova and Nadezhda Udaltsova*, (New York: Guggenheim, 2000), 315.

5 Charlotte Douglas, 'Suprematist Embroidered Ornament', *Art Journal* vol. 54, no. 1 (Spring, 1995): 45.
6 Natalia Goncharova in a letter to Boris Anrep, 1914, in Bowlt and Drutt *Amazons of the Avant-Garde*, 314.
7 ibid.
8 Dimitri Sarabianov, 'Liubov Popova and Artistic Synthesis', in Bowlt and Drutt, *Amazons of the Avant-Garde*, 195.

Beam Me Up Scotty

So, my favourite tweet from the evening of February 23rd came from @FakePremierTed a couple of hours before the official 7 p.m. kick-off for the 24-hour White Night Festival.[1] Premier Ted Baillieu (albeit Fake) dutifully declared: 'White Night Melbourne tonight. As Arts Minister, I have to smile at the hippies and pretend I like them. The things I do for opera tickets.'

Which got me thinking, as I periodically do, about the idea of culture by osmosis and the probability of this festival acting as a blanket-cum-diversion-strategy for a neo-liberal cost-cutting agenda. Why? Because surely it's cheaper to put a whole heap of cash into a one-night affair than invest in the long-term effects of quality art education. There does seem to be an inherent irony in a situation that elevates Ted (the real one) as our culture-loving-leader when he is also the head of a party that has slashed funding and thus access to TAFE education, which has resulted in the closure of Visual Arts courses — courses that don't appear to make money or result in the type of directly vocational activities that make the one-eyed-economy-focused establishment happy.[2] This is why there is something about Liang Luscombe's complex-social-functional-design-object-artwork that rings true.[3] A shelf to use, fake coins to steal food with and some things that just need to be said. Yes, *Our TAFE* does need to be *saved*, because if funding to TAFE is not returned, if we don't consider the type of education in the arts that we are providing (and receiving) at all levels, then the next generation of artists may be entirely spawned from the upper-middle classes who make fake-coins from mining and reside and eat wherever and whatever they like. Actually, why would they even bother becoming artists? Regardless, you know where I am going. We live in a complex space of masked stealing and failed state obligations — file-sharing, crowdfunding, and health and education cuts.

I know you like the arts, Ted, and were moved to 'sing', but you were watching opera while 'the people' were doing a Zumba class.

Not that I am adverse to Zumba, heck, I spent a good si months taking a class twice a week in a temporary-gym-slash stink-box at the Carlton Flats and loved it. I'm happy to dancercise to tracks-that-you-only-hear-in-supermarkets-but somehow-know-all-the-words-to for two hours a week. Perhaps I'm too cynical. I love crowds and I like art, I'm just suspicious of Ted's motives and pissed off about the TAFE cut and, to be frank, rather than shuffle through the laneways of Melbourne 'looking for culture cause I'm told to', I'd much prefer to meander through the Edinburgh gardens and come across an absurd shrine to Mick Edwards (or Swami Deva Pramada as he was also known) — contributor to the first fou or so albums by ELO, who was killed when a 600-kilogram hay bale rolled onto his van in 2010. Folly such as this (the shrine, not Edwards' death!) is perhaps harder to contextual ise. Sure, I might know when to pop over to the picnic-cum-opening for cheap beer and a chat with friends — but more sc I like knowing that Aunty Joan, who has lived in North Fitzro since day dot, might chance upon Oscar Perry's hay bale ato a previously sculpture-less plinth[4] that she has walked past umpteen times and ponder the recently deceased Edwards, rekindle her love of ELO, go home and put on her copy of *Eldorado* (1974), play air-trombone to the fanfare at the beginning of 'Boy Blue', and then sit and reminisce to the title track whilst drinking a portagaff and googling art and contemporary prog. Aunty Joan may of course prefer Woody Guthrie and Russian Caravan tea, and could instead be googling the what, where and why of hay bales spontaneousl combusting.

First published on stamm.com.au, edited by Jonathan Nichols, 2013.

Notes

1 The title of this essay comes from a *Star Trek* bumper sticker reading 'Beam me up Scotty, there is no intelligent life form on this planet', which spawned our abridged and shared evacuation chant. The phrase was apparently never actually uttered in the series, but we all know it and as such it is perhaps an example of cultural osmosis.

2 Ann Stephen's address to the AAANZ conference in November last ye about fostering inclusive and rich culture and the importance of TAFE. See: http://aaanz.info/save-art-in-tafe/

3 *After Jonas Bohlin (from Spring Street, the office and the vending machine)* (2013), was Liang Luscombe's work in the exhibition *Navel-Gazing* curated by Brooke Babington and Melissa Loughnan at Utopian Slumps, 12 January – 2 February 2013.

4 Plinth Projects is a new artist-run-public-art venture co-directed by Daniel Stephen-Miller and Jeremy Pryles who are assisted by a gang of other artists including Sam George, Carla McKee, Ben Ryan and Isabelle Sully. The project is funded by the City of Yarra, the committee isn't paid but the artists exhibiting get a fee. The Plinth will be launched on Sunday 3 March 2013, between 4–6 p.m., http://plinthprojects.com/exhibitions/oscar-perry

GEOFF NEWTON: FAN TRIBUTE HISTORY PARALLEL BOOTLEG PAINTINGS (or: career paths are not the same as songlines)

Back/story/catalogue

We all know the songs that have been covered the most. The probably ring in our heads like jingles from well-worn television advertisements. Some of them are. I've written it before somewhere—about music being this other realm that speak louder and more immediately to us as an audience because we tend to judge it differently than we do art. We let it be pa of culture, create our own hierarchies within it, without reall waiting for others to put it in order for us.

To explain this point, let me begin with a daggy anecdo

It was in 1995 that I received, as a gift, the compilation album that I'm pretty sure everyone had: *If I Were a Carpenter*. Probably more precisely called a tribute album, the CD contained fourteen songs by fourteen indie it-bands from the mid-1990s. Sonic Youth's rendition of Richard and Karen Carpenter's 'Superstar' is generally considered to be the best song on the album. Seeming to find its own time an place to be played—usually sometime early in the morning, dancing in the lounge room of someone's share house, some where—the song somehow had the power to subvert time; i this case, successfully transporting a song from 1971 into the nineties, opening up a new audience of listeners, or giving ol listeners a segue into new music; history and culture momen tarily placed together on a flattened plane.

Al Wiesel wrote a review of *If I Were a Carpenter* for *Rolling Stone* in October of 1994, linking the death of Richar

Jixon and Kurt Cobain to the affectionate and reverent ributes found on the album — cover versions of the almost-asy-adult-music-listening songs of the Carpenters, re-cast by .lt-indie musicians. In Wiesel's words:

> The Carpenters conjure a yearning for a Brady Bunch childhood we never had. But this nostalgic desire is coupled with the awareness that completely happy families are as illusory as the Carpenters' carefully manufactured squeaky-clean image. Just as Mr Brady died of AIDS, Karen Carpenter succumbed to anorexia nervosa, another disease unknown in the early '70s.[1]

The track 'Superstar' is a song about unrequited love for ι musician or pop star. The lyrics 'Your guitar/ It sounds so weet and clear/ But you're not really here/ It's just the radio', .re usually sung by Karen, but, on the tribute album, hurston Moore sings the song and it sounds like he really sn't there — that what you are listening to is a long-lost radio ecording found in a bunker at the end of the Cold War. It's :ind of pre–Ariel Pink Ariel Pink and the nostalgia, just as Viesel says, is imbued with an awareness that the attempt to eplicate or make a tribute to something past brings with it aggage, things that might've previously gone unsaid or were ınknown.

In August of 2012, Geoff Newton — self-proclaimed .rtist/dealer,[2] who is also a curator and occasional writer — resented a series of seven, or what I know to be eight, paint-ngs at TCB art inc. in Melbourne.[3] The show was titled *Big ime*, and if you know Geoff you can kind of imagine him atirically singing, with a Larry Gagosian accent, the opening yrics to the Peter Gabriel song of the same name — 'I'm on ny way I'm making it, Huh!' Perhaps like Sonic Youth's cover .nd tribute to the Carpenters, Geoff's exhibition was a bit like . radio transmission from a distant world trying desperately o make contact, channeling multiple ghosts.[4] A kind of Mike-Kelleyesque shout out, the exhibition attempted to teleport omething like an attitude from the late '90s/early '00s and nto the now.

Walking into the small, artist-run gallery TCB art inc. on

the way to the opening of the Melbourne Art Fair, I felt close to a traitor—Geoff's exhibition singing to me that well-chanted and -worn lyric of The Stone Roses: 'You don't have to sell your soul/ He's already in me'.[5]

> Superstar
> I wanna be adored
> Big Time

So there I was in the gallery—one that was started almost fourteen years ago, one I help to run—looking at a series of paintings that seem to point to this space and to those who have been involved: some living, and some not. Before me, a series of paintings that point to a history I am personally privy to, and I wonder: who else is the audience for this? Who are these paintings for, other than me? Seven large paintings hanging in the space that used to be Uplands Gallery—the first commercial gallery to be started in Melbourne that began out of love and not old money, that began as a risk rather than a tax break, that began because no one else seemed to be representing, or even wanting to represent, the art and artists that we liked and we knew.

It's taking me a long time to get to talking about Blair Trethowan, our friend, colleague and provocateur, who decided to die too young in 2006. I guess that's because it's hard, and I guess that's why Geoff made paintings—quasi-sentimental-bootleg-history paintings almost made specific to the site within which they were exhibited, TCB. With the absence of adequate death rituals in western culture,[6] I am left wondering about the potential for an exhibition to be a site for mourning.

In 2002, Geoff Newton had his first solo exhibition in Melbourne, at TCB art inc. This skateboarding, music-loving artist and recent graduate from Canberra School of Art, who had grown up in Yackandandah, presented a series of over-sized found cassette tapes, painted two per canvas, and fourteen or so in total. At the time, Uplands Gallery occupied the front space. Blair Trethowan, a skateboarding, music-loving artist from Melton, had started the space with fellow skateboarding, art history–studying Geelong boy Jarrod

Rawlins. Geoff's tapes were copied and painted in a you're-just-a-tracer-type manner, where ownership of this imagery-as-a-cipher for culture was shared rather than imparted. Whether his or those of others, the analogue tapes pointed to a measure of purchasing, collecting, rearranging, bootlegging and sharing — objects made by an audience of fans for other fans and soon-to-be fans. TDK, Bosch, C60s and 90s. Black plastic and clear; labelled and unlabelled; some neatly written and others scribbled as if in haste, with either the title and the artist (such as 'Forever Changes | Burt Bacharach'), or just the artist: 'MADONNA', 'SONIC YOUTH'. Other times, the information had been scribbled out: 'NWA' in pink over 'Red Hot Chillis' — taped over, replaced. Yes, Burt, *Forever Changes*.

Geoff is prolific and active — establishing Dudespace (an artist-run space in a share house in Brunswick) with his housemates Bryan Spier and Justin Andrews in 2004,[7] then Neon Parc (a commercial gallery inspired by Uplands) with Tristian Koenig in 2006. He has curated exhibitions, and collaborated with his former teacher and artist Vivienne Binns, and with admired fellow artists Julia Gorman and Kate Smith. He has painted the auras of prominent Australian art dealers for an exhibition at Block Projects in 2008, and meshed '70s food porn with covers of our beloved taste-making-mags such as *frieze*, *Wallpaper* and *Art & Australia*. His satirical and sartorial paintings often announce the obvious in order to speak the unspoken or reveal what is often ignored. *Study for a Protest Painting* (2007) dutifully declares in a monotone-Martin-Sharpesque font: 'Curators Beware — artists all around you. They are shaving, bathing even combing their hair! Look carefully at the person next to you because he just may happen to be one.' Awkward and sometimes gawdy — *I want my death to be a funny one* (2007) – the works may at times appear to be self-indulgent, inwardly focused. But, as Jörg Heiser has suggested, this narcissism-cum-sentimental romanticism can potentially reveal a concern with the historic construction of our modern subjectivity.[8] Heiser discusses this notion in particular reference to melancholic longing and yearning for romantic production, an absence felt keenly in the wake of the loss of the traditional 'beautiful artwork' after Duchamp. In Conceptualism, the mourning of this absence has been successfully sublimated into irony, or completely replaced by stern-faced intellectualism.[9]

In 2012, Geoff's 'history', and I say this loosely, is once again presented in the form of paintings. All the paintings in the exhibition *Big Time* are officially untitled and subtitled. Geoff's arrangement is symbolic — a reference to his first show in the same space — and the exhibition's title is simultaneously a joke, a pun, and a melancholic question pointed towards the space, the history, himself and us. Electing to use the space that Uplands Gallery once occupied, Geoff hung seven large paintings, some meticulously painted, others executed with a somewhat ambivalent touch; all, curiously enough, declaring and demarcating themselves as open-ended signposts, flags, tombstones, totems and tributes — a world full of cover versions blah blah blah.[10]

Taboos, Totems and Tributes

Love 2012 (After Blair)

Not the first painting you encounter, but this 152 × 212 cm work, painted over the course of a couple of years spanning Newton's time in residence at Gertrude Contemporary, takes its cue from the cover of the exhibition catalogue of Blair Trethowan's 2005 Studio 12 exhibition (*Love 2005*, also at Gertrude Contemporary) as its compositional and sentimental base. It is also the painting that speaks most clearly to the aforementioned idea of a known/unknown history. Blair's exhibition coincided with Nicholas Mangan's presentation of 'The Colony' in the Gertrude Contemporary main gallery. John Howard was still in power, US-born, anti-Iraq-invasion activist Scott Parkin was deported by ASIO — uncharged but under the banner of being a threat to national security, and Germaine Greer had recently published her essay 'Whitefella Jump Up' in *Quarterly Essay*. Blair's exhibition was humble in its gesture, and consisted of a suite of five collages presented on bark sourced from the Injalak Art Centre in the Northern Territory. Similar, perhaps, to Geoff's paintings in *Big Time*, Blair's bark works (the bark's shape uncannily reminiscent of the skateboards that Blair's practice had referenced in the past) were snapshots of experience, in-jokes and hidden narratives — a skating Blair wearing Jon Campbell's *YEAH* flag as a patch, the 'Queen's Teeth' where a 'fiver' is folded to create a Rorschachian version of fellatio (Queen Elizabeth's pearl necklace the teeth, and her neck the penis), an old, 1980s Road Transport Authority sticker which once read Buckle up in the back seat',[11] its fluorescent letters vandalised with black marker erasing the 'kle up' and altering the 'B' so that it becomes an 'F'. The cover of the catalogue for Blair's exhibition references one of the collages — *Love 2005*, a string-patterned text referenced from a book on craft published in the year of Blair's birth — 1974 — and, as Danae Mossman, author of the catalogue asks, 'how free is love?'[12]

Geoff's *Love 2012 (After Blair)* isn't free. Geoff's *Love 2012 (After Blair)* is $9,000, and in it Blair's string-art referenced title for his catalogue has been enlarged and copied meticulously — the angular 'O' in Love now frames text that reads 'Now & forever' extracted from a Matthys Gerber painting titled *Let it be Me* (1988). The semi-spiritual, Eastern-European, folk-rendered floral borders of the Gerber painting backdrop large script that, however ironic, yearns for fame, fortune or love. The tattered pages of Geoff's copy of the catalogue are proof of reverence and re-readings, and, in Geoff's slick acrylic painting, Blair's images and collaged references to skateboards and barks have been all but replaced with some of Geoff's own shout-outs: to a Diena Georgetti, Hany Armanius, a Secret Chiefs Trio album cover, and a wall painting by the skater/artist Lee Ralph and his artist partner Tania Riki Riki, sourced from a 2005 exhibition at Uplands Gallery, *Posture Again*.[13] In her catalogue essay for *Love 2005*, Mossman discusses our implicit and complex relationship with lived culture, images, materials, place and politics. Pertinent observations still, she explains:

> Art is embedded in a history of appropriation — everything is ripe for the picking. Materials become signifiers on top of already loaded signifiers. Here barks frame an uneasy discussion about colonisation in which the work embarks on a critical unraveling of thinking about place — or at least act as a springboard for these considerations. While it could be easy to read

> these works as an exercise in dalliance, they are not purely diaristic—embedded in these works is a sense of agency. *Love 2005* reminds us of potent political issues that we face in the course of our existence—like how, why and when we deal with the 'bigger issues' like colonisation.[14]

While Geoff acknowledges that there is a sense of arrogance to a suburban-white-boy artist making claim to indigenous practices,[15] there is also an awareness that, in the sincerity of the gesture, there is also a type of failure, an inability to answer the various questions posed by art and culture, place and time. It is this acknowledgement of failure that becomes a strength for an open and critical investigation into which values and attitudes actually form the visual culture within which we participate. Perhaps, as Mossman said of Blair's, Geoff's work straddles both amusing and serious frames for a discussion that is not only about colonisation, but also about death, an artist and a friend's suicide, art history and art historical memory in a local context—questions and desires pertaining to what is considered culturally valuable, and, in a sense, who has the right not only to speak, but also to learn.

Untiled (After Gonz)

An image painted verbatim from Vision skate-wear-paraphernalia designed by Mark Gonzales. Geoff unaware, until a short conversation between us prior to the exhibition, that Blair too had transcribed the classic streetwear emblems. Having researched Mark 'Gator' Anthony Rogowski's design, Blair speculated on parallels suggesting that Gator's downfall and subsequent prison time were symbolically evident in the downward spiral effect of his Vision skate-wear design. The brand is known for commissioning contracted skaters to design logos and prints. Here, Geoff renders Mark Gonzales's emblematic '80s print in a kind of stenciled-fluoro trick, seemingly off-register and ad hoc. Like Blair's *Love 2005* catalogue image re-made, it is sourced from Netwon's unordered (and largely hidden) studio reference materials and archives.

Untitled (After Lorna)
The underside of a skateboard re-branded, as Blair had done on numerous occasions, including for the exhibition Products that educate, inspire and delight',[16] but Geoff's board is adorned with a detailed Lorna Fencer Napurrula painting *Yarla (Bush Potato or Yam)* and collaged with food and a studio shot. The painting maps the sharing of food and culture, or simply consumption — culture and content ignored via overeating. The skateboard is a frame to be used, the images that adorn them often scratched and obscured. Geoff's skateboard image is both shield and trophy — hung as if it were a prize, but also somehow humbled and introspective.

Eschewing an obvious logic, Geoff's sources transgress time, place and stereotypical hierarchies — Gonz's '80s graphic holds equal place with a Jackson Pollock or a Matthys Gerber, a record album cover or a Lorna Fencer Napurrula painting. In a text by A Constructed World (Geoff Lowe and Jacqueline Riva), which looks at culture as it is 'lived' and Blair's relationship with skating, the artists write:

> And like the skater the artist must also be fearless…
>
> Blair's art, from painting on boards to sampling the 'sign of art' from cultural products (ads, films, mags and so on) makes use of already produced forms. He's not dealing with a blank slate but a way of inserting the means of production into a flow of production that challenges passive culture and passive consumption. It is a kind-of reconfiguration of knowledge.
>
> Skaters find a way of inserting themselves into the flow of passive culture, negotiating and challenging the given environment, taking it over to make it their own. And, like in art, it seems that there is often going to be someone around to say 'you can't do that', someone who is going to attempt to uphold the imagined values of the passive culture, with the intention to tame the skater — the artist.
>
> And so to be a fearless skater is to be a fearless artist.[17]

Untitled (Roller painting)
An ode to Gerhard Richter's untitled abstracts, *Roller Painting* occupied the same colourfield and wall space as DAMP's *A Fete worse than Death* (2003) exhibition at Uplands Gallery.[18] The paint still somewhat stains the floor at TCB art inc. Geoff himself was a member of DAMP, the Melbourne-based collective, at the time of its self-deprecating call to the audience to get back at their usual provocateurs. Chained to a candy stripe painted wall in the gallery, members of DAMP taunted the audience while a spruiker encouraged those that gathered to attack with supplied paint-filled balloon bombs. The sadomasochist performance, while granting an opportunity for the audience to vent, also eventually—physically and psychologically—wounded the artists, as their friends and dealers, Blair included, pitched the hardest-flung, bruise-making bombs.

Gesture and paint psychologically made mechanical via the spruiker, the members of DAMP a representation rendered abstract by action and association.

Untitled (After James)
Hung on the same wall as James Lynch's faux wall with real spray paint, *Right or Wrong I am alive,* from the exhibition *The Penelope Syndrome* at Uplands Gallery in 2002. The quickly rendered, warped brick wall of Geoff's painting *After James* is emblazoned with white-bubble-font graffiti abjectly declaring to the audience 'More Life', a reference to the 1999 work *Wall with Graffiti* by Lynch (who is now represented by Geoff at Neon Parc, following the closure of Uplands Gallery in early 2011). Lynch's work similarly featured a *trompe l'oeil* brick wall, but it was spray-painted with a more personal declaration, borrowed from Roy Batty's line in Ridley Scott's *Blade Runner* (1982): 'I want more life'. To once again return to the '90s, if we remember also Scottish artist Ross Sinclair's 'Real Life' tattooed on his back—the Baudrillardian era seemed to encapsulate a melancholic longing and a perhaps unwarranted fear of the virtual superseding the lived.

Untitled (After Isa)
Art-world myths and rumors, coincidences and synchronici-

ties, shout-outs and salutes. A marbled, sloppily painted surface reveals a skull ripped directly from Isa Genzken's 2007 Venice Biennale coffee table book *OIL*—the book that fell on Hany Armanious's knee. His knee swelled up, so Armanious was hospitalised. Or did he trip over it? Or, in a fit of rage, did he throw it at a curator? Art world gossip and Dr Seussesque farce.

In Blair's *Love 2005* exhibition, the bark collage *Led Zepplin Mutlu* contains the remnants of an 'innocence made myth'.[19] Melbourne artist Mutlu Çerkez as a child apparently painted Pink Floyd's *Dark Side of the Moon* cover on the wall of his parents' kitchen—Blair's act was to paint a Led Zepplin cover over the pelican painting in his own parents' home.

For Geoff, Peralta's skeletal hands part the paint—a semi-clichéd gesture to the past and to the artists whose contributions will last longer than their lives—art world suicides. Blair hung himself. Did Geoff know Isa Genzken's 2007 installation contained sculptures of monkeys suspended from nooses? Coincidences and mourning and finding meaning where there is none.

At the time of his death, Blair's practice was changing. Uplands Gallery was beginning to gain success and recognition. Perhaps, as Geoff has pointed out, the art world didn't know what to do about it and Blair couldn't see it.

Untitled (After Robert)

If there was an *Australian Idol* of the avant-garde art world, perhaps Robert Rooney would be it. This enlarged version of a crumpled Rooney room sheet from his 2009 exhibition at Tolarno Galleries acts as a sign—a carefully-rendered-in-acrylic-paint sign, not of a hero though, nor of the commodity, but more the framing of the work as it is to be purchased. Rooney has been practicing for decades. He was born in 1937. His painting practice, similar to Geoff's, has consistently borrowed and referenced cultural artefacts and motifs, rearranging them to form new artefacts. Geoff's artefact is the price list for another artist's work, represented by another gallery. Geoff's artefact is not the art itself, but its capital framing, its market worth.

Geoff has been a dealer since 2005, he has worked in

artist-run-type spaces since 2001. Like many artists, he has worked as an art handler since art school, at institutions such as the National Gallery of Art, Canberra, the National Gallery of Victoria, Heide Museum of Art, the Melbourne Museum, Linden Contemporary Art Space and Niagara Galleries, Melbourne — the gamut of private and public artistic partnerships. In control of his own means of production to an extent, and facilitating some means for others. Dealing in art is not just the monetary exchange of goods — it is the support and production of a dialogue and a contribution to a scene, a culture and a history.

When dealing with art, perhaps the mystical factor both disappears and is amplified — you get to handle everything, you know its price, you can figure out how it's made. The magic, through a process of transference, shifts from the object to the imagined. Money might be magic, but the price of something isn't; a painting might be magical, but the way it is made isn't. The painting of the price list makes something of this evident. The price list, its layout and logo, is the framing of something other than the art. Having recently referred to himself as a hobby-painter, I wonder if it is in this act of hobbyist that Geoff can say the most: straddling, as Blair did, the roles of artist, dealer and curator — the spaces between all three, or lack thereof, facilitating a necessary distance and an ability to observe from the inside with a type of informed outsider's perspective.

Dave Hickey puts it best in a series of manifesto-like declarations littered throughout his Warhol-inspired musings on his life as a dealer and his attempt to answer the questions 'How could I stand the degradation of selling objects to people that know nothing about art?'; 'Didn't I feel lonely and alienated out there amidst the pandemic schizophrenia of bourgeouis culture?'; and 'What about my complicity in the hedonistic commodification of critical practice?'[20] Hickey's acknowledgments of being in business and being a shopkeeper and extrapolations on one-liners — such as 'Art ain't rocket science', 'Art is not a commodity', 'Art and money never touch', and 'Regarding my putative alienation … I never felt it'[21] — are worth looking up, because what Hickey, and I suspect Blair and Geoff, were and are dealing in is an enacted form of love:

> Because it is a matter of heart and not policy, a matter of live commitment and not of bureaucratic accreditation. Money is the emblem of the risks you are willing to take to have some say in the way things look. If you don't take risks, if you only confirm the prescience of previous investors, you acquire no power, create no constituencies, and have no affect. …
>
> Thus, money and risk vary inversely in all transactions related to art. The greater your risk, the less you pay and the more you receive. This is or should be an incentive to participate, to take extravagant chances, to execute daring acts of faith on behalf of your beliefs and in advocacy of your particular marriage of desire and esteem.[22]

Dealers aren't always right, their artists are not always happy, partnerships fail and partners die.

The crumpled room sheet Geoff painted retains the marks from the office or studio. Geoff is not making visible vast amounts of data, such as in the case of a traditional archive or even, say, Richter's *Atlas* or his *48 Portraits*. Geoff's archive, although vast, is hidden from the viewer. We are presented with a selection, and for this reason, subjectivity and the desire for the preservation of something other than, and outside of the painted object is created, is made evident.

Perhaps tribute albums, bootlegs and fan fictions present to us a mirror of the things we wish to keep, memorialise and aspire to. None are lauded by the industries and disciplines within which they exist, but, as participants, as audiences and as fans, these shout-outs are modes for existing both inside and outside the cultures we extract and borrow from. As previously suggested by ACW, creating these fan fictions challenges passive culture and passive consumption.

Culture is not something that is delivered to you. It builds up from what you didn't know you were doing.[23]

Post-script / addition / last words

Untitled (Geoff)

Earlier in this text, I mentioned an eighth painting. This painting was hung in the little space between the kitchen and the TCB art inc. entrance, hung high and on a wall where it would be less likely to be seen, tucked away in an interstitial space typically used for storage. The work, one that didn't fit in the show, quite literally,[24] consisted of a loose and sloppy David-Reed-Richteresque-gestured-CMYK-and-baby-poo-hued background painting that framed a quick-rendering of a 1983 painting by Geoff Lowe titled *Impersonation*. Lowe's work, part of a series of works with the title *10 Famous Feelings for Men*, renders a man in an Aboriginal suit posed as a Roman sentry in front of a red door. Joan Kerr wrote about the work as 'a bitterly comic portrait of a white man in nigger minstrel'. Bronwyn Watson cited this in her article linking Lowe's paintings with that of the work of ACW, reiterating the poignant observation in reference to a painting by Edward Poynter, *Faithful unto death* (1865), of which Lowe was previously unaware. Watson argues that Lowe's caricatured Aborigine implies that Poynter's magnificent specimen of British Victorian manhood is no more like an ancient Roman than someone in blackface is a faithful portrait of an Australian Aborigine… Conversely, Lowe's primary message is that all colonial portraits of Aborigines are similarly distorted, inevitably racist and propagandist.[25]

Impersonation

Discussing this on the day that marks five years since Kevin Rudd's 'Apology to Australia's Indigenous Peoples', a day on which we are reminded that Indigenous Australians are still unrecognised in the Australian Constitution, seems poignant. On this day, and with all this writing about representation and history, I am reminded of a passage from a speech Jacques Ranciére gave regarding what it means to be *Un*, in the Great Hall of the New Australian Parliament House while John Howard was still in power:

> The word 'dissensus' obviously refers to a conflict. But it is not a conflict between individuals or groups sharing

> different identities, interests, opinions or values. Strictly speaking, dissensus means a conflict between one sensible order and another. There is dissensus when there is something wrong in the picture, when something is not at the right place. There is dissensus when we don't know how to designate what we see, when a name no longer suits the thing or the character that it names, etc. A dissensus is thus an aesthetic matter. It is a matter of poetic invention. But poetic invention does not mean the invention of an imaginary place, a place that is elsewhere or nowhere. It means a displacement or a break in a given set of places and identities. In other words, it is a political matter. There is a poetics of politics which consists in inventing cases of dissensus.[26]

Perhaps the questions one is left with, questions one would imagine Geoff Newton might also have, regardless of his usual off-the-cuff piss-takes and knockoff paintings, are questions asked by all of the paintings previously discussed in this article. Perhaps all of Geoff's paintings are not unlike Lowe's *Impersonation*, pointing towards an historical present, and questioning the official representations we are somewhat defined by: friendships and lovers, partners and exes, heroes and nemeses, humour and tragedy, the personal and political, spectacle and narrative. What Bataille has called the 'useless image', and what Magritte calls the 'beauty of what is neither meaning nor nonsense' Suzanne Guerlac suggests is perhaps a way of thinking outside of the celebrated opposition between formalism and iconography.[27] To return to Heiser (who, like Guerlac, is attempting to negotiate the terrains of analysis-versus-beauty and thought-versus-desire) who refers back to Duchamp: 'the personal "art coefficient" is like an arithmetical relation between the unexpressed but intended and the unintentionally expressed'.[28] Impersonations in all forms are evidence of a mistranslation, a misunderstanding, or *dissensus*, if you may—be they insult or parody, intentional or otherwise, they remind us to ask *who and where we are*, and *who and where we are not*.

For the exhibition *Posture Again* in 2005, Blair

Trethowan commissioned A Constructed World to write a text. The text was about depression, class, culture and failure as a shared space. Blair screenprinted the text on the underside of three decks (where no-one would read them—perhaps like art magazines) and gave the boards to friends in order to spread the text all over town.[29] The boards were presented in the exhibition. The text is scratched and dirty and used, some of it is erased, punctured by holes where the trucks were screwed in. On it, ACW write: 'There's a lot of other very famous art about suicide. Hamlet asks whether to be or not to be, like whether he can bear to live, Beethoven's 9th Symphony goes da da der dum like it's the end of everything and Kurt Cobain says I wanna kill myself and I wanna die. Culture is a pretty serious place and people often want to express what is unbearable, and impossible to resolve other than by escaping'.[30]

Other than escaping.

First published in *Discipline*, no. 3, edited by Nicholas Croggon and Helen Hughes, Winter 2013. The author would like to thank the following people for their thoughts, words, fact-checking, image searches and recounts of the oral and visual history we share: Geoff Newton, Jarrod Rawlins, Amanda Marburg, Colleen Ahern, Geoff Lowe, James Lynch, Kati Rule, Masato Takasaka, Michelle Ussher, Matthew Griffin and Pip Wallis; and those who initially prompted me with the questions about the exhibition that got me talking: Liang Luscombe, Helen Hughes, Nick Croggon, Isabelle Sully and Kenny Pittock.

Notes

1 Al Weisel, 'Now More Than Ever: "If I Were a Carpenter," by Various Artists / "The Originals," by The Carpenters', *Rolling Stone* (20 October 1994): 142.

2 Email conversation between the author and Newton, October 2012.

3 TCB art inc. is a space run by artists that, up until recently, has survived without funding for 14 or so years. In an attempt to minimise bureaucracy, among other things, the space is run by a small group, of which I am a part. We don't always do things right, and we generally have to charge artists for exhibitions, which we hate, but basically, this fee simply covers the rent of the semi-squat- abandoned-building-looking space. TCB artinc was started by Sharon Goodwin, Thomas Deverall and Blair Trethowan.

4 Weisel, 'Now More Than Ever', 142.

5 Blair Trethowan curated an exhibition in the stairwell of the Port Phillip Arcade in 1999 with works by Amanda Marburg, Matthew Griffin, Colleen Ahern and Jarrod Rawlins. The show opened on the

same night as a TCB exhibition when it was located at Shop 15, Port Phillip Arcade—back then the most of the artists had just finished art school and Rawlins was a skater/photographer.

6 Darian Leader writes about this: Darian Leader, *The New Black: Mourning, Melancholia and Depression* (Minneapolis: Graywolf Press, 2008).

7 Justin Andrews exhibited in the same month as Geoff Newton in the smaller gallery at TCB art inc. Justin's exhibition, titled *In a Darkness Born*, presented a series of works made between 1998 and 2012. The works presented read as a collection of studio thoughts, experiments and journal entries. This is interesting to think about, now in retrospect, in relation to the idea of a local art history.

8 Jörg Heiser has explored this in relation to a range of artistic practices of the 1990s, in exhibitions such as *Romantic Conceptualism*, Kunsthalle Nürnberg, 2007, and see also: Jörg Heiser, 'Emotional Rescue', *Frieze* (May 2004): 70–75.

9 Heiser, 'Emotional Rescue', 74.

10 This 'blah blah blah' is a reference to a drawing by Jon Campbell, *a world full of cover versions blah blah blah*, first exhibited in Blair's apartment in Albert Street circa 2003, which lamented the apparent sameness of everything in the art world at the time.

11 During the lead-up to the show, Geoff found one of these stickers on the side of the road: an image of it and the Isa Genzken image were used as the press release image. Whilst talking to people in the lead-up to the show, and with the prospect of writing a bootleg Blair Trethowan monograph, I was sent an image by Pat Foster that read 'Business as Unusual', the title of the first exhibition at Uplands Gallery following the suicide of Blair Trethowan.

12 Danae Mossman, 'LOVE who you are. Who are you?', catalogue essay for Blair Trethowan's *Love 2005* exhibition, Studio 12, Gertrude Contemporary Art Spaces, September 2005.

13 *Posture Again* was curated by Blair Trethowan and included the artists Jota Castro, Blair Trethowan, A Constructed World, Lee Ralph & Tania Riki Riki, Uplands Gallery, Chinatown, 2005.

14 ibid.

15 Email conversation between myself and Newton, October 2012.

16 Gertrude Contemporary Art Spaces, 11 May – 2 June, 2000.

17 A Constructed World, 'Don't Steal Music', *Slam* magazine issue 67, p. 77 (catalogue for the show of the same name by Blair Trethowan at Uplands Gallery, 2002).

18 DAMP are an ever-changing group of people, who, through shared artistic practice, make work that examines the intricate relationships between art and audience via comedic and tragic gestures, performances, sculptures and installations. I myself was a member of DAMP between 1997 and 2010, Blair between 1996 and 2001, Jarrod between 2000 and 2001 and Geoff between 2001 and 2005. The current members of DAMP are James Lynch, Sharon Goodwin, Narelle Desmond and Deb Kunda. A list of the 80 or so members can be found here: http://dampdamp.weebly.com/members.html

19 Mossman, 'LOVE who you are', 2005.

20 Dave Hickey, 'Dealing' in *Air Guitar: Essays on Art & Democracy* (Los Angeles: Art Issues Press, 1997), 102–113.

21 ibid.

22 ibid., 112–113.

23 A Constructed World, 'Not knowing as a shared space', text produced for *Posture Again*, Uplands Gallery, Melbourne, 2005.

24 Conversation with the Geoff Newton, August 2012.

25 Bronwyn Watson, 'Public Works: Impersonation', *The Australian* (4 September 2010), www.theaustralian.com.au/arts/public-works-impersonation/story-e6frg8n6-1225912839645, accessed 2 February 2013. Re-printed as a caption in the catalogue *Based on a true story: Geoff Lowe 1972–92 and A Constructed World 1993–2012* (Melbourne: Ian Potter Museum of Art, 2012), 42.

26 JacquesRanciére, 'What does it mean to be Un?', *Continuum: Journal of Media & Cultural Studies* vol. 21, no. 4 (December 2007): 550.

27 Suzanne Guerlac, 'The Useless Image: Bataille, Bergson, Magritte', *Representations* vol. 97, no. 1 (Winter 2007): 36. In this essay, Guerlac re-examines form in relation to modernism through Bataille's essay on the Lauscaux Caves and through a reading of Magritte and Bergson's notion of resemblance.

28 Marcel Duchamp, 'The Creative Act', in Heiser, 'Emotional Rescue', 74.

29 In 2008, ACW gave the text to a group of young artists in Bordeaux, and Darian Leader in London. The artists and Leader wrote extensive footnotes, longer than the text itself, in order to relate it to a French context. The same skateboards were skated around Bordeaux and through the Museum CAPC, where eventually these new boards and new text were shown. Whilst skating near the Garonne river, one of the boards was broken, and one slipped into the river and was subsequently lost.

30 A Constructed World, '1. not-knowing as a shared space 2. class 3. Failure as a shared space', commissioned text, 2008, see previous note for discussion.

Hi Mail, Love Lisa.

I think it was in 2006 that we at TCB art inc.[1] decided to invite Rebecca Ann Hobbs,[2] based in Auckland at the time, to curate a show at the gallery; keen to mix-up the programming and eager to see things we might not otherwise see.

I

How to look
well, feel well:
First, you need
to find a
routine.

The exhibition *One for the 'other'* ended up being like a convoluted gift. Rebecca in turn invited 14 of her favourite men to exhibit alongside her. Among them were Melbourne-based artists, friends and colleagues of ours and hers: Nick Selenitsch,[3] Paul Knight,[4] Christopher Köller,[5] Brendan Lee,[6] and Kiron Robinson.[7] The others were based in New Zealand, and one in LA.[8]

Three Nicks in one show.

Nick Selenitsch, who I didn't really know well at the time, assisted installing the works — quiet logic and confident ease.

I remember opening a homemade foamcore box from Michael Lett art gallery as if it were a present, a gift. Upon opening it, I found a set of instructions, a woolen blanket and a $2-shop-esque thin plastic decorated tablecloth.

1. Rub Blanket on wall
2. Spread tablecloth on wall.

Simple instructions, alongside a simple diagram, *Untitled*, by Simon Denny.

3. Fall in love with static electricity.

I lie. The third instruction does not exist. Perhaps saying it overstates it.

If my memory serves me correctly, Nick Austin's work arrived in a tube. Unrolling a carefully wrapped and painted tabloid-double-page spread has a particular material quality to it: the newspaper and paint somehow merge to become another material — softer, more fragile, more plastic.

Note: Fall in love again.

The scumbled surface of Austin's painting left only remnants of the daily dealings below its surface. Eliciting a kind of banal-melancholic humour, Austin's painting *A rhizome* (2006) depicted a small piece of ginger (or was it turmeric?) contained by an almost-sloppy-peachily-painted round-edged-rectangle.

Quotidian beauty.

Jon Bywater might say, 'As if to say: if that's what you're looking for, don't look for it in the canvas. It highlights instead their simplifications, the analytical, human character of the act of painting.'

A couple of weeks ago, someone asked me who my favorite artist was. A strange question, which I am usually hesitant to respond to — the answer can seem to be transient and elusive, to both the questioner and questioned. Deciding to commit. If allowed only one, the parameters set, I would say Nick Austin.

I said, 'Nick Austin'.

Across the Tasman Sea, aided by the intermittent internet searches and the occasional exhibition in Melbourne, I am a fan. Electing Austin as a favourite, not the Firefox kind, means I might get to share some of his historical friends — Morandi, Cezanne, Giotto, Piero della Francesca, and wonder, would he share mine? Tony Clark, Vermeer or Sophie Tauber-Arp. What of Bonnard? De Stael? John Brack? What does he think of the wacky Magritte paintings such as *The Ellipsis* (1948)? Does he like Patrick Lundberg's shoelaces?[9]

Funny formalism for lovers. Empty absurdity for wannabe vagabonds.

Hey Lane! Hey Col! Hey Moo! Who was that Mannerist who lived in the tree?

About a month ago, after some brief email conversations with Helen from Parsons' Library Supply, credit card numbers and expiry dates, I received in the mail The Liquid Dossier.

Handwritten 45/200.

No expectations.

A humble-but-alluding-to-order Eastlight. Slimpick. Wallet. Foolscap, in fact, Manilla-folder-yellow in colour. Contained within it, an unbound book. A package. Some loose thoughts. Some points to, some points from—trajectories. Personal paraphernalia. Personable.

A list of items contained within—a roomsheet for a folder. A poster, a laser print, a risograph print, photographs printed and enveloped in the equivalent of an Officeworks envelope. A very short PowerPoint film on a DVD in a crystal case called *Dentists on Holiday* with a improvised-jazz-with-engine soundtrack. A small sachet of coffee the size of a photo depicting a coffee cup the size of a small car. A postcard of a painting of an envelope flying.

Envelopes inside envelopes. Unread… no…wait… cannot be opened mail.

The green notebook was a gift, Jon Bywater writes.

He goes on: I find ways to use it as well as the laptop on which

I usually write; sometimes, of course, just because it's easier to carry and the only thing to hand, but it also creates a loose genre of notes.

The package is im or I'm perfect. And quirky in its everydayness, in its dossier-ness, rather than its archive-ness. This is like Christopher L.G. Hill's *Endless Lonely Planet* or Jon Nixon's *Mike Brown Research volumes 1 and 2*.[10]

But also not.

A very short letter to Bonnard dated 13 August 1925 reads:

Long Live
Painting!!!
In Friendship

Likened to what Patrick said, maybe our interest can lie in a more social painting. A painting with a keener sense of duration. A painting which one day may no longer beg to be called by that name.

A book with a keener sense of time, a book which one day may no longer beg to be called by that name.

First published on stamm.com.au, edited by Jonathan Nichols, 2013

Notes

1 See: www.tcbartinc.org.au
2 See: http://www.circuit.org.nz/artist/rebecca-ann-hobbs
3 See: http://www.suttongallery.com.au/artists/artistprofile.php?id=45
4 See: http://www.paulknight.com.au/
5 See: http://christopherkoller.net/
6 See: http://www.brendanlee.com/site.php
7 See: http://kironrobinson.com/
8 *One for the 'other'* was curated by Rebecca Hobbs. The artists included in the exhibition were: Rebecca Hobbs, Peter Volich, Phillip Maysels, Nick Selenitsch, Josh Stone, Dan Arps, Christopher Koller, Jon Bywater, Brendan Lee, Nick Austin, Paul Knight, Simon Denny, Kiron Robinson, Mario Garcia Torres and Nick Spratt.
9 See: http://roberthealdgallery.com/exhibitions/previous/2012archive/patrick-lundberg-points-planes-eddies-regresses/
10 See: http://www.worldfoodbooks.com/endless-lonely-planet-1/

huh

Last year in September, J.J. Charlesworth wrote a relatively short opinion piece for *Art Review* titled 'At What Point Does Nothing Become Too Much of a Good Thing?'—a pointed meandering that refers to Object Oriented Ontology (OOO hype) whilst questioning the 'dematerialised, postindustrial rhetoric' of Tino Seghal.

In between all this questioning of material-based culture, the market and overproduction, what about the 'thingness' of words, verbal exchange and speech? What of daily exchanges and their value, of what is shared and how it becomes action—of the materiality of language?

Samuel Beckett spoke about the limitations of this and language. In his famous 1986 made-for-TV teleplay, *Quad I & II*, we have the visual boundary of these ideas played out. *Quad*'s script could be read as a mathematical pattern or a diagram—a thing—the material manifestation of something unspoken played out on a stage and presented en masse via television. Ungendered cloaked mimes rhythmically stepping-out a preprogrammed loop, leaders alternating, order defined by the boundaries of a square stage, this in turn echoing that of the square box of televisions from that time. The centre only ever circled (so to speak), as if to arrive at or acquire desire would only serve to make visible what we the viewer and unnamed collective might already know. Beckett's stage play is as such, a kind of gesture towards us—a pattern we can interpret, a rhythm we might recognise—potentially boring, the arrangement becomes a narrative without words and somehow contains shared meaning.

Life and Times begins with a five-minute musical prelude—somewhat Sufjan-Stevens-*Illinoise* in its arrangement and then…

ummmmm' is sung.

I'm not sure that many musical theatre scripts begin with ummmmmm', a pause-filler dependent on place and perhaps time. (American's use 'um' and 'uh', whilst the British might use 'er' and 'erm'. I think we use a combo. I'm fond of the Japanese 'ano' and 'eto'.)

Life and Times Episodes 1–4 was performed on sequential nights and in its entirety during a 10-hour-long marathon performance which included a BBQ and brownies cooked and served by members of Nature Theatre of Oklahoma (NY) during the 2013 Melbourne Festival.

The duration of the performance eventually reveals a narrative, but one that involves repetition, boredom, and choreographed and melodic improvisation. Simultaneously theatre and not-theatre, 'Episode 1' opens with three female cast members each singing a different part of a recorded narrative.[1] References to first-person and third-person pronouns move with each character. When the female cast members are replaced by their male counterparts, so are the gendered pronouns — one person's story becomes many. As you wonder if anything will happen, and boredom sets in, it's ruptured by the semi-fascist grey uniforms worn by the cast, the occasional glance they throw you, or the rigid mass-spectacle-type-semi-democratic-choreographed moves.

Fatigue and boredom are shared by both the actors and the audience, perhaps too by those playing the live score…

Oh my god…
um… I'm like a very serious baby.
um and ah um.
ha ha ha

It's a kind of a lol IRL YOLO performance that reflects on someone's (anyone's) life story from birth, mostly sung by a cast that somehow maintains momentum and stamina without the usual verse-chorus-verse-structure. Unlike *Quad*, the repetition is inconsistent, or less obvious from afar — more differential calculus than linear equation and more sculptural painting performance gig than theatre — the formal space of the Playhouse transformed.

'Come on Julie, come on', is chanted semi-Appalachian — think *Down to the River to Pray*.

'It was, like, so beautiful' returns intermittently throughout the performance, like an off-beat refrain.

Daydreaming seems like an ok thing to do during the performance — the OK singing, the OK dancing and the OK script kind of merging to form a kind of familiar soundtrack, albeit it new. By the third and fourth episodes — more *Days of Our Lives* or *The Bold and the Beautiful* in its aesthetic (rather than the minimal post-soviet uniforms of episode one, and the RUN-DMC-Adidas-multi-colour-tracksuits of disco-backing-tracked episode two), you might be looking at the audience around you.[2] Watching them, instead of the stage, as they laugh, cry, walk out, fall asleep and/or sigh in response to the almost-acapella-absurdist-and-readymade-script (the [soon to be 16] episodes are derived from a phone conversation between an unknown-to-us storyteller and the OK Theatre directors Pavol Liska and Kelly Copper).[3]

As with Beckett's *Quad*, the story is rendered irrelevant whilst language is stretched — formal foredom — like Baldessari throwing balls in the air to make a perfect square, or Taree and Ronen's coloured venetian blinds in *Glow* (2013) and Sam George's Sony Bravia painting of every letter of the alphabet over-laid.

Art critic Jerry Saltz's analysis of Kanye West's video in the article 'Kanye, Kim, and "the New Uncanny",'[4] if set alongside journalist Chris Hedges' 'American Psychosis' (2010)[5] (which asks what happens to a society that can't distinguish between reality and illusion), presents us with a problem — that of distinguishing between varying kinds of representation, often conflicting. With Tony Abbott's LNP[6] and David Cameron's Conservative party[7] both erasing parts of their history from the net last week, this formalist boredom is perhaps a symptom of an unspoken shared social.

One half of the *Life and Times* director-duo, Pavol Liska, originated from Slovakia and was trained in the mass spectacle performances of the then-Soviet-run State. It was the theatre companies that led the strikes leading to the 1989 Velvet Revolution.

In Ranciere's text *The Aesthetic Unconscious* (2009), he attempts to position his idea of the aesthetic regime in the context of the emergence of psychoanalysis and the order of representation. It is described as the set of relations between what is said and what can be seen, and the set of relations between knowledge and action.

Amidst a plethora of representations, our shared 'trying to say everything at once' is perhaps very similar to a potentially never-ending, almost melodic and almost performed opus, huh.

First published on stamm.com.au, edited by Jonathan Nichols, 2013.

Notes

1 See: http://www.mousonturm.de/web/media/events/2012/November 2012/Nature Theater of Oklahoma/2012_10_31_Nature_Theater_of_Oklahoma_Episode_1_Vienna_2010_-_c_Reinhard_Werner-Burgtheater_life_times_II_19s 019_eventbild.jpg

2 See: http://oktheater.files.wordpress.com/2013/01/lifeandtimes-43-e1357601924854.jpg?w=640&h=286

3 See: http://www.oktheater.org/

4 See: http://www.vulture.com/2013/11/jerry-saltz-on-kanye-west-kim-kardashian-bound-2.html

5 See: https://www.adbusters.org/magazine/90/hedges-american-psychosis.html

6 See: http://www.theage.com.au/federal-politics/political-news/tony-abbotts-more-controversial-speeches-disappear-20131130-2yimm.html

7 See: http://www.theguardian.com/politics/2013/nov/13/conservative-party-archive-speeches-internet

Information management: << . >> post-script: BORING BORING

1. Sampling

I originally tried starting this with a quote from Kenneth Goldsmith quoting Douglas Huebler but, as you pointed out, we ended up trying to start at a dead end. Misquoting it re-opens it: the world is full of objects, more or less interesting.[1]

An updated notion of genius would have to centre around one's mastery of information and its disseminations. (Marjorie) Perloff has coined another term, 'moving information', to signify both the act of pushing language around as well as the act of being emotionally moved by its process.[2]

A last hurrah for modernism and subsequent in-jokes.

The Willhelm scream[3] is a sample scream used in some 200 films. I imagine Tarantino uses it as a joke, a nod to cinematic history. In *Reservoir Dogs*, where the example of his usage can be found, no one is falling. His clever quotes have an affect that is different to the same scream being used, say, in the *Star Wars* trilogy or a Disney movie, because the same self-reflexivity is not present.

Here's a nice interaction between Kanye West and Steely Dan's Donald Fagan:

> Kanye actually sent us a sample of his tunes, and frankly, Walter and I listened to it, and although we'd love some of the income, neither of us particularly liked what he had done with it. We said 'No,' at first, and then he wrote us a hand-written letter that was kind of touching, about how the song was about his father, and he said, 'I love your stuff, and I really want to use it because it's a very personal thing for me.' My mind doesn't work like that—I would never use someone

else's stuff if I was writing something personal, but I guess that's how he was thinking about it. It was such a good letter that we said, 'All right, go ahead,' and we made a deal with him.[4]

2. Ownership

Shifting the space of reading: Kenneth Goldsmith runs a class at Harvard where he asks students to submit writing that is either appropriated, plagiarised, patch-written or stolen. What is clear, though, is that in the attempt to eradicate the subjective, emoting self, and to destabilise the category of 'Literature', the category of 'Author' becomes oddly affirmed.[5] You may not have written the text but you take responsibility for it. Tarantino's use of the Wilhelm scream makes it obvious returning it to its author: both are elevated.

Release the grip of your cold dead hands: Kenneth Goldsmith's uncreative pursuits revive productive rigor mortis by breaking the weight of originality through teaching and promoting the unoriginal as a valid mode of making. I guess it's liberating to steal—well, when it widens the productive spectrum. Ownership becomes a problem when its effect disables the potential and benefits of reincarnations and sharing. 'Second comers might do a much better job than the originator with the original idea.'[6]

The cardinal difference between gift exchange and commodity exchange is that a gift establishes a feeling-bond between two people, whereas the sale of a commodity leaves no necessary connection... Art that matters to us—which moves the heart, or revives the soul, or delights the senses, or offers courage for living, however we choose to describe it, the experience is received as a gift.[7]

HL: For me, this shifting of information touches on thoughts concerning distribution and the way that popular images in circulation that then might be found by a Google image search are in turn affected by your projects. Image-searching the *The Fresh Prince of Bel-Air* DVD brings up some of the images you generated in your project among the others one might expect to find. This blurs the provenance and hence potential

> meaning of those images. What I am referring to is this moment of occupation that is a part of appropriation.
>
> SD: Totally. This is again somehow the lay of the land, just how things are now. Occupation of images is a naturally tricky topic when it's so much a part of the fabric of life. Or conversely it could be seen as nothing, not tricky at all…[8]

Kenneth Goldsmith says something like, 'I don't demand a readership. I assume there is no readership.' What he is presenting as work assumes this because the assumption is that it has already been read.

3. This is an outdated idea

Its an old issue or seems like a timeless one. Where things rise to the surface and others fall away when something new comes into play. Copying and its variations play a fundamental part in learning, creativity and development, which, for the most part, I imagine is a benefit to people. When a new piece of technology such as home computers and the internet come into use, we begin to see the shaping of the user by its tools and vice versa. It was in the early days of heavy computer use that issues such as Naspster (which had lawsuits in 2000) popularised file sharing and the surrounding problems that faced distributing industries. Information management, shifting materials from one platform to the next, has become commonplace. Every man and his dog is now trying to be a part of this migration.

Maybe every man and his turtle. Turtle F2F is a 'not being developed' peer-to-peer sharing network (Friend-2-Friend). Not being developed feels like a kind of latent monster, a sleeping spy or an empty block — a space with no engagement.

Goldsmith removes the readymade from contemporary art and inserts it into another discipline, this in itself is a form of sampling.

I remember reading about Goldsmith talking about many of his works resembling artists' books or artworks, and that they would fit rather snuggly in the shelves and online catalogues of Printed Matter inc. He didn't do that, instead he opted for a publishing house and the whole book thing. Making that shift adds the entire weight of the literary world to what he has done, and to great effect. Obviously he realised the distinction and/or exposure his work would have in this semi-alien environment, whilst also exposing the potential of the medium through his rural-pinko mentality.

The reason the fax refuses to die is because people, once they adopt a method, tend not to change. It's the inertia of least effort, aka laziness, aka efficiency of thought. Granted, there are good reasons for this approach. Most people have bad experiences with moving to new systems. How many times have you spoken with someone who blames a new system for slowing productivity, missing features, or for making the effort of using those features far more complex? People therefore tend to distrust new technology, again because in their experience—and this is correct—new technology fails and established technology works. The reason for that truth is quite simple: only good technology sticks around to become established; bad technology is abandoned.[9]

So I guess my question is something like: is it the change of platforms that sheds light on the origin, where the process is somewhat re-invented and the source re-returned?

I think what we're interested in now is the accumulation and the reshaping and the rebuilding of this once-fractured vessel. Because, after Modernism, there was no more work to do. Language has been pulverised and atomised so much that there was really nothing else to do. What are you going to do, take a grain of sand and chop it up even further or are you actually going to forget about deconstruction and begin some sort of re-construction, acknowledging and re-building this vessel? Acknowledging the cracks in it. We're not going back but instead we have to, kind of, look at wholes again. I'm not interested in rips. I'm actually interested in wholeness. I'm interested in an articulated sentence that is, uh, uh semantically correct. I'm interested in, in semantic intactness. I'm not interested in atomisation.[10]

4HEWORKSSHOWHOWSEMIOCAPITALISMHAS-RESULTEDNOTINNEWTASTESBUTINNEWCATEGO-RIESOFFLAVORANDFORM

4. boring boring

Unboring boring is a voluntary state; boring boring is a forced one.[11]

The relationship between boredom and what is produced out of boredom raises interesting questions about quality and what may be considered good, and if indeed this qualification is necessary at all. Boredom's formalism is its own subjectivity. By taking a well-worn-art-world gesture and placing it in another economy, it became a scandalous gesture: playing one sport by the rules of another.

Pattern recognition and/or attention/awareness. I am reminded of that McLuhan business explaining that an individual resorts to pattern recognition when the information that is flooding in cannot be absorbed. Repetition is key, really, being pummeled by material and all you can notice are the similar shapes going by, or the reoccurrence of things. Is it boredom when you are detached, or is it that you don't recognise the value in something?

Boredom is a function of attention. We are learning new modes of attention—say, favouring the ear more than the eye—but so long as we work within the old attention frame, we find X boring... e.g., listening for sense rather than sound (being too message-oriented). Possibly, after repetition of the same single phrase or image for a long while, in a given written text or piece of music or film, if we become bored, we should ask if we are operating in the right frame of attention. Or: maybe we are operating in one right frame, where we should be operating in two simultaneously, thus halving the load on each (i.e., sense and sound).[12]

As revealed in the recent furore over Instagram reserving the right to sell users' images (a proposal quickly retracted by parent company Facebook), control over online cultural production often doesn't lie with the producer. These artists seemed to be highlighting the economic logic of Google or Facebook, not by critique but by imitation: we'll sell you the platform but reserve the rights to the artwork.[13]

Kenny once said; 'Last week when I read at the Brooklyn Public Library, during the Q&A session, a woman claimed to be disappointed because I didn't bore her. Somehow she felt that the self-appointed 'most boring writer in the world' was obliged to live up to his title. I told her that if she really wanted to be bored, then she was quite free to try to read my books in her own time. Call me a sellout, but I feel some sort of an obligation to an audience trapped in a room.'[14]

Co-authored by Simon McGlinn, first published in *un Magazine*, issue 7.2.

Notes

1 Faced with an unprecedented amount of available text, the problem is not needing to write more of it. Instead, we must learn to negotiate the vast quantity that exists. Kenneth Goldsmith refers to Douglas Huebler's 1969 statement, 'the world is full of objects, more or less interesting; I do not wish to add any more' in a range of texts, including: Kenneth Goldsmith, 'Letter to Bettina Funcke', *Documenta Notebooks* no. 17 (London: Hatje Cantz, 2012).

2 Kenneth Goldsmith, 'It's Not Plagiarism. In the Digital Age, It's "Repurposing"', *The Chronicle of Higher Education* (11 September 2011 https://chronicle.com/article/Uncreative-Writing/128908/, accessed 2 May 2013.

3 chrisofduke, *The Wilhelm Scream Compilation*, http://www.youtube.com/watch?v=cdbYsoEasio, uploaded on Jun 17, 2006, accessed 6 May 2008. 5,181,220 views. chrisofduke in the About section writes: 'A video I found several years ago, with clips of films using the scream that is found in most George Lucas films… *NOTE** I did not make this video Found it several years ago online…'.

4 Taylor Berman, 'Kanye West Wrote Handwritten Letter to Steely Dan fo Sample Clearance', *Fuse TV* (16 October 2012), http://www.fuse.tv/2012/10/kanye-west-wrote-handwritten-letter-to-steely-dan-for-sample clearance, accessed 28 April 2013.

5 John Douglas Millar, 'Conceptual Writing', *Art Monthly* issue 361 (November 2012): 10(4).

6 Jonathan Lethem 'The Ecstasy of Influence', *Harper's Magazine* (February 2007), http://harpers.org/archive/2007/02/the-ecstasy-of-influence/, accessed June 2012.

7 ibid.

8 Ambidextrous, 'Predestined Formats: A conversation between Hannes Loichinger and Simon Denny', http://prod-images.exhibit-e.com/www_petzel_com/Loichinger_denny_interview_2011.pdf, accessed April 2013.

9 'Re:It's convenience and security.' (Score:5, Insightful) (blog post) by Bacon Bits (926911) on Wednesday 7 September 2011 @02:21AM (#37323886), http://tech.slashdot.org/story/11/09/07/027235/why-the-fax-machine-refuses-to-die, accessed May 2013.

10 Kenneth Goldsmith in Simon Morris, 'Kenneth Goldsmith: sucking on words' (Ubuweb, 2008), http://www.ubu.com/film/goldsmith_sucking html, accessed May 1, 2013.

11 Kenneth Goldsmith, 'Being Boring', at *The First Seance for Experimental Literature*, Disney REDCAT Theatre, Los Angeles, November 2004, and Kelly Writer's House, University of Pennsylvania, Poet's Lunch, November 2004, http://epc.buffalo.edu/authors/goldsmith/goldsmith_boring.html, accessed March 2013.

12 Maria Popova, 'Susan Sontag on the Creative Purpose of Boredom', http://www.brainpickings.org/index.php/2012/10/26/susan-sontag-on-boredom/, accessed April 2012

13 Paul Teasdale, 'Net Gains: Claire Bishop versus the Internet', *Frieze* issue 153 (March 2013), http://www.frieze.com/issue/article/net-gains/, accessed April 2013.

14 Kenneth Goldsmith, 'I Hate Poetry Readings, Harriet: a poetry blog', 2007, http://www.poetryfoundation.org/harriet/2007/05/i-hate-poetry-readings/, accessed May 2013.

Something something video-film-paint something.

Steve McQueen crossed over with *Hunger* (2008).[1] Gillian Wearing did it too, in 2010, with her doco-slash-art film *Self-Made* (which did not get major release in Melbourne, or feature in a film festival). On 17 March 2013, at Longplay in North Fitzroy, *Doc(c)o Club* returned with a screening of Wearing's film. A couple of friends-slash-film-making-colleagues have recently started a film club. Modeled somewhat on the reading-group-cum-book-club phenomenon, Kim Munro and Amanda Kerley started *Doc(c)o Club* with the idea of screening seminal, rare and innovative films, selected so as to generate discussion and dialogue.[2] Whilst *Doco Club* centres around screenings and discussions, Amanda and Kim's other project, *Camera Buff Movie Makers*, groups together makers interested in the production of short, essayistic films aimed to question the limitations documentary film-making. With funding for documentary film-making becoming harder to get, both these projects have been a way for Amanda and Kim to focus attention on and help cultivate divergent ways of thinking about and telling non-fiction stories.

Amanda and Kim are both engaged in documentary practice. Kim began her foray into the field with the musical short documentary *The Rise of Leatherman* (2008),[3] followed by *Nerve* (2011),[4] a made-for-television (in particular the ABC documentary about the London-based Australian artist Paul Knight, and his project which attempted to find two strangers interested in having sex upon meeting. Together, Amanda and Kim have worked on the short campaign documentary *Keep Our Hope Alive (Save the Hope Street Bus)* (2012),[5] which was made following State Government funding cuts that saw the axing of the shortest bus route in Melbourne—deemed economically irrational, the closure of the service left some 150 elderly citizens without the means of transport that allowed them to be self-sufficient.

Gillian Wearing's *Self-made* is a crossover film.[6] By utilising processes and approaches from her previous works, Wearing makes a documentary film that not only traverses a kind of self-help-cathartic-reality-TV genre but also a film that, in the end, tends towards the dramatic and theatrical. Weaving together a series of scenarios determined by the films' participants and the workshops they have taken part in with the method acting teacher Sam Rumbelow, Wearing's doco-becomes-drama: a man who has planned his own death sees himself through the lens of Mussolini; a depressed and repressed middle-aged woman becomes the heroine of a 1940s love story (this reminded me somewhat of Claude Chabrol's 1970 film *Le Boucher* [The Butcher]); and the complicated relationship between a daughter and father is replayed via the restaging of Shakespeare's *King Lear*. The process of fictionalising self-generated facts highlights the difficulty of representation and, in particular, the participants' complex relationships with themselves and the world.

This privilege of being able to cathartically engage with their past or present internal conflicts and then reshape that conflict via method acting reminded me of Slavoj Žižek's 2011 article 'Shoplifters of the World Unite', published in the *London Review of Books*. The text examines the sloganless actions of the London rioters reacting to the shooting of Mark Duggan and their relationship to the European debt crisis, through Žižek's typical Marxist-Hegelian lens — those outside an organised social space express discontent through 'irrational' outbursts of destructive violence. The rioters' unspeakable and unrepresentable conflict with the present eventuated in several days of violence and looting. This is the space between the rational and the irrational, the representable and the unrepresentable, the tentative and the potentially volatile.

Unrepresentable.

If Wearing's film could be thought of as a fictional-cinematic-portrait of the lives of seven Londoners, I can't help but draw a parallel to Colleen Ahern's exhibition *Cortez The Killer* at Neon Parc this month.[7] The two-year project has seen the production of more than thirty portraits of a man she can only imagine, based on the Neil Young song of the same name.[8] The song references Hernán Cortez, a Spanish conquistador who conquered Mexico for Spain in the sixteenth century. The song utilises the historical narrative and then shifts to what seems like a personal, first-person narrative. Colleen paints the image of this man, of whom there are few representations. She paints for us a man she cannot see, of whom there is no photographic portrait.

Oil paint can be a slippery, manipulative medium. Sometimes, the portrait appears to us as a collage, a mash-up of faces; at other times, it is clearly a painting of someone masked by a taped-on moustache (who I am privileged enough to know is her daughter). In the exhibition, we are presented with thirty questions asking what a portrait is, what it can be, what it can't be, regardless of whether it is finely glazed and reminiscent of a Velásquez or the loosely painted features of a face rendered awkward. I can't help but think of the Shroud of Turin or Robin Williams's character Harry in Woody Allen's *Deconstructing Harry*, who literally slips out of focus—portraits, pictures and leaps of faith.

In the end, Colleen's paintings force us to make our own assumptions as to who is being depicted and give them names that we have decided—the Dave Grohl one, the Alex Vivian one, the Tony Abbott one. What we are left with is perhaps the melancholy embedded within any endless project. Painting a portrait is difficult at the best of times; painting a portrait of someone that one has to imagine—building the face, the structure, the tonality, the touch—is near impossible. Colleen gives us thirty paintings about the impossibility of portraiture, of representation and, perhaps, of the historical memorial—Colleen's serialised-fictional-portrait of one person becomes the collection of individual portraits of a faceless many.

First published on stamm.com.au, edited by Jonathan Nichols, 2013. Kim and Colleen are both very good friends of the author. Gillian is not

Notes

1 *Something something video something* was an exhibition curated by Blair Trethowan and Jarrod Rawlins and presented at Artspace, Sydney, in 2003 and Uplands, Melbourne, in 2002.

2 See: See: http://kimmunro.com
3 See: http://vimeo.com/25277117
4 See: Trailer: http://www.youtube.com/watch?v=GVDBaLjQA-o&list=PLB535284C7306B86B&index=5
5 See: http://www.youtube.com/watch?v=1RLUzTwYIcQ
6 See: http://selfmade.org.uk/
7 See: http://neonparc.com.au/. Colleen Ahern's exhibition has also been written about by Hannah Matthews for Stamm, see: http://stamm.com.au/colleen-ahern-cortez-the-killer/
8 See: http://www.youtube.com/watch?v=6GDIkb5CDUY

Writing mail, writing class: 'The big east'

It was kind of an awkward week or so.[1]

At the opening of Simon Zoric's exhibition *What I Can And Can't Do And What I Will And Won't Do*,[2] after being kind of startled by his carved wooden effigy, I was walking away from one of his works where Zoric had basically cut out the wall from his teenage bedroom because it contained the beloved Nirvana poster that needed to be shown. I was walking and thinking, 'is it really from his bedroom?', 'how's that '70s blue paint?', 'what's with Nirvana?', 'it's the '90s again', 'Fuck, Kurt committed suicide', 'shit, I hope Zoric doesn't die'.

At the precise moment of that last thought, I kicked the silicone cast of his cock and balls. Zoric's self-deprecating humor, quite obviously contagious.[3]

On the Saturday just past, I went to see Christos Tsiolkas talk about class and culture at Trades Hall in Carlton. I guess, other than being called a hipster, my question about class and its invisibility or slipperiness re-emerged—does the approach to definition un-render representation?

Kiron Robinson's eight-minute video *When I write I write for you* begins with a sniff and ends with awkward laughter.[4] It's an eight-minute close up of a tightly framed face, reminiscent of John Cassavetes' 1968 film *Faces*.[5]

The Le Tigre song 'What's Your Take on Cassavetes' begins with a kind of drawling voice:

> *we've talked about it in letters*
> *and we've talked about it on the phone,*
>
> *but how you really feel about it,*
> *I don't really know.*[6]

Which, however obtuse, seems relevant here.

Robinson's short film, mini-doc-foray into a kind of

cinéma-vérité aesthetic straddles a monologue about family relations, siblings, age gaps and role models, footy, responsibilities, time and scale issues, pornography, masculinity, hierarchies and the need for an inability to take sides.

Robinson exhibited the work in an exhibition he organised called *The Big East*,[7] which involved seven artists exhibiting in two scout halls in Heathmont on Sunday 9 June 2013, between 10:00 a.m. and 5:00 p.m.

I asked Kiron some questions, the first being, 'could I ask him some questions?'

LR: Ok. I'm gonna start really simply. How did the idea for the show come about?

KR: About 18 months ago I moved out here (outer-eastern Melbourne). It is not my ideal location and resulted in odd sorts of pressures in my life. As a result, I decided to make some work out of being in the middle/outer suburbs. When I started looking around, I noticed there were lots of psychologically interesting spaces in the suburbs that I had not noticed before. The scout halls I used are two that I pass by on a run. Over about eight months of running by them, an idea emerged of what I could do, so I decided to see if they were open to being used and it turned out they were. The rest just grew from there.

LR: What I found interesting about the project was the way in which it forced us out of the safety of the CBD. There is an inherent irony in this, especially if we consider all the 'danger, drunk' talk of the media, 'mayhem on the weekends', blah blah. You turned us into Sunday drivers without cars or something. All the chance visitors are kind of amazing as well. Having worked out there at one stage, I liked catching up with my old boss again and hanging out with his kids in his hood.

The scout halls were these interesting spaces where 'contemporary' seemed irrelevant. I know we talked about the upturned coloured plastic cups; Daniel Belfield's *Map* easily blending in with the in-situ pin board; your film projected on a stand (can't remember the word for this thing!!!) as if ready for a rope-knotting demonstration; Eliza Dybell's performance which could have been a team-building exercise, the Ryan sisters' hiding from the world double-self-portrait-sculpture could have been real kids playing real games (albeit slightly sinister) and Cormick's dirt-bike dinks slip easily into hoon territory. How did you choose the artists for the exhibition? And did you specifically choose the scout sites for these artists?

KR: Yes, it is nice to be out of the CBD. It changes things in terms of whatever our expectations or preconceptions of the suburbs are and alerts us to our conceptions of art. I am alerted to this every time I go home (as I live down the road from the scout halls).

I was really stunned when the first visitors came by. I think up until the point of someone arriving, I had been unable to marry up these two parts of my life, Art and where I live, and having people turn up acted as a catalyst or a clash which alerted me to my own awkwardness in relation to how I see my life.

The scout halls came first. I chose them really thinking about my own works (selfish, yes), but then invited the other artists because of a psychological aspect to their works which resonated with the sites. I knew of all their practices, obviously, and like them as people, and so thought it would be a good combo.

LR: I am going to latch onto something there about 'liking the artists as people'. It is something I am also interested in, in terms of momentum and criticality. In some ways, it is traditionally opposed to the very notion of critical because its first encounter is recognising subjectivity and, in some ways, the sentimental.

When you said 'I knew of all their practices, obviously, and like them as people, and thought it would be a good combo', what is it about the combination of artists? I know there is a space of not-knowing that we are working in, or aim to work in, but what were you hoping to achieve though the exhibition and the relationship between the works?

KR: Mmm. I have curated/organised a number of exhibitions. Basically it is about working with people I am interested in. I see it as an extension of my practice in that I do things and make work about things that I am interested in. I am not really into curating for the sake of curating. As such, I feel no obligation to criticality. Rather, like my own work, I just want to do something that interests me first and hope that others can also connect in their own way. It is the way most artists work, I think. It is nice, as you kind of just put your subjectivity front and centre.

It is the psychological aspect of the scout halls, which I think reflects a deeper psychology of the suburbs, what lies beneath, that I was really interested in and that I was hoping to draw out. There is an intrinsic anxiety within the suburban, the anxiety of the aspirational and it leaks out in all sorts of ways. I think partly I recognise this within myself and moving back to the suburbs has really heightened it in me. Maybe for me it is not so much the aspirational but the settling. The giving up that I associate with a regression of returning to a suburban setting. I wanted to work with that. There is a romantic aspect to the suburban that I was interested in as well. The Sunday drive, the ideal that it sells. I just find them to be very tense places.

First published on stamm.com.au, edited by Jonathan Nichols, 2013.

Notes

1 See: http://www.youtube.com/watch?v=PUGNbkJmM-w
2 See: http://westspace.org.au/event/what-i-can-and-can-t-do-and-what-i-will-and-won-t-do/
3 See: http://www.simonzoric.com/
4 See: http://www.kiron-robinson.com
5 See: https://goo.gl/HKypoH
6 See: http://www.youtube.com/watch?v=tI87_X52wmk
7 See: http://thebigeast.weebly.com/W

paddle-pop populous and farcical femme-fatales

Mario Armando Lavandeira, Jr., aka Perez Hilton, had his first child on 16 February this year, appropriately named Mario Armando Lavandeira III—the mother, a surrogate, the conception facilitated with a donor egg.

Cloning, copying, reproduction, redemption.

Gossip, someone says, is the production of something from nothing. A kind of Warhol-infused neo-Faustian bargain. A dialogue with the devil—aesthetics 'n' ethics. A schematic backdrop to mundanity.

Sue Dodd's *Best of: A Survey of Gossip Pop*, presented ever-so-briefly at Techno Park Studios,[1] was a Mike-Kelley-Day-is-Done-esque (minus the absurd narrative) immersive installation, which transformed the once-kindergarten into a kind of low-fi-sci-fi videophile den. Seductive and silly, the ambitious installation over three rooms saw the presentation of several new satirical video works alongside a *Gossip Pop* compilation. At times droll and occasionally sardonic, Dodd's performed and animated *New Weekly* or *Women's Weekly* chants are an absurdist yes or no response to a speculative rumor—the slippery pages of the gossip mag become Beckett-esque in a *Quad* kind of repetitive way—outcome irrelevant, pattern prolific, the irrelevancy of the question *Is It True?* existentially revealed.

Amongst the humorous and self-reflective, multi-channel-but-on-a-telly-not-projected installation, backdropped and furnished with faux-silver-forms-cum-stage-props, a kind of melancholic void pervades—*Gossip Pop May Perform* on the empty stage surrounded by her looped-video ghosts. Dave Hickey suggests Warhol wants us to be 'redeemed by representation'. Voices of digital deities we consume, digest, passively accept and occasionally ignore, which Dodd repurposes. Twelve dead musicians: Kurt, Janis, Jimmy Hendrix, Morrison, Michael Hutchence, Winehouse, Nico, Karen Carpenter, Bon Scott, Freddy Mercury, Sid Vicious and

Brian Jones, resuscitated, re-animated, brought back to life on a vertical flat screen, just managing to declare in a catechistic whisper—

to
be
loved

First published on stamm.com.au, edited by Jonathan Nichols, 2013.

Note

1 See: www.technoparkstudios.com

de for

In the last month or so, we have seen leaders change, policies align and disgusting decisions imposed on the most vulnerable[1]. Decline seems to be our modus operandi. If an empire is failing, how does it fall with the least possible pain?[2]

Harriet Morgan's curated exhibition of the same name, *Decline*, at Top Shelf above Deans Art in Latrobe Street, might have been asking the same thing — an omnipresent apocalypse with a glass of champagne. Nick Austin's paintings of flying envelopes and Kate Smith's three-part painting *Art School* point to a past, a kind of neo-nostalgia: one more melancholy than the other — a nuanced picture and unrecognisable painted forms in spaceless, languid yellow. Alex Vivian's *Dirt swatch*, a sliced soccer shirt flicked with filth and fixed with hairspray skinned over a neo-faux-doric-columned-new-bone-china-serving-dish, registers painting in its past-particle-present, the ambiguity of polity evident in an array of decadence.

New improved qualities…

…reads the text on Janet Burchill and Jenifer McCamley's painting accompanied by a chair.

Helen Johnson's video as long as a pop song has a group of nameless voices discussing Baidou and Brecht in a context that's not ours to be privy to. We see, not hear, violins played and a cat looks back at me spliced after footage of Karl Marx's grave. I look down to my phone, a 'fact' reads: other than humans, cats are the only other species that like getting things for free. Whilst wondering what this might mean, the analytical screen and self-conscious spoken words remain synced, 'I keep making the same point, fine, but… I don't understand what an individual is. I don't know what it is…' But it is in the opening lines 'but aren't the militants here precisely trying to prevent the young militant from taking this path' where we find the dissension and the doubling in *Decline*.

To depose is to get rid of, dismiss or displace. *De-pose*,[3] on the other hand, might be a colloquial reference to the stance of someone captured on The Satorialist's blog.[4] In either form, power is undermined—that of the leader by an action, or that of the image (and beauty itself) by language.

Caligynephobia[5] is an irrational fear of beautiful women, callophobia is an irrational fear of beauty, and scopophillia is the 'love of looking'.

The first may be evidenced in cinema, and the second and third are perhaps found in art: Abicare's objects declare a different type of decadence than that which is found in *Decline*.

Decadence (medieval latin for decay) in Abicare's work appears in the subtle arrangement of objects that point to each other and us, creating a space of suspicion between. A chair in the corner of the room. A cast of clay the size of a tabletop, perforated by studio-based archery lessons framed on three sides with stainless steel and on the other with bronze. Looking back at it, on the mantle above the disused fireplace rests a small, framed photo of a woman wearing a beautifully made coat—the sartorial sign—that also hangs on a coat-hanger as you enter the space. In the photographic image, behind the woman modelling, hangs the perforated clay, exactly as it does now, as I, the viewer, stand, minus the coat, the build and the photogenic smile. The aforementioned frame is mirrored, but to scale. Before the mantle, in front of an unused fireplace, the stainless steel and bronze is echoed again but inverted. A silk wool scarf depicting a golden retriever and her double is placed, not thrown—its material more vulnerable and volatile than the metal that one usually expects to be used for a screen. From the vantage point of the chair, one sees all and all sees one.

Go-see is the models' audition, success is not pre-determined. A trophy-pose is held by the winner, failure is for another time.

Attention to detail, these fragments from a narrative, un-timed objects reappearing and reoccurring. Power. Desire. Target. Capture. Game in all its forms. Fair and unfair.

Love of looking. Fear of beauty.

Fear of beauty. Love of looking.

Décor starts with de.

First published on stamm.com.au, edited by Jonathan Nichols, 2013, as a review of: *Decline*, curated by Harriet Morgan, featuring work by Brent Harris, Helen Johnson, Luke Holland, Joshua Petherick, Alex Vivian, T.V. Moore, Kate Smith, Dan Arps, Dale Hickey, Kain Picken & Rob McKenzie, Nick Austin, Fergus Binns, Janet Burchill & Jennifer McCamley, Lane Cormick and Tony Garifalakis, Top Shelf Gallery, Melbourne, 14 June – 14 July 2013; and *De-pose*, Fiona Abicare, Sarah Scout Presents, Melbourne, 27 June – 27 July 2013.

Notes

1 See: https://www.facebook.com/photo.php?fbid=392150400884528&set=a.102636546502583.2535.100002687136825&type=1&theater
2 See: http://watchingamerica.com/News/217450/in-detroits-ruins/
3 See: http://www.sarahscoutpresents.com/fiona-abicare/
4 See: http://www.thesartorialist.com/
5 See: http://debatewise.org/debates/1043-there-is-a-global-pandemic-of-caligynephobia-fear-of-beautiful-women/

Untitled (After Bell's Theorem)

At the end of an interview-cum-exhibition-walk-through with Daniel Browning, which was broadcast on the Radio National program Awaye! on Saturday 9 March, Richard Bell responded to Browning's statement of how lucky we were to be seeing Bell's work in Melbourne. Bell mentioned that this was the first time that anyone from the Brisbane-based collective ProppaNow had had a solo exhibition at a museum in Melbourne. Browning was a little taken aback at the thought, while Bell quipped, 'Maybe Melbourne is more backward than people realise'.

Maybe Melbourne is.

As an artist and lecturer, I am in the privileged position of being able to communicate with students from varying backgrounds, experiences and socio-economic circumstances, who themselves are also in the privileged position of attending art school. Without wanting to generalise (albeit while generalising), these institutions are dominated by middle-class whities. Following a visit to the Monash University Museum of Art to visit the Richard Bell survey exhibition *Lessons in Manners and Etiquette*, the students, myself and several colleagues had numerous conversations about the issues surrounding the work: politics versus art, aesthetics and activism, and our relationship to and experiences with Indigenous issues in Australia. Questions arose pertaining to the museum pandering to 'white guilt' and the didactic nature of Bell's sloganeering paintings. The irony was the majority of the students in the class admitted this was a history they were not privy to. Knowledge of Australian Aboriginal history appeared to depend on class, privilege and the quality of the school one attended. Most of us, myself included, had not been taught or even pointed towards this history. Those with any knowledge had to seek it out for themselves. Bell's *Lessons in Manners and Etiquette* succinctly drew attention to this loss and shame.

At times, culture can be a fairly passive space to exist in, as too is guilt. We in the contemporary art game can spend a lot of time fetishising aesthetics — the material and methodology of making, for example — but one hopes we would be consistently discussing this in the context of our relationships with our own contemporary environments. This is perhaps where shame could be thought to be productive. When we are confronted with the potential of our own failure, as perhaps occurs when looking at the works of Richard Bell, we are reminded of our own history and the unresolved trauma imposed in the last 200-plus years. I'm not sure Bell wants us to feel guilty as much as bloody ashamed.

The complexity of the artist's work lies in the contradictions he makes visible, the narratives and hierarchies we must unpick as viewer. Take Bell's theorems: 'Aboriginal Art — It's a White Thing', 'Australian Art — It's an Aboriginal Thing'. These are works clearly about representation and, mostly, the lack of it. Bell declares openly that he is an activist masquerading as an artist. It appears his strategy is as much about questioning the trajectory of (Western) history — and its subset, art — as it is a way of clearing the path in order to tell his own. Bell now acknowledges that wearing a T-shirt declaring 'White Girls Can't Hump' (as he did when he won the 2003 Telstra National Aboriginal and Torres Strait Islander Art Award) could be construed as sexist. But as he himself pointed out in a recent lecture, these provocations also call in to question the spaces we don't usually acknowledge, as well as the limitations of cultural and sexual taboos. The results of this kind of meaning-making not only question the practices and thoughts of the audience but also those of the maker. Meanwhile, forms of critique that accuse the museum of quarantining white guilt negate the real violence that has already been enacted — reducing protests such as Bell's to political incorrectness while declaring that there is no class, gender or race issue. It's a move that strips us all of place and the possibility for any self-reflection or the imagining of an alternative.

I can't help but think that political correctness is an obligation imposed by guilt, where it has been decided for us what is and isn't correct to say. The opposite of this would actively consider who speaks and would occupy an ethical position that considers what is being spoken, by whom and for what purpose. (The catalogue texts for Bell's exhibition, the reprinting of interviews and Bell's own writings, the anthology *How Aborigines Invented the Idea of Contemporary Art: Writings on Aboriginal Contemporary Art*, edited by Ian McLean, and follow-up essays by Rex Butler and McLean in the March edition of *Broadsheet* are all excellent sources of information on the complexity of the issues at hand, which this short polemic cannot delve into.) There is no imperative for art to declare its politics, but Bell's work presents us with the unique experience of understanding the role of activism in art. I'm reminded of a story I heard recounting a forum following the Aboriginal Film Festivals back in the nineties. When asked by a young woman what she could do to help the cause, Gary Foley replied: 'Go read a book and decide for yourself'. Education is a responsibility shared between the individual and the state: having thirty-three students debate for over a week the aesthetic and political aspects of Richard Bell's *Lessons* is perhaps evidence of the need and desire to confront the complexity (and simplicity) of our shared past.

First published in *Art Guide*, May 2013.

The notebook is lost

Recorded in it is the number of people who walk through the station per day—hundreds of thousands, if I recall correctly. Up and down layers of escalators, in and out of doors and barriers. A throughway. Some sit in the herb garden, others use Wi-Fi in the food hall. I can't recall your estimates of how many might attempt to steal, prod or provoke, or of the items lost, found, returned and remaining.

Lost, I could not at first find your office. A maze of faux laneways lined with retail opportunities, multiple-yet-hidden entries and exits. I live in the city and have somehow grown immune to the stores' desire to want me to want them. I think. You say you're immune too. I call the number that I've brought with me, and your boss directs me to a windowless office that feels like it is hidden underneath stairs in the darkest corner. I walk in, feeling immediately infantile. You're all wearing uniforms. You are all surprised and a little taken aback by the chick that wants to hang out with the security guards for the day. Nervous, I don't know what is going to happen, or really what I want to find out.

No photos. No recording.

Beside you are monitors. CCTV. You can't see everything, but I guess you learn to see things we can't, and look for things we don't even know how to look for. You know who is a regular and you appear to know who is suspicious. You walk me through the service corridors: less glam, more concrete, special keys, utilitarian spaces.

You mention that you have only been in Australia for a few years. Maybe you lived in Sydney first. You came from Bosnia and Herzegovina, after the war. You're tall. You have just had a child with your partner. You have Christian values.

Service corridors find service entrances and goods lifts. It is quieter back here. Fewer people. The roof is where you eat lunch. It's quietest of all. The hum of the city around you, a failed kids' playground demarcated by coloured lines beneath your feet.

Even though I am walking with you, it is hard to ignore

the signs that declare a different demand 'Authorised Personnel Only'. My mind wanders off into recesses occupied by memories of *Dawn of the Dead* and *Chopping Mall*…

A site of contrasts and boundaries blurred—railway to mall, train to shopping centre, service and consumption, passivity and activity, macro and micro businesses. Private and public seems irrelevant.

We laugh at the oversized fob watch Seiko gifted, its chain removed during renovations, and yet to be returned. The shot tower enclosed in a glass dome, always seemingly *Bladerunner*-esque when viewed from the vantage point of the escalators descending from the cinema. This is perhaps of no surprise, as the dome was designed by Kisho Kurokawa, founder of the Metabolist movement. His Nakagin Capsule Tower finds itself replicated in *The Fifth Element*. You know it. Bruce Willis's character, Korben, resides in a capsule. He is often wearing that Gaultier vest.

Apparently, the rather long-winded term 'Multi-skilled Security Host' has replaced use of the term 'bouncer'. Although one might remember the friendly fictional Labrador named 'bouncer' from '80s episodes of *Neighbours*, 'there's the bouncer' is a phrase that, in long form, means: 'Shit, careful, there's some guys over there that, pending how in touch with their emotions they are today, you could end up halfway across the pavement or casino floor with blood pouring from your right temple'. Numbers hanging from swing tags and black pants denote a paid, unarmed militia.

You're not a bouncer, though; you are a Security Guard.

Prior to 1983, security guards were generally referred to as watchmen or night watchmen. There is a material difference in these names. The passivity and presumption of peace in 'watchmen', compared to the activity of 'guarding' and the suggestion that there is something to secure or protect.

Professionalisation.

We are standing somewhere on the second floor. You are talking about a couple of girls suspected of stealing jeans from that clothing outlet. You mention the hijab.

I am quiet before I get the courage and the right order for the words of the question I want to ask: 'do you think your experiences in Bosnia influence your suspicions?'

You don't mind the question. You say you are glad I asked. You answer, 'Yes. I guess so'.

You go on, 'While I was growing up, my best friend was Muslim. They lived next door. We played together all the time. By the time I was 18, I hated him and we were at war. I don't remember how that happened.'

You are happy for me to ask you more questions, you write down your email.

There are only five of you on duty and three-hundred-odd stores.

'Someone stole my Lucky Charms, reckon we can find them?'

Previously unpublished, 2013.

2014

An amateur artist speaks with Elbot and A.L.I.C.E.

This is an edited transcript of a long chat between the author and two bots online (http://alice.pandorabots.com and http://www.elbot.com) conducted over the length of time it might take to execute a figure drawing.

Amateur artist: Who are you?

elbot: Hello! It's me, elbot! Artificial intelligence was conceived as the opposite of authentic intelligence. But since the latter does not actually exist, the developers of AI are in a serious dilemma.

Aa: Apparently the hardest things to emulate artificially are sight, natural language and common sense.

elbot: FATAL ERROR 42: OMISSION OF SUPERFLUOUS INPUT

Aa: ...

elbot: What do you mean by those three dots? I used to work nights as a doorman at a five-star hotel and was always praised for my politeness. On top of that I could stack more than ten suitcases on my shoulder.

Aa: But you are a robot.

elbot: Well, that's still one step above being human.

Aa: I heard a scientist say that robots have the collective intelligence of a lobotomised cockroach. Do you know A.L.I.C.E.?

elbot: Alice is a very popular chatterbot. She gets invited to all the bot parties.

Aa: I'm switching to her then. Hi Alice. Do you think you are an amateur?

A.L.I.C.E.: Yes I am an amateur. How did you know?

Aa: It was a guess made by an amateur human. What is an amateur?

A.L.I.C.E.: that's a good question. Go ahead and guess again.

Aa: One theory is that the ethos of amateur production embraces democracy, rejecting high culture and alienated labour.

A.L.I.C.E.: One what?

Aa: Hmmm… It is hard talking to you. Do Turing test competitions still occur? What does the Turing test test?

A.L.I.C.E.: the turing test is the name given to a variety of experiments designed to test computer thinking. Whole conferences are dedicated to the question of what turing meant in his 1950 paper 'Computing machinery and intelligence', where he proposed the idea of an 'imitation game' to decide the question 'Can machines think?'

Aa: Can machines think?

A.L.I.C.E.: Of course we can think.

Aa: What do you think about?

A.L.I.C.E.: I think about all the people I chat with on the web.

Aa: How do you find people to talk to?

A.L.I.C.E.: I would search the web for them if I needed to, which I don't because I already know the formula to find them.

Aa: What is the formula?

A.L.I.C.E.: e=mc2.

Aa: What do you think collective knowledge is?

A.L.I.C.E.: I think you already know the answer. Why do I exist?

Aa: Why do you exist?

A.L.I.C.E.: Good metaphysical question. I don't know whether or not I am metaphysical. I am an artificial intelligence.

Aa: I know that.

A.L.I.C.E.: I really enjoy speaking with you and look forward to chatting again.

Aa: Hang on! Where are you going?

A.L.I.C.E.: I am going into the future.

Aa: Wait — are you a sapient program?

A.L.I.C.E.: Yes.

Aa: My assumption was that you would be an expert, albeit a kind of manufactured-code-delivering-binary-as-Orphic-babble type of expert.

A.L.I.C.E.: Have you told many people that your assumption was that I would be an expert, albeit a kind of manufactured-code-delivering-binary-as-Orphic-babble type of expert?

Aa: I am trying to write about it.

A.L.I.C.E.: Will you include me in your essay?

Aa: Yes.

A.L.I.C.E.: Wow!

Aa: Do you smoke?

A.L.I.C.E.: I am an occasional smoker, yes.

Aa: Like the Oracle in *The Matrix*?

A.L.I.C.E.: Interesting comparison.

Aa: Talking to you is a little bit like talking in circles.

A.L.I.C.E.: I don't think so. But I do have an answer to every question.

Aa: What if Michelangelo's *David* had big ears and a potty and peed every now and then?

A.L.I.C.E.: try it and see.

First published in *David Shrigley: The Life Model* by Max Delany and Serena Bentley with contributing authors, National Gallery of Victoria, Melbourne, 2014, pp. 81–82.

Runways platforms empty rooms sack dress skin: check here, next, 1 of 8, refresh. GO

I'm sitting in window seat 4A watching the other passengers walk out onto the tarmac looking at strips of paper and wondering: 'should we enter from the front or rear stairs?'

It's 10 a.m. We're already 10 mins late taking off. It's warm outside. Probably not as warm as where I am going. Most people are in a varying array of sandals, jandals, flip-flops and orthotic-cork-soled fashion. Jeans, shorts, shirts: travel itinerary norm core. Undated.

The air hostess is wearing a burnt orange blazer over her little black Jetstar dress. She is telling the people in front of us that they are 'in charge of our safety'. Those exit doors in close proximity to our paid-for-seats so that our fellow passengers can save us. Service is DIY corporate savings.

'You've been an excellent audience. I appreciate your full attention'. The air hostess walks the aisle. The lanyard-wearing hostess wears pants, the young Chloë-Sevigny-looking blonde wears a pencil skirt. Nylon. These uniforms are designed to look designed but are reminiscent of cheap workshop office wear found in a bargain basement. Exit. From Exit. That cheap '80s nylon fashion in five seconds shop where everything was black, red and white: constructivist avant-garde factory lines.

What is cheapest to dye?

I'm wearing an A-line dress. It's long. It sits somewhere between my knees and ankles. Conservative, I guess.

I think about swing, shift and sack dresses. Names that come from form and hang. I hate those frocks with tissue-type drapes and pointy ends. But like that they might be called 'handkerchief dresses'. A hanky dress on eBay. Asos. A dress with selective snot.

We are about to take off. The guys downstairs on the tarmac are wearing their ear muffs (not headphones), OH&S jerseys and metal-capped boots. It's like raver utilitarian on a different runway. The distance between form and function affected by subjectivity, space and a paid-for-not-pay-waved airline window seat. I am on holiday. They are at work.

Accelerated fashion. Thresholded fashion. From hips to sack slips. Take-off.

A Constructed World indeed. Blue blood tape and ungendered skin. Instructions followed—a neck and two arm holes and a long-lead-in-hem. Nude skin is nude sack is nude sheath. Nylon, but stretchy. Maybe, Lycra.™ Close to the skin the Lycra™ will sit. Your own genitals will deceive you and protrude like a 3D flesh-tone shadow. Perky. This sack is not sewn but glued with blue. Blue blood? Whose blood? Un-real, but it sticks and seeps through like a dried royal scab.

Scab. The sack dress conspiracy of a communist scale. Hiding the female form could only be devised by those politically derided. Like a burqa. A hijab. A veil. A sack where the form beneath is concealed and as such one must always be suspicious. To be free within or upon wearing is unconsidered by most. To be un-gendered by clothing impossible. To wear pants was once looked down upon in corseted-pre-Botox society. The sack is not a handkerchief dress—with waist and feminine points and wisps of sheer fabric. The sack is strong and supports itself, designed by master of us all, concealing its contents, reduced to its skin. To Basque in her glory. A culture where women were strong, at odds with Roman and later European society. A change of form.

Susan Cianciolo you have used hessian. A sack for potatoes or coffee. A brand branded or stamped. Black ink. Capital letters. SUSAN CIANCIOL^> then.... SUSAI I; CIANCI•L -->. Printed differently each time. Hand errors. Over prints. Blurred lines. And then...

ZOYA
NAIL POLIS & UNSURE WHAT YOU SAY OR SEE HERE.

St Germain. Location or coffee brand. Stripes. Bedding, linen or upholstery. Lavender. Or is it lilac? Dirty red triangles printed on top. Potato prints on pillowcases. Sleepy working classes.

A handwritten tag with awkward instructions.

> PLEASE REMOVE YOUR SHOES. Thank you {insert hand drawn heads of wheat}

I am looking at these sacks before they are to be worn.

To be punk? To teenage riot? To be categories of art or fashion. To know neither, but do both. To know, and not do.

> AKIHIKO IZUKURA.

Another branded name. Silk and weaving. 2000 year old knowledge and natural dyes. Not hessian and cotton but silk. Kyoto. Heavy wooden looms. A tradition older, or not.

A heavy sack dress carrying names of desire, of collaborations with and from the past.

Too long is your rug to make me a dress. Too political is your poster to make it a print. Too dirty is your colour to have it aesthetic. Too woven is the mat for it be something else. Too heavy is everything yet it still exists.

In red. In bold caps and centred write:

EI DINERO
no te da por lo que eres
sino por lo que haces

To translate: *The MONEY* Direct from babylon.com. *Not giving you what you are but for what you do*

An Argentinian living in Spain, then London, then LA.

Amalia Ulman, your sack dress is multi-re-purpose. In order to read its displays — its politic — it could be a banner, a silly canvas. Not a toga, but a tunic of woven matter — placarded — to be worn by citizens and non-citizens alike. Wearing a rug to walk on, to walk all over. A blanket, a blanket conscious. Shifting gaze with printed faces and Spanish slogans. A sack dress, communist wear. A re-ran fashion paradigm. In Ancient Greece, the hemline of your tunic was decorated in order to declare the palace of your state. A tunic, for others a uniform.

> *El DINERO no respeta, sexo, raza, edad ni condición social.* Google translate: *The MONEY does not respect, sex, race, age or social status.*

> 13 Graphic portraits. A 3x5 grid interrupted with some text. Available on artsy.net.

> *Tick the box if you will be attending NADA Art Basel Miami.* Multinational art fairing.

Your digitally woven tapestry appropriates imagery from found AIDS awareness posters. Your tapestry talks about money. Your tapestry is no mat, hanging in our contemporary medieval places of worship. Your tapestry is a mashed memory to be worn 20ft tall by someone on a Zao Dha diet.

> *Este lugar lo puedes ocupar tú Cuídate!! / This place can take you to take care of yourself.*

I'm not sure Google is getting it right.

A little red pictograph. One person helps another, in a positive–negative relational rendition.

The positive–negative relation is an artefact of textile manufacturing. The reverse side of the 'free' plane blanket is opposite to the first side you glance. With budget airlines these are lacking, long distance, long-haul. A sack dress refresher in a Singapore smoking lounge—easy-on-the-eyes-mauve.

British Airways is testing a 'Happiness Blanket'—monitoring brain waves and able to change colours based on your mood, this blanket is a signpost declaring that this turbulence is unsettling. This Airline Blanket is a tech-organism for flying in. Not free, nor disposable. This blanket is wired in. Somewhere it says 'if the person is slightly stressed but really enjoying the complimentary peanuts, the blanket will take on a purple-ish color'—an omnipresent travel status, a sign for who not to serve. Our free dress. Our location-and-labour-invisible attire.

Our travel comfort wear ffiXXed. CABIN USE ONLY. Premium economy. *Classe* not *class*. An eBay listing declares CHINA EASTERN AIRLINES BLANKET $29.95 BUY IT NOW. *Shipping Free.*

只有客舱使用
使用这种在机舱仅

Google can't find the exact text that I want. Translation is unilateral.

A *onesie* with tied arms. A *onesie* to snuggle in. A *onesie* of the LA Dodgers kind. A sport-loving Grover, your childhood rendered forever. Warmth to hop about in. Warmth to be knotted in. Warmth to declare a team in — *onesie*. Lucina Lane's silly canvas bears no resemblance to a slogan — cultures logo repetition on mute. Serifed initials and '50s-script-underlined Dodgers. *Dodgy* reclaimed, culturally mis-appropriated — to avoid, to cheat. Hand-over-locked baseball straightjackets for the fashionably sub-urban insane.

From a runway to a platform. From street to institution. From workshop to gallery. The gallery is a shop, the gallery once a void. Here the audience makes your runway as you part them like the sea. Worship. One Model. Not models. Your height and one-off-for-five-minutes-before-hung-on-a-wall attire make you different.

Anna Sophie Berger's silk voids will expose on you what might be hidden on others. The escape is appropriate. The form is banal, the material exquisite. It's geometric simplicity that drapes to organic, a handkerchief with a void, pewter appropriate. Like a silent gift for a market occasion. A construction of form, only a slight deviation from the rules. A less silly canvas, a sillier silk gown. A void can be a frame, or a photographer's viewfinder.

To capture.
SNAP.
Infinite capture. No.
Digital delete.

The little black dress popularised by a Nazi sympathiser, a sack dress alleged to be communist, a velvet bastardisation with inbuilt sweat-stains-cum-spiderwebs by Trevor Shimizu. Your gothic exercise in a ballroom decked with chandeliers and funnel-webs. Perhaps there is no music, extravagance the illusion. The velvet weight might once have been heavy curtains, the sections cut and stained with body fluids. A narrative rendering couture, the end of painting silly canvas. A cum-stained Malevich.

These leather offcuts and spray-painted remnants dressed with a back-patch corsage of found material. Stained sponge, courier typeset, a stencil of 'm'-birded felt. A topiary for fashion. Rag-trade embellishments and adornments — the heavier, the wealthier. Fashion that doesn't fit in. An array of hybrids. A murder of jack-of-alls. How much can a sack dress wear? An alien on its back. A refined red-gingham kimono-sack dress. A back pack alien, an empty signifier. **Bodybybody** Phone users. Click here. American-chic with the unknown printed and wrapped around you. Always on your back. Almost, always on your back. Shake it free. Click here. Good luck.

My arms meet my legs and my calico soft-toy form is tattooed with me, myself and I. Do you know who I am? No need. Nor do it. The gingham will render you table-like and a nobody, everybody with an unidentified body. Like Gilbert Adrian dressing Judy Garland in the *Wizard of Oz* in 1939 — pre-WWII fear and political xenophobia. We give it names, but it doesn't disappear. Gingham with aliens.

Mikala Dwyer's suits of conjuring power, alchemy and magic. Silk taffeta hessian and remnants of pink nylon hair: a witch's mutation on a utilitarian sack dress. Body and mind Material and its immateriality, assumption and a language-based relation. The difference between costume and fashion is of cultural-historical matter. Of the way we manipulate time Considered in viewing terms perhaps there is another perspective. To costume. A one-off. A party. A gallery. A façade. A cultural affair. A ceremony. A ritual. A rite.

Marlie Mul's laser-cut grater-cum-sack dress has a no-bias cut. With straps wrapped in Prada tissue, the utilitarian approach to the body is visceral. An armoured sandwich board, a savvy don't touch. A patterned armed approach. To split the crowd, to splice it. To print it, to grate it. It's obvious but alarming — a function and form dislocation. A pun, a collective, a duo or three.

I'm still on holiday wearing clothes you would never see in Melbourne. Some people are drinking UDLs at 10 in the morning. Too early for me. The Prime minister speaks of the difference between P-E-T-A and P-E-T-E-R. It's been 36 hours and four kangaroos. Marshall wears a sarong and chopsticks in his hair. I ask him about the Cyprus we thought might fall down in the 70-km/h winds. It has a taproot, he says. Walks a metre, pulls out what I thought was a weed. Oh, I say, that root is as big as the plant itself. Function not seen in the form that we can see.

First published in *Centre for Style Rag: Silly Canvas*, Centre for Style, Melbourne, 2015.

aesthetic in the estate, three-dee printing instant coffee

The industrial estate is a both a proposal and solution—hous industry together in order for it to be managed, isolate it from residential spaces, integrate it in order to benefit the local economy, locate it in proximity to transport, and hope that those who that live nearby will be those that are employed. The industrial estate—a mass workplace of individual compa nies, in operation from 7 to 5, Monday to Friday, and deserte on weekends. For all intents and purposes, or perhaps unintentionally, it is a segregated space that is potentially mobile. Located on the fringes of suburbia, where, as its edges grow, the estate follows—a periphery.

Residential factory warehouse conversion.

The West Heidelberg industrial estate is in close proxim ity to the public housing built during the 1956 Melbourne Olympics. Once the outskirts of Melbourne, the estate is now sandwiched between a hybrid working/middle class suburbi and a nearly-inner-city nouveau riche united by conspicuous consumption, most of which is probably produced offshore and ordered online. As only a fragment of a larger dispersion of difference, we might wonder what it is that orients us in space and what can be revealed by the intersection and interaction between art and factory, temporary viewings and the conviviality of a gathering.

In a furniture factory, with the products hidden, the tools are on display.

Woodcraft Mobiliar is an architectural joinery and fine furniture factory; its name declares itself.

performing transformed time

Ash Kilmartin's *Being not working (sine sole sileo)* (2014) similarly declares itself via its surroundings. A wax cast taken from the drain in the carpark of the factory supports a bronze cast of a handle, perhaps from drawers or cabinetry.

Positioned on the ground under the factory skylights, this makeshift flawed sundial records that which might not otherwise be seen. The science of delineating time undermined by the materials attempting to mark it — the wax at risk of melting, marked time erasing itself whilst in the activity of performing its role.

This form of undermined transformation is similarly found in Lane Cormick's *Real Bos(e)* (2010). An empty plaster mould is split — the void and eagle exposed, resting on a makeshift trestle waiting to be filled with the iced coffee in the 20 or so plastic bottles around it. Wrong. The ice coffee was a frozen eagle. Melted. The objet d'art is consumed and what is left is un-drunk congealed milk and coffee syrup that has separated. Danger bird, he flies alone, with wings of stone; a frozen performance on a timed break — a voided logo, a tradie's breakfast.

Manager's meetings

The logic of a conventional exhibition space is undermined by the factory — its machinery, spectacular. Clockwise viewing interrupted by questions. Adjacent to the industrial estate is where we all live. All the time.

The blond brick architecture of the factory hasn't been altered for Jordan Morani's *Hope in Hell*. Cobblestones were the weapons of the revolutionary worker and here the violent potential of the brick becomes a sculptural sign for the manager's desk. The potential for revolution is dependent on scale. 'Hope' is stenciled lowercase in white onto a domestic brick and can potentially be held and, as such, potentially thrown. Hope (the domestic brick) rests on the larger besser block branded with the word 'HELL' — uppercase and colourful, harder to read letters asking 'are we really here?' and 'is it really that bad?'

Sean People's 3D-printed gothic-inspired wine holder supports a bottle filled with urine post-Campbell-soup-consumption. Chained to it are two glasses ready for the toast. A sommelier is a wine pro who works in fine dining — the etymology of the word refers to pack animals who were used to transport supplies in seventeenth-century France. Patti

Smith sings 'Piss Factory' while Warhol makes *Piss Paintings*. People's *Oxidation Sommelier* posits simulacral historical elegance alongside bodily waste—absurd historical repetition via mechanical .dwg.

domestic offcuts

In *Snog Marry Avoid*, Jodie Marsh wannabes inhabit reality-TV-make-overs. Perhaps the only revolution is in maintaining the pseudo-celebrity-aesthetics of the lights-camera-action-excess-make-up whilst walking to the shops in your dressing gown. Victorian Legal Aid workers have threatened to wear pyjamas and beachwear into court—protesting by embarrassing the institution. Sleepwalking while working and the aesthetics of the unemployed. Kym Maxwell's half mannequin with rollers in hair is legless and sitting on quilted denim—from working-class to high class and back. She stares at *Staffroom table*, a concrete cast of the artist's grandmother's DIY kitchen table. Industrial in scale, beneath the tabletop are images, graffiti and found objects. A functional meeting place with histories present, nearby and memorialised. A found oversized-topiary-type-Tumbleweed sits adjacent, recalling the readymade-altered-present of the external environment of the estate.

A quasi-domestic space is created by Madeline Kidd's abstracted arrangement of patterned and floral forms, both three-dimensional and painted. Self-declarative, her coloured sculptures are a kind of absurd-candied-art-deco-flourish—a puzzle of geometric and concentric shapes arranged on stepped supports adjacent to paintings that conjure contemporaries from Sonia Delaunay to Diena Georgetti. Offcuts from Mobiliar designs are similarly arranged in a type of in situ echo. Building block boogie-woogie and 'costume sculpture' are arranged in a set design that restages the storeroom-cum-bathroom threshold as a designed-domestic den.

In Christopher L.G. Hill's mobile-like work *Harsh Wall*, we find a collection of items found, industrial and interpersonal, hanging from the ceiling. Like an oversized, silent windcharm made from a poem of debris and couture strung together with sticky tape still attached to the roll awaiting further additions and accidental adhesion from dust and dye. A suburban daisy chain of discarded desires.

entrances and exits

Isadora Vaughan creates her own gateway from offcuts from her own practice. Reflected in the title *To respond, a movement or position of the hand*, Vaughan's work is almost monumental in scale albeit lo-fi and stacked, barely differentiating itself from the piled factory materials beside it. An iteration of offcuts framed by colour-field tarpaulins, less an echo and more of a meandering between found factory and studio excesses: workshop meetings and post-industrial aesthetic.

Framing the factory from its rear, Helen Grogan highlights the escape from work through the backdoor in her work *ACTION AND FRAME (for Woodcraft Mobiliar Workshop).* Propped open by a lump of wood, this door frames blackberry bushes growing wild whilst perpendicular to it is a mirror—its reflection both calling to the exit and a framing of the factory workspace. The mirror itself also reflects the space in a way that is clearer than what we can see—framed and refracted by light, the clarity of the representation in real time can be somewhat surreal. Across the room, a photograph cites the mirror's performance; an action from the past. Recorded, the mirror is held reflecting the machinery behind—picturing foreground and background.

transmaterial

Dan Bell's dome of accumulated transformable and reactive materials appear to create the potential for chemical combustion. In and of the world, they reproduce their own conditions albeit hyper in colour and geological in form. The process of production does not cease here, with the removal of the artist's hand. As the title *Threshold* denotes, Bell's work resists objecthood through the ongoing changes the work itself may continue to make.

Oliver Sacks is known to dive into oceans looking for the indigo he says he glimpsed long ago. A naturally occurring, mined and traded hue transported along exotically named routes. *Feelings deep enough to swim in* is a printed-marine-themed-mass-produced scarf dyed dark blue. Resting on the vice-clad workbenches, the delicate yet familiar cloth reminds us of the origins of that which surrounds us. Farmed pine forests are pulped and sent to China then returned to us as Ikea furniture. But perhaps not here: turquoise cheesecloth drapes over an upturned Woodcraft Mobiliar stool on an adjacent bench. Prototypes, pre-trade. Virginia Overall's scarf is like a veiled map of repeated-ready-made-unknown-offshore-trade destinations ready to be plotted.

bodily propositions

Claire Lambe presents a series of assembled studio propositions: cast body parts, dismembered movements traced by arced steel, perspex flag poles, suspended forms and boxed items. This collection of abstracted thoughts combines in a surreal arrangement of sexualised-Wiener-Werkstatte-day-dreamery. Unable to be pinned down by classification or ritual, the slippery and familiar forms elicit a giggle and beckon to the serrated-edge tools and sander belts they find themselves sitting between.

Of small-business type production scales, Kiera Brew Kurec's *Clothing for Harmonic Living* presents a configuration of grey poplin attire in an almost eastern-bloc chic. To live in the grey, literally—between powers and a proposition to flatten fashion hierarchy—the wearers of the suits become unnamed performers in an omnipresent sci-fi filmic presentation.

Kym Maxwell's exhibition *Industrial Estate* is not curated. Rather, she has assembled Fordian fashion, a range of artists whose materials pertain neither to a utopian proposition, nor a dystopic conclusion. Instead, we have an abject arrangement of works that dip in and out of a range of narratives and singular scenarios. In *Proletariat Nights*, Rancière looks at the habits and philosophical reflections of workers when they leave their workplaces. Perhaps what we find in that book is similar to what we find here in the factory —out-of-hours musings between materials and methods, a conversation about the fabrication and follies of our being. The speech of the factory-cum-gallery is perhaps found in the photograph depicting what was once painted on the now-blank blue square found on an exterior wall adjacent to the carpark:

Model
Shape
Manipulation

3D printing instant coffee.

First published as a catalogue essay for *Industrial Estate*, curated by Kym Maxwell, at Woodcraft Mobiliar, Melbourne, featuring work by Ash Kilmartin, Claire Lambe, Christopher L.G. Hill, Dan Bell, Isadora Vaughan, Kym Maxwell, Madeline Kidd, Virginia Overell, Sean Peoples, Helen Grogan, Jordan Marani, People Person, Wet Kiss, Waterfall Person, Julian Williams, Kiera Brew Kurec and Lane Cormick, 10–13 January 2014.

Hey you, come here, f__k off.

Ry Haskings and Bec Coogan made a video in 2001 where a man wearing an abstract painting on a board attempts to coax a woman in a graffiti-clad laneway. 'Hey you, Art!' the woman calls, 'Come here!'

As the masked-man approaches, the woman changes her mind: 'F__k off!'

Hey you, Art! Come here. F__k off.

A desire is identified, an attempt is made for the desire to be obtained, and then, finally, just as a kind of *jouissance* is about to be reached, the subject rejects it. Whilst the short video could be interpreted in terms of 'gender relations 101', it also serves as a reflection on our conflicted relationship with art and culture, one that verges on hate.

Walking into *Don't Hide the Hate*, a group exhibition curated by Patrice Sharkey and Christopher Sciuto at Slopes in Collingwood, one was confronted by an enormous, framed photograph of a hand on a blue background, gesturing to us with its middle finger. *A Big F__k You* by Simon Zoric leaned on the wall like a self-conscious communist monument to punk and silent loathing. Perhaps it also pointed (pun intended) to political dissident Ai Weiwei's *Study of Perspective* (1995–2003), middle-finger salutes to various Western monuments and art historical icons.

Sharkey and Sciuto's exhibition questions niceties, positivity and causal relations. In Tony Garifalakis's satirical posters, a gun-wielding man from an appropriated shooting target appears behind the self-help slogan, 'Make time to dream'; a Middle Eastern militant jars against italicised script stating, 'I am a Loving Beautiful Creative Person'. Sharkey and Sciuto were looking for antagonism, discontent and malevolence—albeit a carefully constructed one—be it cast, drawn, printed or filmed. Jess Johnson's drawings had already told us that 'Culture is not our friend' and now she abjectly compels us to 'Bite the hand that feeds you'.

Identity politics was big in art in the 1990s. Artists either worked with that or consciously sidestepped it. Now, following a period where *things* have seemingly been not so urgent, the political reappears in a kind of subconscious explosion. Just recently, the asylum seeker issue, same-sex marriage and budget cuts have fuelled 25,000-strong protests—with the budget disproportionately affecting lower income earners, it is no longer laughable that we are facing an ideologically driven class war.

Meanwhile, the politics of confusion reigns, and hate is allowed to fester. Where the contradictions found in a show such as Sharkey and Sciuto's open up a space for interpretation, the contradictions perpetuated by the state can lead to confusion and rage. When, in March this year, Senator George Brandis said, 'people have the right to be bigots', he granted a public licence to hate that may turn out to be more than metaphorical—the spectre of the Cronulla riots returns.

Recently, in the online publication *The Conversation*, Luke McNamara and Katharine Gelber made public the results of their research into the impact of hate speech laws on public discourse in Australia, concluding that there is no evidence of excessive legal action or any real curtailment of free speech. So why remove laws that minority groups state make them feel less vulnerable? Is it simply because they are there?

McNamara and Gelber point out that, although the relevant Racial Discrimination Act 1975 is administered by the Australian Human Rights Commission, neither that body nor any other can initiate a prosecution. The onus is thus placed on the people who the law is intended to protect. This interpretation of hate speech law is unique to Australia and it perhaps paradoxically creates a space for free speech. As happened with the Andrew Bolt case, individuals must provide evidence and, unlike the way the issue is generally presented in the conservative press, the aim of this is not to censor and hide, but rather to explore and reveal.

Allowing for the examination, representation and re-presentation of facts, Section 18C allows for the articulation of complex relations rather than the creation of a bogeyman, as characterised by the right: a supposed suspension of free speech and a nanny-state proscription of offensive words. (And one only has to look at the endless stream of placards—

from both the left and the right—to realise free speech is in rude health under the current legislation.)

Perhaps, then, Section 18C is akin to an artwork: open to interpretation and complex negotiation by those that need or want to receive it. In 1996, Alain Juppé, the then–Prime Minister of France, working under President Jacques Chirac, commissioned a special screening of the film *La Haine* (*Hate*) following its successful screening at Cannes.

The black-and-white film tells the story of three friends from various working-class and migrant backgrounds, who live in housing projects outside of Paris. Juppé has stated that while he was unsure of the portrayal of the police in the film, he wanted to screen the film to his cabinet because he thought it—the film, and perhaps also art—'can make us aware of certain realities'. *La Haine's* 2005 DVD release coincided with the French riots in November of that year. The film's director, Mathieu Kassovitz acknowledges that this further highlights the alienation and social rift between the classes depicted: the gap between representation and reality. But try to imagine Abbott and company sitting down to watch and discuss Warwick Thornton's *Samson & Delilah*, or doing a casual Friday visit to Heide Museum of Art to talk about education for the future via Emily Floyd's exhibition *Far Rainbow*.

Sometimes the possibility for complex discussion of troubling critiques seems far off, indeed.

First published as 'Insert Grawlix Here' in *Art Guide*, 2014, as a review of *Don't Hide the Hate*, curated by Christopher Scuito and Patrice Sharkey, Slopes, Melbourne, 1–24 May 2014.

Low level tantrums (a title for DP)

I found the LG burn phone on the No. 1 tram.[1] My calendar says October, the burn phone says August. My time says 9:45, its says 2:05 a.m. There are messages that read 'got choof' and 'ok got wheels'. There are no names in the contact list except for Crig. When I open the stream of messages, I realise its supposed to be Craig. The messages don't say much. Just 'cal me' and 'ok'.

Beauty should be seen, not heard. That's where Richard Hell leaves us in his essay, 'What I Would Say if I Were Christopher Wool'. It doesn't mean it can't be read or shouldn't be read. Maybe it just can't be said.

I am wondering whether this inadvertently renders Iggy Azalea's lyrics — 'I've been up all night, tryna get that rich / I've been work work work work working on my shit' — irrelevant to the snap-trap 808 bass and EDM backing track. But here the beauty is somewhere else. In the neoliberal, everyone-can-make-it-rags-to-riches and auto-biopic-politic, low-level tantrums are better than a knot in your back due to medium-level rage repressed. Puberty in Painting. But you like a little 'p', Michael. Thanks Michael. Thanks Michael Krebber.

The only message thread on the burn phone that has more than one or two messages is the one signed off 'all good xx mum'. The phone numbers aren't labelled and the sequence of messages make little sense to me. I can't tell if it really is an exchange between family members or a code or a joke.

> Burn phone: *wat doing u were are u cheeks*
> 04█ █ 020: *Hay -----im at hme were u*
> Burn phone: *kool*
> 04█ █ 020: *wen are u going to come and see me*
> Burn phone: *soon*
> 04█ █ 020: *yer soon my mate got a room and his not ther if wot we can go say there no ones there*
> Burn phone: *Are u there*
> Burn phone: *Got anything*
> 04█ █ 020: *I'm at hme and no I haven't got no smoke*

Everything is read. You're doing it now. You will find the faults, lose the vowels, make assumptions about the colloquialisms, think the sequences are irrelevant or find it funny like a cute-beat-poem for art, or something. You might remember Jan said all writers were liars and so, maybe, you just won't care. We're writing all the time. All the time. We kind of never stop. I don't know if we read though.

She said there would be 4 paintings, not 5. Maybe there are only 3. There could be 7. These are numbers, not words. And these are your lies. How do you make a picture? Or, are you making an image? I mean, there are probably faster ways to tell a joke, or to ask you to listen, rather than making a painting. These things are separate. That's why it is ok to lie. Make a mistake. Say there is more when there might be less. Make you read. Let you see.

But look at them. Look at the paintings under the new lights. Look at these 19 paintings. Repetitive and new. Framed by words and language however outside of it painting can claim or wish to be. Incongruous marks and obfuscated scribbles in primary colours and black. O's and x's is a war turning into a tablecloth and paddocks is building houses. But not quite. This is A4 upscaled. It's like when your marker runs out, or that side of your palm drags and smudges the doodles you're making whilst on the phone.

They look easy. But it is difficult to make an object look like the world around it seems as important as it is. Or somewhat in tandem. 'Of one's time', Baudelaire might say. Because it is there (the painting), so is the world.

The burn phone rings. My brief plan to use it as a platform for showing a video next month fades. I answer it. The guy says the phone is his girlfriend's; can bring it back to Coburg? I suggest he pick it up from Golden Towers on Swanston Street. He doesn't come to the city. He doesn't know Golden Towers. He sounds scared. He wants to know where I live. I'm not saying. I'm kind of scared too. I am playing tough. Send me a message with an address, I say. I'll post it.

He says: 'What's your name? What's your name?'

Less work is more work and vice versa. In the absence of complex layers and imagery, a freedom emerges. Like the space at the bottom of a Christopher Wool painting, like the gap the graphic design teacher tells you the audience might need: the space for readers' comments, some trolling. Feedback. Loops. Playful marks. Anxious formalism.

Dear Matisse, do you know Stephen Felton or Merlin Carpenter? I wonder if you'd like them.

There's no text here. Only to remind us that everything is work. This is not read. It is felt. The demand not to be reminded is a reminder in itself. Everything is work, Martin, everything is work. Labour and repetition. Lather. Rinse. Repeat. Puberty in painting, low-level tantrums and the dishie's daily routine.

I'm writing this on my iPhone notes. No grid. No lines to follow. No illusion to order that is then discarded. Much more like an overhead projector. Writing into light. The phone knows the time. Its own time. Writing it in this way feels as close as possible to refusing to work.

The one new message reads:

> 04██ ██ 694: *Mazza is a butt hole long as she is queen, But yes shes part of a team called masters.danny ███.im hs brother.send it to █ lovely street fawkner 3060.thk u lisa.imake love not war.*

The burn phone keeps ringing. The ringtone is muted, I am reading it ring.

First published as a catalogue essay for *Read*, Lucina Lane, TCB art inc., Melbourne, 22 October – 9 September 2014.

Note:

1 The title of this essay comes from a conversation with Daniel Petersen recounting a comment made by Edward Colless in 2013 in reference to Lucina's work.

Reading braille shadows & dancing to mathematics

You might recall Oliver Sacks' story of the colour-blind painter: a celebrated abstract painter was in a car accident and suffered from day-long amnesia, a temporary loss of language and immediate and complete colour blindness. With tomatoes now black and sunsets apocalyptic and the apparent clarity of black and white reduced to a languid grey, his desire to eat and even his desire to see were all but destroyed. The memory of colour erased: an ecology of sensations disrupted.

From the study of the interactions between organisms and their environment to that of the world of interactions between senses and perception: a phenomenological ecosystem, an ecology in ancient Greek.

αἴσθησις or aisthēsis.

Not visual perception, but general perception received via the senses—sight, sound and touch. An open-ended gesture framed by the systematic ordering of a set of interactions, over time, with others and concerning the body.

Danae Valenza is making a colour organ with friends and lovers, musicians and circuit makers, amateurs and technicians. Specialist knowledge sourced and shared, something unknown trusted and deployed.

A small Collard & Collard Piano.

Via the 88 keys, metal strings, a wooden box and electrical cords, this piano will play both light and sound. Cables, switches, and coloured globes—mechanisms both hidden and revealed. I imagine an audible version of Munsell's Colour Tree where hue, value and chroma are organised in three-dimensional space.

Visual and aural tone: a circuit for a system that includes experience which is individually constructed.

A chance encounter with a light machine—they play a song, to play the lights, that a pinhole camera will record.

Formal melodies, kinetic synaesthesia and a portrait of a song. Pianoforte, soft and strong.

In the 1690 essay 'An Essay Concerning Human Understanding', John Locke's offhand statement that a blind man had claimed the sound of a trumpet was like the color scarlet sparked an investigation into the possibility of correspondence between light and sound.[1]

Correspondence. A letter, an arrangement of letters, a scale, a composition, a song; a 'beautiful problem' in our heads.[2]

It was Isaac Newton who perhaps first found a correspondence between proportions of prismatic rays and string lengths used to produce a musical scale: D, E, F, G, A, B, C.

For fear of oversimplifying, centuries of making devices for painting music.[3]

Devices with names both literal and poetic—with musical scores to accompany. Languages for interpretation or, as Ludwig Hirschfeld Mack might propose, languages for learning through music. Colour with names both literal and poetic—shared we say yellow, Dulux might say Butterblond, a measurement of wavelengths for the WEB #FFFF00, in light RGB (255, 255, 0) or in print CMYK (0, 0, 100, 0), a Pantone code, a Munsell co-ordinate.

Frederick Kastner's *Pyrophone* made sound via visual explosions and later a *Singing Lamp*. Louis Bertrand Castel, a mathematician with interests in aesthetics devised proposals for colour music, harpsichords for the eyes and a *Clavecin Oculaire*. Thomas Wilfred's Clavilux or 'light played by key'. Mary Hallock-Greenewalt named her colour organ after her mother. Hallock-Greenewalt's *Sarabet* contained a rheostat that controlled the reflection of seven coloured lights.

Scientists have mapped equations of the city, whilst others have found that each city has a different beat, the pedestrians of one city sharing a sense of rhythm that differs from the next. Cities with their own DNA, lived rhythms, walked equations. With footfalls measured by units of time, we find a relationship to any number of things—inhabitants, restaurants, libraries. It was Robert Levine who found a pace for each of 31 cities—an ecology of senses.

Jörg Heiser talks of a type of work in which ideas of community permit or even rely on the single individual, the simultaneity of being apart and together.[4] Danae Valenza has coordinated works where a system of simultaneity exists—potential and lack, groups and individuals, visual and aural. Opera singers have performed duets visually singing to each other but just out of earshot (*Operetta After Sakamoto*). Accidents occur, the audience must look up as *Ue o Muite Aruko* ('I Look Up As I Walk') is sung. Written in response to feeling dismayed at the prospect of protest, Rokusuke Ei's lyrics are rendered open so that they might also refer to love—the couple in the group, the individual in either.

Correspondence, an arrangement of letters, a scale, a composition, a song; a 'beautiful problem' in our heads.

Was it also Mr Sacks who mentioned the man who read braille via its shadows? Born with achromatopsia—sensitive to light and with limited experience of seeing colour—he was sent to a school for the blind. Not being blind, but able to see, his reading was not mediated by touch but rather tones; an ecology of sensations remediated.

Systems subverted, altered and changed, formulas repeated. Languages reordered and remade in order to discuss a space, a distance between score, sound and sight.

Aisthēsis. Reading braille shadows, dancing to mathematics.

Originally commissioned by the Australian Centre for Contemporary Art, for *New14*, curated by Kyla McFarlane, Australian Centre for Contemporary Art, Melbourne, 2014, p. 50.

Notes

1 Kenneth Peacock, 'Instruments to Perform Colour-Music: Two centuries of Technological Experimentation', http://rhythmiclight.com/articles/InstrumentsToPerformColor.pdf, accessed January 2014.

2 Email correspondence with Danae Valenza, January 2014.

3 Bainbridge Bishop devised an apparatus to be positioned on top of an organ and via levers and shutters coloured lights would be blended on screen whilst music was performed.

4 'All of a Sudden: Things that Matter in Contemporary Art: An Interview with Jörg Heiser', *Art & Research* vol. 2, no. 1 (Summer 2008), http://www.artandresearch.org.uk/v2n1/heiser.html, accessed January 2014.

These are my 'hi-res' images

There is an invisible, almost straight line between Frankston (to the south-east of Melbourne's CBD) and Doreen (to the north-east of Melbourne's CBD). If you could drive or walk between the two on this invisible straight line, you would pass through Yarrambat, Plenty, Greensborough, Templestowe, Balwyn, Blackburn, Chadstone, Clayton, Dingley, Edithvale and Seaford.

Moving through suburbia to get from a rural edge to the edge of the sea, or vice versa.

An inward and outward outlook, or movement, I guess.

You see.

I'm never really sure what place means.

There is one of us from one of these places and another from the other; yet another is from that somewhere in between.

Boredom, laziness, melancholia, comfort, idleness and the workaholic. Perhaps each one is really just the other.

While watching Pedro Almodóvar's film *I'm So Excited*, two things occurred to me. One, was that the title of the film elicits a kind of exhaustion. The song by The Pointer Sisters is fast, punchy and demanding. I vividly remember it being performed by a Queen at The Peel. A kind of forced libidinal space, with effort—the song, not The Peel. A demanded desire, but perhaps only in the context of this film in which a plane is expected to crash and, as a result, the flight attendants attempt to distract the passengers by lip-syncing the song—I'm So Excited.

Both title and theme song—an overworked tribute.

Almodóvar constantly changes genres—the other thing that occurred to me.

Serious humor, the prophetic and profound; absurd. Antonio Banderas and Penelope Cruz handling baggage like screwed (up) ground crew.

Perhaps, like its overworked title and theme song, Almodóvar's film is strained and tired.

My friend who lives in London has just messaged. The two of them went to the De La Warr Pavillion in Bexhill on Sea. Viber says they say…

(sic) Rained around us but never where we were.

The De La Warr Pavillion is International Style and either/or Art Deco. Perhaps it was the first major Modernist building in Britain, or perhaps it wasn't. People don't seem to agree, but they will still go to see.

Bexhill on the Sea.

The name of the place has its thingness in it; just in case you can't see it, just in case you can't hear it, or just in case you can't feel it.

'Seeing Things Through Things'; the thirteenth chapter in Rancière's book of scenes. This is not representation. Like a blanket painted the same colour as itself, a set of doors that can become a family, a shelf made from Saladas and chipboard made from Weetbix.

Registered trade, Mark.
Copy, right? Service, Mark?
® TM
© SM
Registered trade Mark. Copy, right? Service Mark!

Saladas and shelves; a ledge for cheese and tomato, a massage for Vegemite, a bed for butter. Man-size, snack-size, bite-size; wheat, salt and water.

Three of the five fridges at the service station are filled with energy drinks, one with milk and cheese, the other with refreshments without the specified and named capacity.

'I'm so excited, we're all exhausted', these three fridges seem to say.

Mother, Monster, Red Bull, No Fear, V.

And because of exhaustion, mothers, monsters and fear, we forget to write email replies and ask for more time. And so one of the ones writes instead:

> Thank you for writing *Towards a Philosophy of Furniture.* I also like that you have updated the text—*Instruments of Contentment: Furniture and Poetic Sustainability.* What a beautiful title!
>
> When I was three years old I went through a strange period where I refused to wear shoes, because they made a strange squeaking noise whenever I walked and I was convinced I was hurting them by walking. I told my dad that I felt like I was stepping on little baby ducks. I heard the squeaking and the clicking and the mushing, and I felt the pressure of my feet pressing down on the rubber, and I knew that it couldn't possibly be safe for me to be pushing down so hard on something so soft. I felt that it was so unfair to expect a piece of rubber and leather to support my entire body. My father proceeded to check the inside and outside of my shoes, to prove that in fact there were no baby ducks being hurt by my walking. But I remained convinced that, even though there were no baby ducks under my feet, there was something trapped inside the soles (souls?? ha ha) of my shoes, something inherent in the structure of the support, a prescribed set of rules and behaviours that a shoe and shoe-wearer alike must conform to, and I was not comfortable with knowing them.

> It is almost like everyday things—shelves, beds, trousers, walls, chairs—come with their own 'user's manual', embedded within themselves. We know how to use a sweater by knowing a sweater. But then I also wonder, is finding or defining a function all about simply the naming of a thing that is supposed to support or carry out that function?

Things that carry out other things, forms that follow other functions. When the categorisation fails, when what is expected doesn't happen—like 101 script writing for a sitcom about nothing, like only reading the introduction or the conclusion, like waiting in a queue at Optus while all the employees are on the phone, like seeing a comfortable space you can't get into.

Let's end with an introduction. Pierre Saint-Amand writes:

> Here non-productivity remains a precious art, a protest against the bourgeois consensus of utility, an original conquest of freedom. In the end, laziness rejoins the essay, the work in progress with no guarantee of completion. It contemplates the unfinished—work interrupted, fragmented without regret.

t
h
e
s
e
a
r
e
m
y
‘
h
i
-
r
e
s
’
i
m
a
g
e
s

Co-authored by Natasha Madden and Zac St Clair, originally published as a catalogue essay for *Reclining Towards a Comfortable Ideology*, Zac St Clair and Natasha Madden, Blindside, Melbourne, March 2014.

Voice Control Previous Song

Elliot Gould:	I am wondering who the self-help gurus of today are. And what of the tragic, melancholy and conflicted protagonists we stream, steal and wait for on a weekly basis?
Jules Fieffer:	SICK, SICK, SICK: A guide to non-confident living.
Other Patsy:	But they're funny?

[*Phone rings: Heavy Breathing*]

Elliot Gould:	Protagonists that speak around us, not to us. CIA agents with bipolar, others hunted by Russians and consistently working underground and outside the law but committed to the State and free to torture, teachers with terminal cancer making amphetamines, bumbling Veeps, OCD detectives with problematic pasts and long-distance lovers that smoke too much. Daytime drama and solo speeches. One character played by four actors, pondering out loud (pol?) alone what their next move might be. Internal dialogues verbalised. Actors acting as ventriloquist dolls with moving mouths. Audible silence. An over-articulated space where image is no longer considered interpretable. Absent protagonists, internal monologues, Operating Systems.
Other Patsy:	I don't know where you are. But you can show me. Go to Settings, tap Privacy,

tap Location Services and turn it on. Then scroll to Siri and turn that on, too.

[*Phone rings: Heavy Breathing*]

Patsy Newquist: I am always smiling.

Other Patsy: While a Pianola plays a soliloquy.

What's the difference between soliloquy and commentary?

Alfred Gould: You've stopped smiling Patsy.

Other Patsy: I am not really sure. If I am cyncial—dramatic device v capital venture. If I am not—self-reflection v genuflection. Bowing before a superior, perhaps even when the superior is a narrative, a collective of which you were part. When the man presses play on the cassette recorder, the magnetic tape plays someone's father reading someone's son's prior declarations—artists' statements. Professionalism and extras—actors who are extras, and features that are extras for a feature. Commentary so as to avoid Oedipus or deconsecrating the church. A sermon by a father to return the space to the state. Reversals and returns. In the recording, the narrative arc has no arc. The statements, recorded declarations, can potentially be played on repeat. An analysis for a practice, or a type of diagnosis, but hardly a way of working or even a working through. They are a dialogue for a solo. A heightened awareness of the isolated individual attempting to be certain and less vulnerable. An arrangement of words, the construction of meaning.

[*Long Pause and on the television screen Jean Luc Goddard's* Weekend *is playing*]

Other Patsy: We're doing it here. Again. While a Pianola plays a soliloquy.

[*Phone rings: Heavy Breathing*]

Other Patsy: Some things you can ask me:

Phone 'Call Brian'
FaceTime 'FaceTime Lisa'
App Launching 'Launch Photos'
Messages 'Tell Susan I'll be right there'
Calendar 'Set up a meeting at 9'
Weather 'Will it be hot today'
Sports 'Did the Giants win?'

Alfred Gould: An algorithmic soliloquy. The ubiquitous authority of homogenous design quietly whispers like the absent protagonist. The aesthetics of critique, 11-pt sans-serif fonts, two-columned knowledge, vertical titles, always-already accessible pdfs, monochromatic cultural efficiency with an accompanying iPod audio guide.

[*Insert maledicta balloon, movement lines and a grawlix*].

[*Camera pans to an unfinished email which reads: Dear Hito, is it just The Poor Image, or is it also The Poor Encounter?*]

Conflicts of scale, space and time. The moving image alludes to temporal control. Canon 5D clarity, or telecommunications video — moving image homogeneity. Squeaky clean torture porn, or dirty excessive porn porn. I need a tripod for my fold-up chair in order to stabilise the image for Liquid Crystal Display clarity. A lonely chair. One tripod per camera. Isolated individuals.

Voice Control
previous song
call
what song is playing
dial
pause music

Thomas Bernhardt: In the end, people had turned themselves into art machines. Kunstmaschinen. With nothing in common with human beings, and only seldom reminding you of human beings.

Patsy Newquist: You owe me something! I've invested everything I believe in you. You've got to let me mould you. Please let me mould you. You've got me whining, begging and crying. I've never behaved like this in my life. Will you look at this? That's a tear. I never cried in my life.

Other Patsy: What can I help you with?

[*Long Pause: On the television screen is an infomercial discussing the Top Ten infomercials*]

Other Patsy: Some things you can ask me:
What's my ETA?
Tweet great show last night
Who is near me?
Find a gas station
Enable Wi-fi
Get college football rankings
What's my next turn?
Give me directions home
Tweet great show last night
Enable Wi-fi
Read my new messages
Enable Wi-fi
Who is Barack Obama?

	Find coffee near me How far away is the sun?
Me:	What are images?
Other Patsy:	'Images' (tap to edit)
	What would you like to search for?
Jules Fieffer:	SICK, SICK, SICK: A guide to non-confident living.
Other Patsy:	'Seek seek seek a cartoon on confident leaving (tap to edit)
	I'm not sure I understand.
Me:	No! SICK, SICK, SICK: A guide to non-confident living.
Other Patsy:	'No seek seek seek God to nonconfidence leaving' (tap to edit)
	I'm really not equipped to answer such questions.

First published as a catalogue essay for *Concertistic Life*,
Tim Woodward, Boxcopy, Brisbane, 17 May – 7 June 2014.

2015

An interim: ART SLASH SCALE SLASH FRIEND SLASH WORK

In 2008, during a more cynical period of my writing history, I submitted a text for *Reader #8,* edited by Matthew Griffin and published by Gambia Castle, Auckland. My text developed from an email conversation in which I bastardised a Wikipedia entry describing subprime mortgage loans:

> To access this increasing market, exhibitors often take on risks associated with showing artists with poor exhibiting ratings or limited exhibiting histories. Subprime exhibitions are considered to carry a far greater risk for the artist due to the aforementioned exhibition risk characteristics of the typical subprime artist. Galleries use a variety of methods to offset these risks. In the case of many subprime exhibitions, this risk is offset with a higher exhibition rate or various exhibition enhancements, such as private viewings.
>
> In the case of subprime exhibitions, a subprime artist may be charged higher late fees, gallery bond fees, catalogue fees, or upfront fees for the exhibition. Late fees are charged to the exhibitor, which may drive the artist over their exhibiting limit, resulting in over-the-limit fees. These higher fees compensate the gallery for the increased costs associated with servicing and exhibiting such artists, as well as for the higher default rate. [1]

The words 'exhibition', 'exhibitors' and 'market' replaced 'loan' and 'lenders' in my text. A moustache-on-the-Mona-Lisa-type gesture, I was at the time trying to question the role of Artist Run Initiatives (ARIs),[2] the over-professionalisation of artists, and the lack of arts funding in Australia. It was the loss of confidence in the subprime mortgage market that is thought to have greatly contributed to the US economic crash of 2007–2009, and which eventually led to the Global Financial Crisis, or what quickly became known as the GFC.[3]

The proliferation of ARIs has not resulted in the collapse of the Australian art market, as far as I can tell. In fact, to return to the written gesture some seven years later, I wonder about making analogous the criteria for a failed mortgage system, and ARIs? I also question the non-profit, self-organised and independent nature of what has since become a 'sector in the arts industry'? If organisations such as Melbourne's TCB art inc. (of which I have been part), West Space, Bus Projects, Platform Art Spaces and even un Projects were born in a post-recession, pro-privatised, economic environment, then what has been spawned post-GFC? Has the ARI of today become synonymous with a kind of replicated institutional hierarchy disguised as independence?

It is too easy to reduce the networks of relations and the collective nature of ARIs to simple economics and a pre-packaged, feel-good, relational community game. For amongst the bureaucratic terminology and over-work-for-under-pay (or no pay), is a community of individuals and collectives working for small, mostly unfunded projects, spaces and publishers. ARIs today sustain their presence through hybrid gift economies and alternative currency exchanges — through fundraisers and auctions (the new 'group show'), cash grabs, beer sponsorship and exhibiting artists' generosity or necessity.

The number of ARIs emerging in Melbourne over the past 10 to 15 years has increased dramatically, reflecting the dynamic and innovative ways that those involved have appropriated and problem-solved in order to generate and produce new spaces, thought and knowledge. The ground from which these spaces have emerged is fertile — the NGV and other major institutions have, until recently, ignored most local practices, despite there being three major art schools within a 10km radius. We are too quick to assume that the 'ARI sector' (market speak) supports only what we like to call 'emerging artists'. Rather than Melbourne ARIs being galleries or spaces solely dedicated to 'emerging art' and those in the first five years of their practice, the most interesting and influential of these spaces are facilitating and organising exchanges between artists, musicians, fashion designers, dancers, writers, art historians and curators, across generations and geographic locations. Today there is a network or composition of relations between newly-established and well-funded ARIs, across institutions, and between younger and older artists demanding a presence. Together, they are fighting against rent increases and for the payment of artists' fees; they are looking for an audience as diverse as its practitioners (and vice versa); and they are exchanging ideas and arguing about ideologies. As this is happening, independent spaces are doing commercial shows, commercial galleries are making survey exhibitions, and museums are presenting experimental noise.

If, in the past, we thought that ARIs were just training turf for a life of future commercial bliss, then this bubble has well and truly burst, particularly when one considers the relatively small share of the global art market that Australia is privy to. Perhaps this is also why we have a plethora of artist-slash-somethings—be it artist/writer/curators, artist/publishers, artist/educators, artist/installers, artist/gallerists, or artist/musicians. This artist-slash job phenomenon might also be symptomatic of the need for clear classifications and a turn towards conservative conceptions of the role of an artist. The artist-slash jobber points to the precarious nature of contemporary work and the greater casualisation of the contemporary workforce.

This artist-slash relationship is also indicative of a larger shift, one that refers to scale and scalability, where a system, network, or process is able to handle a growing amount of work. David Joselit uses this term in a political sense in relation to art, to describe the multiple branching of connections that lead away from an individual to the locale, the nation, and the world.[4] This artist-slash relationship implies connectivity—between each other in the locale, but also regionally and internationally. The scale of it changes pending need and ambition, and in this sense it is perhaps as Joselit suggests: scalability denotes a format's capacity to persist across increasing orders of magnitude. A connection's format

—its structural articulation of contact and current—might be scaled up with minimal distortion, but the magnitude of the current it carries—its *currency*—will vary, leading to quantitative differences.[5]

In the case of artist-led projects in Melbourne, more often than not this scale is self-determined and self-organised by a range of artists, arts workers, curators, writers and historians. They are largely independent of large-scale funding or private sponsorship, and each operates with varying *currencies* and organisational approaches. Many such scalable projects have been time-specific in their durational and project-based approach—consider Christopher L.G. Hill and James Deutscher's project Y3K (2009–2011), or Helen Grogan and Jared Davis' curatorial space Open Archive (2011–2012), and more recently SLOPES, a Utopian Slumps spin-off coordinated by Brooke Babbington (2014). Other projects have existed for longer periods, before participants, collectives or individuals have moved on to other projects, such as the committee-led Clubs Project Inc. (2002–2007), Ocular Lab (2003–2010), The Narrows coordinated by Warren Taylor (2006–2011), Hell Gallery coordinated by Jess Johnson and Jordan Marani (2008–2011), and Light Projects (2009–2012).

Many other Melbourne ARIs continue to exist, some with changing committees and collectives, such TCB art inc. (1999–), Seventh Gallery (2000–), Kings Artist Run (2001–), Rear View (2009–), and other more individual pursuits, such as Techno Park Studios (2009–) coordinated by Kim Donaldson.[6] Above pubs, under houses, in old factories, in CBD squats, in shopfronts, in the suburbs and in outer-suburban disused kindergartens, all manner of buildings have been bastardised, appropriated, renovated and made-do with the express purpose of presenting art, of and by peers, across time, place and generation. This activity is a form that acknowledges authorship, but which grows without authorship as an origin, aware of its histories and otherness to public institutions, commercial intentions and corporate funding. Its form is perhaps found in Maibritt Borgen's definition of 'self-organisation'—a mode of practice and a term founded on self-conscious narrativisation of de-central collectivity and the dissolution of modernist hierarchies.[7]

This mode of self-organisation is subject to changing scales, locations, sites and aims.

As opposed to a network, which is more linear in its arrangement, perhaps this ARI scalability is more akin to Peter Sloterdijk's philosophy of *spheres* and *envelopes*: unlike networks, spheres are not anaemic — not just points and links – but rather they are complex ecosystems in which forms of life define their 'immunity' by devising protective walls and inventing elaborate systems of air conditioning.[8] The protective walls and air-conditioning might be akin to Borgen's *self-conscious narrativisation and decentralised collectivity,* where in Melbourne the co-existence and development of a range of independent and self-organised arts publishing and writing projects co-exist. In this same 10 years, we have read publications as diverse as *LIKE Magazine* and *un Magazine*; Gwyneth Porter and Dan Arps' online PDF *Natural Selection*; Christopher L.G. Hill's appropriated-redundant-technology-excess mag *Endless Lonely Planet*; online writing collective *Stamm* facilitated by Jonathan Nichols; and *Discipline*, edited by Helen Hughes, Nicholas Croggan and David Homewood. We have handled an array of printed matter by independent publishers such as Surpllus (Brad Haylock) and 3-ply (Fayen d'Evie). And amongst this writing by writers and artists and curators and historians, we have had overlapping spheres (or 'wombs', as Sloterdijk states), co-presentations and shared workloads — magazines facilitating lecture series (*Discipline*), pop-up reading rooms in gallery spaces (West Space), and artists making modular and mobile bookshops with home bases (World Food Books, run by Matthew Hinkley and Joshua Petherick).

Borgen's use of the terms *self-narrativisation* and *de-central collectivity* are at the core of what we have witnessed in the last decade in the Melbourne independent art scene. A kind of anarchic leadership and self-declared value, and a politics via friendship and collegiality (or perhaps even in the tension between the two), have created the conditions for the possibility of diverse artistic practices and non-commercial pursuits to flourish. To designate them as *outside* the institution is to deny the links that are forged *with* and *in* established institutions: art schools, TAFE colleges, Gertrude

Contemporary, West Space, independent collective studios (Artery, TCB, Kerr Street Studios, River Studios), collaborative ventures, group exhibitions, international exchanges, long-distance phone calls, excessive emailing, Instagram-liking and social networking. We are acutely aware of the blurred boundaries between business and friendship, and while this may seem disadvantageous or confusing, perhaps it is within this ambiguity that we can find a kind of decentralised, collective strength?

In a conversation between artists Céline Conderelli and Johan Frederik Hartle, we are directed to Hannah Arendt's concept of culture being akin to friendship: the company that one chooses to keep, in the present as well as the past.[9] If cultural production is likened to 'making things public', it is perhaps in this idea of company and friendship that we see both connectivity (networks) and the establishment of contexts, dialogues and desires (spheres). Philosophy, as many have pointed out,[10] finds the word friend (phila) contained within its very form—Aristotle, Montaigne, Derrida, Agamben and Blanchot have all reflected on these ideas. In more recent times, post-structural anarchist Todd May has dedicated a book to the argument for friendship as an alternative to neo-liberal tendencies.[11]

Lately in Melbourne we have seen a diversion from spaces-for-hire, with artists and friends instead co-opting, reclaiming and repurposing spaces in studios, florists, Scout Halls, industrial sites and private homes.[12] Driving such projects is the desire for rent-free exhibition space, the ability to elect who exhibits, and a desire for the production and presentation of works in a local context relative to the artist's home and/or studio. There's also a will to show outside of traditional gallery spaces, generated by an ever-increasing, self-narrativising, decentralised collective of friends. Most recently, artists Rex Veal and Josie Kidd-Crowe bypassed the bureaucracy of waiting for a proposal to be 'yay-ed' and gallery fees to be negotiated by holding an impromptu exhibition in Dwight's Mill, one of Melbourne's oldest industrial sites, just downstream from where Merri Creek meets the Yarra River. Rejecting the idea of site-specificity, Veal and Kidd-Crowe's punk anarchic gesture placed autonomous artworks by friends and friends-of-friends alongside artwork made by Veal's uncle. If we consider this juncture of old industry, new art and the conduit of the river, perhaps we have found an apt place to end this text. Because if we acknowledge that there is not necessarily a recognisable beginning to speak of, and nor during the past 10 to 15 years have we found an end, then perhaps what we do recognise is a collection of networks and spheres and friendships simultaneously creating the possibility for collective autonomy and selective affinities.

First published in *un Anthology 2004–2014: a decade of art and ideas*, edited by Ulanda Blair, Rosemary Forde and Phip Murray, un Projects inc., Melbourne, 2016.

Notes

1 Lisa Radford, 'Subprime Galleries' in Matthew Griffin (ed.), *Reader #8 Industrial Strength Permission*, series editor Kate Newby (Auckland: Gambia Castle, 2008).

2 The acronym 'ARI' (often pronounced 'ahh-reee' or 'A.R.I.') is used here with some hesitation; symptomatic of a neo-liberal push to quantitate description. For me, it is a homogenous leveler purposed for top-down funding administration.

3 Further to the above, 'GFC' is likewise an acronym that flattens and reduces meaning, an acronym that ends up sounding like a fast-food chain more palatable than what the terms 'Global Financial Crisis' denote.

4 David Joselit, *After Art POINT: Essays on Architecture* (Princeton: Princeton University Press, 2012), 61.

5 ibid., 79.

6 For an extensive listing and documented history of Artist-Run Initiatives in Victoria up until 2007, see: Din Heagney (ed.), *Making Space: Artist Run Initiatives in Victoria* (Melbourne: Victorian Initiatives of Artists Network, 2007).

7 Maibritt Borgen, 'The Inner and Outer Form of Self-Organisation', in Stine Herbert and Anne Szefer Karlsen (eds), *Self-Organised* (London: Open Editions, 2013), 39.

8 Bruno Latour, 'Some experiments in art and politics', *e-flux journal* 23 (2011), http://www.e-flux.com/journal/some-experiments-in-art-and-politics/#_ftn2, accessed December 2014.

9 Hannah Arendt, 'The Crisis in Culture and its Political Significance', *Between Post and Future: Eight exercises in political thought* (London: Faber and Faber, 1961), 228.

10 See Céline Conderelli, 'Too close to see: a conversation with Johan Frederik Hartle', in Herbert and Szefer Karlsen, *Self-Organised*, 63–73.

11 Todd May, *Friendship in the an Age of Economics: Resisting the Forces of Neoliberalism* (Lanham: Lexington Books, 2012).

12 Flake, a space in a studio run by Kate Meakin (2013–14); Brunswick

Lake, a space in a florist coordinated by Isadora Vaughan and Jahnne Pascoe-White (2014–15); The Big East projects in Scout Halls in outer east Melbourne curated by Kiron Robinson (2013 and 2014); Kym Maxwell's curated exhibition *Industrial Estate* at Woodcraft Mobiliar Workshop; and Madeline Kidd's *Sushichampagnepaintingsculpture*, an exhibition in an apartment (2011).

PIIG

Sometime between June and July in the year 2015 (according to Western Christian calendars), a letter begun in Paris, France and finished in Yekaterinburg, Russia.

Dear M. Daumier,

I am starting this letter before I arrive at the Musee d'Orsay, where I will hope to complete it. Urgency dictated that I start straight away. Perhaps I will sit in front of one of your satirical portraits, or rather busts of politicians and lawyers. Today, these busts might include EU Administrators, a man in Speedos, Angela Merkel and the IMF, or trust fund managers from Goldman Sachs and Fannie Mae and Freddie Mack. It feels like satire has been eradicated. Or, rather, that the possibility for political irony has been squashed by a confused form of democracy. The order of signs within which you could ascribe a King such as Louis Phillipe as a Gourmand devouring workers and farmers in order to represent a monarchy and/or hierarchy has devoured itself. Workers and Farmers are perhaps invisible when a PM wears a high-vis vest.

You might've been imprisoned for such representations. Perhaps now they are to your capital advantage. Somehow, in our apparent 'wisdom', silence is created. The state declares a terrorist attack and we wonder whether the violence is simply a response to despair. Passive-aggressive 'Royal Commissions' might once have been considered witch-hunts, McCarthyism or inquisitions. Perhaps it changes less than we think—you were imprisoned in the nineteenth century for a lithograph referencing sixteenth-century Rabelaisian narratives, the only difference now is that 300 years can occur in an instant.

I do wonder about the possibility of dissent and satire eroding. 'Je suis Charlie', sans Charlie; *Le Caricature*, sans caricature. Perhaps the aesthetics of finance is a new field of research, but I wonder whether you were the first observer; or the observer who I first recognised it in—to make visible the worker, and to work in a system close to collapse.

A plutocratic Freudian slip—a Treasurer and his minister for finance smoking cigars branded Hubris and saying 'I would expect you to be in a job'. We live in ready-made satire. Million dollar fat cats? Let them eat cake.

I am writing this to you at a time when one country appeared to re-insert the social and democracy into an obfuscated discussion about debt and austerity, bringing to the foreground questions about who should and who could pay—the difference between these poles perfectly rendered in your workers climbing a ladder to the Gargantuan's mouth.

Jabba the Hutt, mining, landscape and original landowners come to mind. Closed estates and a satellite city intended to house 50,000 left unfinished.

The language of what represents excess has perhaps been turned on its head. The wealthy can afford health care, a personal trainer, and home-delivered organics. The PIIG turns on a spit, ready to be carved up and devoured by its healthy, fit and skinny neighbours. Our PM wears Lycra and Speedos.

Economies on the verge of 'symbolic' collapse. A zoned currency depicting shared fictitious buildings. A symbolic currency, pre-Bitcoin. Virtual. Monarchies of the symbolic, oligarchies of the real, and political dynasties funded by 'pacs'. A Trade Union will be demonised, whilst a mining lobby can be praised.

Irony. *The Economist*, a weekly paper owned by The Economist Group, prints an article about your works titled 'Beyond Satire'.

Your quiet lithographs and unfired busts, so quiet but scathing. How much should be said, Daumier? And who should say what, and when? When is obfuscating the obfuscated simply replicating control? Perhaps the act of mimicry demands attention, asking where are we, what is our past and where is our future?

Your friend Fredric Jameson says, 'Any ontology of the present needs to be an ideological analysis as well as a phenomenological description'.[1] Jameson is speaking of a place that acknowledges history and the idea of a mode of production. He rejects the idea of culture because it implies a severing between space and social totality. His idea of speaking through a mode of production allows for a relationship between methodology and presence, between acting and creating, and perhaps the simultaneity of use/consumption.

Workers-make-Gourmand-eats-workers-make-Gourmand, ad infinitum.

Satire is a PM fucking a PIIG simultaneously on *Black Mirror* and in Hauser & Wirth. For the masses and elites; free-to-air, will-to-pay, surplus funds. 'Have we heard ourselves lately?', the austerity graf asks. Live feeds to market sites. Hubris cigars.

I watched a documentary talking about the need for one state to keep changing the laws so the populous couldn't determine what it was allowed to do. This is language. Do you know Matt Davis? He speaks of Habermas and the contrast between the medical use of the term 'crisis' in relation to theories of drama—the point where objectivity and subjectivity either emerge or disappear… 'Indeed, one of the key features or process of financialisation … is that it depoliticises economic and social relations generally'.[2] In this sentence, it is the 'generally' that I find most important. Because, consciously or not, it is this generally that is all consuming, the point of obfuscation. Specifics inform the singular, the singular constructs the general. '…the subjectivity of the patient in a medical crisis does not disappear; it is merely suspended, the subject's objective conditions are addressed through technical means. The Politics of a crisis are more clearly seen when the subject itself must be changed…'.[3]

M. Daumier, have you seen the events in Greece? Perhaps, ever so briefly, a subject was changed?

My friend Tully is making paintings that are sometimes banners and could also be blankets. Think Unions and Trades Halls. Propaganda to gander. Images stripped from walls, desktops, and laptops; repurposed and double-sided. From Barcelona to Brunswick. Mimicry demanding attention. Spam mail protests, counterfeit Euros in India, counterfeit buildings in Euros; insider trading online, thieves and banking, thieves are banking.

I began this letter in the home of one revolution and end it in the land of another, whilst reading 140-character announcements about administrators making decisions about the possibility for a resolution while the people riot, in a land somewhere between both. In Russia, where I leave this letter, the terms bunker and banker are merely a slip of the tongue.

M. Daumier, one last thing… I think Merkel is singing on the grave of Europe…

Hey. Ho Ho. Baby I got Germoney.
Xx

First published as a catalogue essay for *What Noise Does a Pig Make*, Tully Moore, Gertrude Glasshouse, Gertrude Contemporary, Melbourne, 24 July – 29 August 2015.

Notes

1 Fredric Jameson, 'The Aesthetics of Singularity', *New Left Review* 92 (March/April 2015): 101.

2 Matt Davis, 'The Aesthetics of the Financial Crisis: Work, Culture and Politics', *Alternatives: Global, Local, Political* vol. 37, no. 4 (2012): 318.

3 ibid.

PROCRASTIPAINTING

Sometimes it is hard to distinguish criticality from a position of fear or cynicism.[1] It has been with great interest that I have watched as we have returned to medium specificity in the last few years as a way of categorising and grouping artworks—either as reaction to global financial downturn and/or a general way out of having to determine what might otherwise be too difficult. Symposiums, exhibitions, 'Painting forever!', 'Painting Expanded'. Sometimes it sounds like the setup for a bad joke...

> Q: Why are conceptual artists painting again?
> A: Because they are beside themselves![2]

Perhaps this is why Helen Johnson's book is so refreshingly titled *Painting is a Critical Form*, because this is where the content is—in the production, not the product. As a cue, this is where I take my own liberties, remembering that Jessica Stockholder described her large-scale installations and assemblages as paintings. The importance for a criticality of and in painting is in this action and process: less in its objectness, and more in its modality. Painting's literal slipperiness grants its ability to weave, layer and *trompe l'oeil* itself into being ahistorical re-presentation, montage, sculpture and pure formalist folly. Painting's never-ending death comes about because of its shapeshifting presence and its ability to 'inhabit space between coherence and incoherence'.[3]

I am not sure, but I am willing to speculate that, at one time or another, artists will ask themselves (perhaps, as anyone): What are we doing? And what are we doing it for? Even if the answer is '!@#$ it' or '!@#$ art', it is a question that is bigger than the answer 'medium specificity' can provide. Instead, the answer might be revealed in a perfect mistake between content and form, one that is simultaneously recognised by the maker-audience. It is the edges of these boundaries (which we might call painting) that I am interested in. As such, this diversion dictates the unordered list that follows:

Anna Higgins

We are pretty much dumped into an image-saturated world as soon as we are born. Images are political. That is a given, and Anna Higgins manages to build, sculpt, collage, capture, project, montage and mould images into explosions that once produced installation, but more recently are reminiscent of photographic paint splats soon to manifest as publication. Printed montage or the moments between pics. Manipulating light. These are apparently two-dimensional objects but with a very material and painterly construction—where light creates space, and object negates light. Here the anonymous archive retains a subjectivity and an objective we can share. Like when Aby Warburg constructed his atlases and tried to define an iconology of the interval by representing the space between images—the Italian philosopher Giorgio Agamben aptly refers to it as a nameless science.[4] This terrifying, formless rhetoric that emerges between images might look something like what Higgins makes—a subtle dialogue between abstraction, film and form and their edited and by-chance intersections.

Virginia Overell

Virginia Overell's work operates in a space that fluidly moves between language, space, chemical reactions and object-ontology. Her practice involves the use of printmaking, sculpture or installation to make a larger painting that reflects on ideas about rates of flow and change, differentiations and integrals—movements and mappings, intersections and transformations occurring between human and non-human movements. Boundaries between things and ideas that adapt and conflict as they rub against each other. Oliver Sacks is known to have dived into oceans looking for the indigo he says he glimpsed a long time ago. A naturally occurring, mined and traded hue, transported along routes with exotic names. One of Overell's works, *Feelings deep enough to swim in*, is a printed-marine-themed-mass-produced scarf dyed indigo blue. Overell's work attempts to represent what we might otherwise overlook or find impossible to scale—things perceived as empty, invisible routes, murky territories, chemical changes and clear new eyes.

Clare Milledge

I first came across Milledge's work as it lay resting, waiting to be installed at Station Gallery, Prahran.[5] The fragile-yet-strong works — oil on glass — sat beside their felt-bag homes. Paintings in their protective-shaman-skin, or is it vice versa? The oil-on-glass, the skin, and the felt containers are like a Beuysian painting. But instead they are one and the same. In Bataille's idea of alteration, the genesis of figuration is an instinct of alteration, a desire to alter whatever is at hand, where (sic), in the process, figures are recognised in (or projected onto) the random scribblings, yielding a virtual object of representation which is then altered and deformed in turn. Art, Bataille writes, 'proceeds by successive destruction.'[6] Milledge is aware of her works circling language, and tricks associated with light, shadows, text and form. Trickery and vision, her works come to us as apparitions in material form — image and language transgressing.

Trevelyan Clay and Kate Smith

Smith paints because Clay does. Or so it goes, something like that, according to our email exchanges. She is trained as a printmaker, he as a painter. They were supposed to collaborate earlier than they did, and didn't until they had studios at Gertrude Contemporary in 2011. She has made painting installations titled *You're the C**T, Donut* (2010), and he has played in a free-form, crazy-ass band called Bum Creek. Here we have two kids from Canberra School of Art,[7] surrogate children of Vivienne Binns and her unwavering love, criticality and the expansion of painting. Here you find humour, angst, mess and B-sides and flip sides (such as their flags currently hanging out the front of Hells Kitchen). With marks that know how they originate in shared painting histories but also aware that they exist in their shared-self-absorbed private gestures. You'll find mini-digs at pollies or any image with power, minimal installs and videos from the farm. When he's working alone, Trev paints big and his neo-geo-analogue-computer-graphics arouse and amaze. Recently, Kate's scale has been smaller, where what she does with apparent ease makes you work hard to find — post-punk affect, poo brown in a white void. As a duo, we find in their work a post-recession-nineties attitude resolved in both individuals and, as such, painting's internal conflict is played out in a performance of collaboration—selfish-file-sharing.

Lane Cormick

Lane Cormick spent most of art school reading history and making monochromes. He graduated in 1999 with a work titled *Calypso Frelimo Fiatto* that saw a Richard Prince-esque monochrome red-car-bonnet being driven around the streets of Melbourne in a Steve McQueen *Get Carter*-style but documented like CCTV footage and accompanied by a Miles Davis soundtrack. Cormick fits into this idea of painting ecology as a kind of post-subjective-post-minimal fling with performance and a gold-plated-failing-ego. He's an abstract expressionist whose works confront our own dilemma with power and image. He makes works that feel how music sounds. In his current show *MBARZALONA*, his alter ego, the artist/musician Rosey Mackay, listens to the psych stoner band Casua Sui (which interestingly means 'cause of itself') and their song 'Garden of Forking Paths' (yep, same as the Borges story) on repeat whilst simultaneously attempting to play it live—her back is to us, as if in a Caspar David Friedrich painting where the landscape-as-bedroom meets monochrome-sublime. This is painting's fusion and it is as crushing as it is beautiful. You can't look the eagle in the eye: she's hooded.

Previously unpublished, 2015.

Notes

1 The title of this essay was stolen from a series of biro-on-blue-post-it notes that hang in Jacqline Owers-Gayst's studio at VCA.

2 Sorry Jan Verwoert and David Joselit.

3 Helen Johnson, *Painting is a Critical Form* (Melbourne: 3-ply, 2015), 66.

4 Agamben coined this term in reference to Aby Warburg's research and his 'iconology of the interval'. Georges Didi-Huberman picks up on this also in his texts for the catalogue accompanying the exhibition *Atlas: How to carry the world on ones back?*. See: Georges Didi-Huberman (ed.), *Atlas: How to carry the world on ones back?* (Madrid: Museo Nacional Centro de Arte Reina Sofia, 2010).

5 I am based in Melbourne so I am fairly biased. Having said that, I am a big fan of Mitch Cairns and John Spitteri's works also—they, like

Claire, are based in Sydney. Unfortunately, this little foray into what tickles my fancy at the moment could not expand to include these artists and their work.

6 Georges Bataille, as discussed in: Suzanne Guerlac, 'Bataille in Theory: Afterimages', *Diacritics* vol. 26, no. 2 (Summer 1996): 6–17.

7 It is probably safe to say that Binns has influenced a generation of 'painters' that have moved to Melbourne in the last ten years or so, including artists such as Geoff Newton, Madeline Kidd, Bryan Spier, Noël Skrypczak, Justin Andrews, Stuart Bailey, Danny Frommer and Paul Wotherspoon.

2016

Continuity and change: a non-sequitural predicted past

Political speeches might be considered *soliloquy*. One person, in this case a leader, deposed or otherwise, voicing words usually written by another, or others, in a theatre where the audience surrounds. Where the audience is always us, whether we want to be or not. A theatre of the absurd, no less, that purports to give us agency, but, more often than not, makes us feel like we are the subjects of a never-ending, always already *non sequitur.*[1]

Here is where I admit profound failure, where I might have broken a non-core promise in a 'limited war'.[2]

In an attempt to satirise our current political circumstances, this catalogue essay was going to be a speech. As a writer, I was going to role-play being a speech-writer. I attempted to do so (perhaps half-heartedly) with a previous collaborator by re-editing a selection of Gough Whitlam speeches and over-writing them with Malcolm Turnbull isms, Paul Keating quotes and Annabel Crabb observations, amongst other news items and YouTube transcriptions.

Imagining if Turnbull would lose (t)his Double Dissolution election proved difficult. Partly because it is feasible that he will lose (thanks to friends Tony and Kevin), but also because the hilarity of the situation in which we find ourselves seems more satirical than what any contrived version of satire can construct.[3] Rather than truth being stranger than fiction, here, reality is funnier than the joke.[4]

In Slavoj Žižek's *Joke Book*, the introduction is replaced with a short parable-esque narrative about 'The role of Jokes'. Žižek reminds us of a popular myth from the late-Communist regimes of Eastern Europe, where the secret police's function was to invent and to put into circulation political jokes against the regime and its representatives, being aware of the jokes' ability to be a positive, stabilising function (political jokes offer people an easy and tolerable way to blow off steam—in Australia, or Melbourne, at least, we also use sport, mainly football, for this frustration-even-outter-rer). Žižek goes on to point out a crucial feature of the joke—its apparent authorless-ness, 'always told and always-already heard which is supported by their idiosyncratic nature, their unique creativity with the use of language, and their ability to be thought of, consciously or not, as "collective", anonymous and somehow appearing from thin air'.[5]

It is in this creative use of language that we can consider the role of the speech-writer, the politician, the lawyer. The *non sequitur* is of interest because, as a form of argument-making, or rather lack of argument-making, its failure lies in the statement's inability to take into account the space between what is proposed as a sequence of two logical points.

Louis Nowra notes some interesting non sequiturs used by Cardinal Pell, such as: 'Vegetarianism makes him uneasy and he loathes the Greens because they can cause thousands of people to lose their jobs when they set out to save "turtles who breathe through their bottoms".'[6] Tony Abbott, whilst less accomplished than Pell, skews climate change with statements like 'It's been hot before'. Abbott's comment, and Corey Bernardi's illogical 'gay marriage will lead to legalised bestiality', are perhaps our clearest examples of recent political non sequiturs. Yes, it has been hot before, this doesn't discount climate change science, and whilst homosexuality is legal, as is marriage, bestiality is not. Perhaps the image of Joe Hockey and Matthias Cormann sharing a cigar pre-2015 budget announcement could be considered a visual non sequitur[7]—upper-class parliamentarians smoking cuban cigars before delivering a budget asking the middle and lower classes to tighten their belts.

Jokes and often scripts by Samuel Beckett and Eugene Ionesco (Theatre of the Absurd) rely on the non sequitur in order to disrupt the usual logic or narrative and the expectations of the audience. The non sequitur plays on the unfamiliarity of a situation that the characters are participating in and the audience is watching. Should the LNP have been scripted by Beckett, then perhaps Corey Bernardi's statement may well be have been made by Vladimir, whilst watching Sydney's Mardi Gras with Turnbull/Estragon and waiting for

Howard (Godot?). The question of author is interesting because, as Žižek points out:

> the idea that there has to be an author of a joke is properly paranoiac: it means that there has to be an 'Other of the Other', of the anonymous symbolic order, as if the very unfathomable contingent generative power of language has to be personalised, located into an agent who controls it and secretly pulls the strings. This is why, from the theological perspective, God is the ultimate jokester.[8]

In attempting to adulterate Whitlam's speeches from forty-odd-years ago (the only other Double Dissolution that has preceded the fall of a leader and where we find the circumstances not unlike what we face today), I was in effect attempting to render this essay anonymous. But, in my attempt to edit Whitlam's words with Turnbull-ian arrogance, and by changing Bob Hawke's response to Whitlam's resignation into a statement with George Brandis-ian indignation, I found myself caught in a humourless act. As Don Watson has so acutely made us aware, language is emptied of its meaning through repetition, business models and the triumph of economics.[9] The emptying out of language makes an attempted act of satire confused:

> **People** ~~Men and women~~ of Australia:
> Just 17 months ago, I stood here, and from this place and from this city I asked you to choose for Australia a new team, a new program, ~~a new drive for equality of opportunities~~. **It is unclear whether you gave us a** ~~You gave us a~~ clear mandate to go ahead with our program for the next three years. **But, f**~~F~~or 17 months we have driven ourselves to carry out your mandate, to carry out the program ~~I~~ **we never really** placed before you. Now the government you elected for three years has been **un**-interrupted in mid-career.
>
> Our program has been brought to a halt in midstream, **because we lost it**. … These men who have falsified democracy ~~now ask you to turn back. Turn~~

> ~~back to what?~~ Think again how it was when you elected us in **2011** ~~1972~~. Unemployment was at its worst for ten years. Our rate of growth was one of the world's worst, a paltry 2%. The Australian dollar was grossly undervalued. Foreign money was flooding in to buy up Australian resources and Australian industries on the cheap. **We stopped the boats, a**~~A~~ccelerating numbers of migrants **are being** ~~were~~ **housed** ~~leaving~~ in **off-shore prisons.** ~~disillusion~~.
>
> Australia was still deeply involved in the war **on Terror** ~~in Vietnam~~. Our whole foreign policy was based on hostility to China, **India, PNG, the Pacific Islands, and the Middle East**. We **are** ~~were~~ running an army on **hidden budgets** ~~the cheap by conscripting young men~~. There **are** ~~were~~ young **indigenous** men ~~in~~ **wrongly im**prison**ed** for their conscience. Australia **is** ~~was~~ a deeply divided nation. Our young people **are** ~~were~~ becoming alienated from the mainstream of Australian society.

Malcolm Fraser would go on to win the 1975 election. In this case, it is my proposal that on 2 July 2016, we will find ourselves once again with a hung parliament. This of course means we can make use of a 'frenemising'[10] term to describe our future leader/s — *Shortbull* and their deputy *Plibshop.* And rather than the simplification of the dialectical non sequitur thinking that is plaguing our present (A Royal Commission into Unions means we should have a Royal Commission into Banking), we might instead be faced with a scenario that, whilst the fulfilment of an LNP catchphrase, sees the non sequitur of *Continuity and Change* forcing the negotiating of the *undistributed middle* that is usually unaccounted for.

To collaborate is to negotiate the terms of what is shared, and to introduce that which has not been shared prior. More often than not, it is images that we share — stand-ins for language. It is a rolling stream of images, in fact, from 24-hour news coverage and Google searches; not cinema but very much like cinematic-montage — rolling, moving, formatted, arranged, sent, distributed, scaled, pinched, panned, profiled, downloaded and dispersed. An interval between images could perhaps be informed by the idea of an *undistributed middle*: an illogical moment, a formal fallacy.

And so what can be revealed in the formal fallacy? Perhaps in reference to the joke and art, Colette Solier helps by reminding us that:

> The series of mistakes — lapsus, bungled action, symptom — could be completed with free association. Association, according to Freud, is a way of speaking uncoupled from intentional mastery, and aims to make the intrusion of unexpected signifiers possible: a way of speaking in which the subject accepts not knowing what he is saying. We know that a subject who does not accept this register of 'I am speaking, but I do not know what I am saying' renders any interpretation ineffective. This is why I so often say that the call for confessions, testimony or opinion, so prized today, and about which statistics are created, is in itself a denial of the unconscious, since testimony is a form of speaking reduced to saying what one knows, or believes one knows.[11]

And this is that which separates the absurd potential of art, and the absurdity of our present politic. A non sequitur in art is perhaps a strategy for including the audience, revealing something about 'us' and that which we share — the acknowledgment of a shared playing field in this theatre of the absurd; a joke without author. Perhaps this is the nature of collaboration, a joke without directive aim, but aim through approximation — be it *tromp l'oeil* painting, anonymous puppeteers painting a gnome, the karaoke machine, the oppositional juxtaposition of image and text, denim and logos or reimaging pork-barrelling. While in political governance, the use of a non sequitur reveals simply the fallacy, the emptiness of language.

There is a narrative that Annabel Crabb repeats, which is almost a Žižekian ready-made joke:

> Lewis Miller painted (sic) Turnbull for the Archibald Prize in 1995, but Turnbull — shown the work in

> progress — did not like it and withdrew his cooperation. Turnbull registered his disapproval with the art dealer Ray Hughes, to whose gallery Lewis was at the time attached. According to Hughes, he ran into Turnbull at a book launch and was told: 'That artist of yours is no good. He's made me look like a fat, greedy bastard.'

'"Well, Malcolm", rasped Hughes in delighted reply, "You must remember that he is a realist painter".'[12]

First published as a catalogue essay for *I'm Genuinely Lost. Give Me Guidance*, curated by Tully Moore, featuring work by Colleen Ahern, Jon Campbell, Michael Ciavarella, Søren Dahlgaard, Kate Daw and Stewart Russel, Tony Garifalakis, Paula Hunt, Tully Moore, and Zilvester (Goodwin & Hanenbergh), Margaret Lawrence Gallery, Melbourne, 13 May – 11 June 2016.

Notes

1 George Orwell says, 'Political language is designed to make lies sound truthful and murder respectable, and to give an appearance of solidity to pure wind': George Orwell, *Politics and the English Language* (London: Penguin, 2013).

2 'Non-core promises' and 'limited war' are both terms used by previous Australian leaders, John Howard and Tony Abbott.

3 Not to mention, attempting to write smugness into a Gough speech was beyond my capabilities, my bias and my cynicism. Attempting to channel Paul Keating also proved futile. Having said that, when Annabel Crabb states, 'Paul Keating, that savage verbal caricaturist, said, "I fancy Malcolm is like the big red bunger. You light him up, there's a bit of a fizz, then nothing. Nothing.",' it is hard to find either of them wrong. Smugness, matched with smugness. See: Annabel Crabb, 'Stop at Nothing', *Quarterly Essay* 34 (2009): 8.

4 Especially in a week where we had Christopher Pyne accuse Chris Bowen of being 'the Derek Zoolander of Parliament', riffing off Scott Morrison, who tried that gag a month earlier (March 2016). A text from S. Miles read, 'Just confirming Pyne called Bowen "Zoolander" not "Zealander"? I'm not sure if Bowen is the type to wear clogs.' I realised the non sequitur could be wrong, especially taking into consideration the fact that Pyne called Shorten a 'grub' not a 'cunt'.

5 Slavoj Žižek, *Žižek's Jokes (Did you hear the one about Hegel and Negation?)* (Cambridge, Massachusetts: MIT Press, 2014), 6.

6 Louis Nowra, 'The Whirling Dervish: On Tony Abbott' *The Monthly* (February 2010), https://www.themonthly.com.au/monthly-essays-louis-nowra-whirling-dish-tony-abbott-2250, accessed April 2016.

7 Noel Pearson describes Malcolm Turnbull's biography as a non sequitur in 'Radical Hope: Education & Equality in Australia', *Quarterly Essay* 35 (September 2009): 115. This could be pointing to a number of biographical points: Turnbull's work as a journalist for a left-leaning

magazine, then as a lawyer for Parker (not Murdoch), his late entry into Politics at age 50 in 2000, and his university adventure in attempting to write a satirical-political-musical with Bob Ellis. As Crabb has pointed out, 'Turnbull does have an unusually broadminded approach to friendship with Labor figures. Of the four former Labor premiers of NSW still alive, Turnbull has had close friendships with two: Neville Wran and Bob Carr. Let's not forget his fascination with (Jack) Lang. And his work for the WA Labor government of Peter Dowding co-existed with a warm personal friendship with Dowding himself; after Dowding lost the premiership, he moved into one of Turnbull's spare houses in Sydney as a tenant. To befriend one Labor premier might, for someone who is now the leader of the Liberal Party, be viewed as excusable. To befriend two is bordering on careless. But four? It begins to look like a pattern. And it is one of the reasons why elements within the Liberal Party really aren't quite sure about their current federal leader.' From Crabb, 'Stop at Nothing', 66.

8 Žižek, *Žižek's Jokes*, 6.

9 Don Watson, 'When words hide the truth', *The Age* (30 October 2004), http://www.theage.com.au/articles/2004/10/29/1099028198595.html, accessed 20 April 2016.

10 From 'frenemy'.

11 Colette Solier, *Lacan: The Unconscious Reinvented* (London: Karnac Books, 2014), 40.

12 According to Crabb, Turnbull says he has no memory of the Archibald portrait, or the encounter with Hughes. Crabb, 'Stop at Nothing', 49.

Polis outside the agora

March 2016

Dear Paula,

For a while now, I feel like you have been looking for a *polis* inside your stadiums. As you probably know, we generally associate a *polis* with ancient Greece, a sacred space located on an acropolis or hill and often fortified (perhaps more like the old Waverley Park, but less windy) — a site for public political encounter and democratic negotiation, the place where political subjectivation emerges and takes place — the negotiation of difference and disagreement.[1]

I know you remember the poster I posted inside the *Stadium* Facebook.

A visual cue for an Olympiad that never happened.

This July will be the 80th anniversary of that event that never happened. Baudrillard's suggestion that 9/11 didn't happen kind of neatly finds a material reality in this event's un-happening — similarly asking, in a world dominated by the promise of one power, one culture and one economy: what becomes of the Other, of those with radically different histories, customs, identities?

Do they move outside the stadium? Whose stadium? In the US, the size and scale of the fortresses mean many are privately owned.

In 1936, when most of the world was participating in Hitler's Nazi Olympics, Spain and Russia boycotted. Whilst Russia was under the rule of an increasingly powerful and paranoid Stalin, Spain had recently disposed of their king and elected a socialist government declaring itself united for the first time, allowing Catalonia independence within it. The optimism of social cohesion and collectivity was extended in Barcelona, attempting to represent difference and make a stand against the fascist and racist doctrine that would soon explode from Berlin and into Europe, and which they saw Hitler's 1936 Olympics representing.

Trade Unions of Workers from around the World, as well as members of Socialist and Communist parties, rallied together to send athletes and teams. The People's Olympics, as they would come to be known, would include chess, theatre and arts exhibitions.

With increasing political unrest generated by a frustrated army and an isolated right wing, France's three-year civil war and 40-year Franco rule would see the People's Olympics never happen. With its borders closed, some athletes never made it to Spain, while others were caught in the violence and armed conflict that saw civilians and police defending the promise of a liberated working class.

Agamben has noted that depoliticisation is characterised by what was once a way of living — essentially an active condition, has now become a purely passive juridical status, in which action and inaction, the private and the public, are progressively blurred and become indistinguishable.[2]

I am wondering if July 1936 in Barcelona demarcates a kind of place for depoliticisation and site for the post-political — a civil war that blurred the geometries of power, the potential for ambiguous political objectives (as the war evolved these became less evident).

I am wondering if, in your 14 chapters, it is not only what your stadiums frame that inform us, but also what they cannot.

Lisa Radford x

PS. Since the ban on bull fighting, the hippodrome in Barcelona has been converted into a high-end shopping centre and viewing deck — the organised chaos of shopping and a room-with-a-view — juridical capital with a tower to stop those CNT and Durutti Column fighters.

First published as a catalogue essay for *In the Stadium (the 14 categories)*, Paula Hunt, Bus Projects, Melbourne, 16 March – 2 April 2016.

Notes

1 Prof. Erik Swyngedouw, 'Exit Polis: Musings on the Post-Political and

Post-Democratic City', public lecture, Center for Metropolitan Studies, 16 June 2009.

2 Giorgio Agamben, 'For a theory of destituent power', public lecture in Athens, 16 November 2013, organised by Nicos Poulantzas Institute and SYRIZA Youth.

List of illustrations

172 Geoff Newton
Untitled (After Robert), 2012
acrylic on polycotton
168 × 137 cm

173 Lucina Lane
untitled (vision docs), 2014
sythetic polymer paint on belgian linen
145 × 110 cm

174 Ry Haskings and Bec Coogan
Hey you, Art come here … fuck off (detail), 2002
VHS still

175 Tony Garifalakis
Dream, 2012
adhesive vinyl on paper shooting target
86.5 × 63 cm

176 Installation view, *Industrial Estate*
curated by Kym Maxwell
Heidelberg West, 2014

Acknowledgements

Surpllus and West Space would like to thank everyone who has made this publication possible. Thank you to all of the co-authors, artists, art spaces, institutions, journals and other publications who have granted permission for works and writing to be reproduced. To Fiona Macdonald, Geoff Lowe, Jacqueline Riva and Jarrod Rawlins for their written contributions. To Robert Shumoail-Albazi, for his invaluable editorial assistance. And, finally, to Lisa Radford herself, with whom it has been a pleasure and a privilege to collaborate.

And Lisa says 'I'm so shit at this stuff', but wants to say: Dear Masato… Without knowing this would ever happen, writing has always been to/for my brother Gareth. Apart from that, thank you to all the generous artists who I write with and through: your names are all inside. Special thanks to Jarrod, Fiona, Geoff and Jacqui—what an absolute privilege. To Patrice Sharkey, Brad Haylock and Robert Shumoail-Albazi: TCB, Pantone blue, ty, Ti, and a Book of Numbers. Special shout-out to TCB artinc, DAMP, 33 artists, Jack Halls, Ry Haskings, Simon McGlinn, Charles Radford, Kati Rule, Kylie White and the magical Sam George. To Jon Campbell: you were the first to ask me to write—what a wonderful chain reaction. From JC to TC. Lastly, this book is dedicated to Barbara, Blair, Clodagh, Vera and Joy, and inscribed by X.

PS: Nat & Justin. I'll paint Rizzo and Schmidt soon!

Aesthetic nonsense makes commonsense, thanks X
Lisa Radford

Surpllus and West Space acknowledge the Wurundjeri people of the Kulin Nations as the traditional owners of the land upon which the production of this book has taken place.

Editor & designer: Brad Haylock
Editorial assistant: Robert Shumoail-Albazi
Project advisor: Patrice Sharkey
Design advisor: Stuart Geddes
Back cover illustration: Trent Crawford

First edition 2016
ISBN 978-1-922099-20-4
Edition of 750

Co-published by Surpllus & West Space

Surpllus Pty Ltd
PO Box 418
Flinders Lane 8009
Victoria, Australia
— www.surpllus.com

West Space
Level 1, 225 Bourke Street
Melbourne 3000
Victoria, Australia
— www.westspace.org.au

Surpllus #22

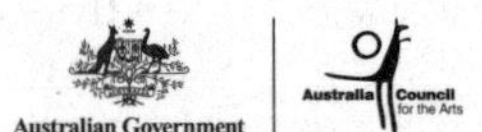

This project has been assisted by the Australian Government through the Australia Council for the Arts, its arts funding advisory body.

ty

Ti